Economic Freedom and the American Dream

Joseph Shaanan

palgrave
macmillan

ECONOMIC FREEDOM AND THE AMERICAN DREAM

Softcover reprint of the hardcover 1st edition 2010

First published in 2010 by
PALGRAVE MACMILLAN®
in the United States—a division of St. Martin's Press LLC,
175 Fifth Avenue, New York, NY 10010.

Where this book is distributed in the UK, Europe and the rest of the world, this is by Palgrave Macmillan, a division of Macmillan Publishers Limited, registered in England, company number 785998, of Houndmills, Basingstoke, Hampshire RG21 6XS.

Palgrave Macmillan is the global academic imprint of the above companies and has companies and representatives throughout the world.

Palgrave® and Macmillan® are registered trademarks in the United States, the United Kingdom, Europe and other countries.

ISBN 978-1-349-38067-1 ISBN 978-0-230-10223-1 (eBook)
DOI 10.1057/9780230102231

Library of Congress Cataloging-in-Publication Data

Shaanan, Joseph.
Economic freedom and the American dream / Joseph Shaanan.
p. cm.
Includes index.
ISBN 978–0–230–61775–9
1. Free enterprise—United States. 2. Capitalism—United States.
3. United States—Economic policy. I. Title.

HB95.S48 2009
330.973—dc22 2009023031

A catalogue record of the book is available from the British Library.

Design by Newgen Imaging Systems (P) Ltd., Chennai, India.

First edition: January 2010

10 9 8 7 6 5 4 3 2 1
Transferred to Digital Printing in 2013

Economic Freedom and the American Dream

Contents

Part V Culture

Acknowledgments

Many people assisted in the writing of this book. From Palgrave Macmillan I would like to thank Laura Lancaster, Kristy Lilas, and especially Laurie Harting for her insightful suggestions and encouragement. I owe a debt of gratitude to many of my colleagues who were kind enough to discuss with me diverse topics related to the book. I would like to thank the students in my "America and the Free Market" class whose comments and views in the debates that took place gave me a better perspective on the subject matter. Finally, my greatest debt of gratitude is to my wife for her advice on an earlier draft and, most importantly, for her patience and support.

CHAPTER 1

Introduction

Economic freedom is the distinguishing feature of the United States to millions around the world. Democracy, liberty, freedom of speech, and the separation of church and state all characterize the United States. However, it is primarily economic freedom that defines America. The present book *Economic Freedom and the American Dream* (*EFAD*) explores the overwhelming effect of freedom to profit on America; so powerful is the effect that it shapes nearly all aspects of American life, including politics, media, culture, and, of course, the economy. The benefits include a general level of affluence and opportunities for attaining the American dream, especially for the well educated, entrepreneurially gifted, and well organized. However, unrestricted economic freedom also inflicts a heavy toll on democracy, economic efficiency, and, paradoxically, economic freedom itself.

EFAD challenges the orthodoxy that our economic system is "free market" as well as the presumption that unchecked economic freedom necessarily enhances the nation's economic well-being and political freedoms. It is proposed that, for the sake of illusory economic gains and a dubious description of economic freedom, America is sacrificing some of its finest attributes. The recent bailouts have brought attention to the topic more so than in the past 70 years. With the socialization of risk for giant financial organizations, and "heads they win, tails we lose" type choices for the public, the bailouts represent striking examples of the consequences of what is described here as unrestricted freedom to profit.

Examined are three economic freedoms distinctive of American capitalism: (1) Best known among them is the individual liberty to pursue personal gain or economic self-interest. This freedom represents the nation's driving force and is at the root of the other two freedoms. (2) The freedom of corporations to pursue profits is less heralded but no less important because giant corporations are the predominant form of economic organization. They command vast resources and possess substantial economic and political power, and their influence extends to all facets of life. (3) The freedom to enter markets and engage in business plays a significant role in America's economic success; in addition, free markets represent the nation's underlying political-economic philosophy. Free markets, specifically competitive free markets, are also used here as a frame of reference with which to evaluate the effects of the first two freedoms.

By studying the effects of the three freedoms, their interactions (such as clashes between individual and corporate freedoms and between free markets and corporations), and their relationships with noneconomic freedoms, the book offers an unusual perspective on some of America's most difficult dilemmas. When those freedoms are studied separately and mostly in the context of a single area, for example, the economy or politics, the scope and the interrelated nature of their effects are obscured. Information from diverse areas allows for a more comprehensive assessment on how the freedom to profit defines the nation and its people and how it overpowers other values.

Discussions on the influence of the freedoms are interwoven with detailed accounts of other topics, including individual opportunity, the culture of materialism, media and the news, politics, government, and economic power. The focus moves from society and the nation to firms and individuals, with the common thread being the ubiquity and cost of economic freedom. Although the perspective afforded is frequently that seen through an economic lens, nonetheless the study is interdisciplinary. Following the traditional approach of studies in political economy, the book incorporates and synthesizes material from different branches of economics and from history, political science, and sociology.

1.1 General Overview

EFAD provides a description of America as a nation driven and shaped by the freedom to pursue profits, where there is an ever-present awareness of business opportunities and a devotion to economic matters, including a willingness to make sacrifices in other areas of life. The book focuses on the high costs resulting from a rather broad interpretation given to economic freedom including, the freedom to profit by circumventing the market, especially, through government help.

A key argument is that, in America, the freedom of corporations to pursue profits is paramount and has priority over that of individuals, and the two freedoms are increasingly in conflict. The unrestricted freedom of corporate giants can harm markets and economic efficiency—the very rationale for laissez-faire and the justification for its unfairness—and has led to a deteriorating quality of life for many over the past three decades. The blame for adverse economic outcomes is usually attributed to the invisible hand of the market—an act of nature beyond human control. In reality, asserts *EFAD*, the deliberate hand of large corporations is often instrumental in bringing about these changes.

It is well known that the freedom to profit plays a large role in modern American life. Less well understood is how thoroughly this freedom shapes the nation and crosses traditional boundaries. America is a land of opportunity, and the pursuit of self-interest and profits has produced a relatively high standard of living and a multitude of individual economic opportunities. It is here that economic freedom shines brightest. Immigrants have a better chance at the good life than in most nations. In the more competitive sectors of the economy, the price mechanism prevails. The economy is famous for its flexibility and dynamism. Consumers encounter an astonishing variety of goods and services. More generally, in line with other industrialized nations, nutrition levels have improved, rates of mortality for birthrates have declined, and education levels have increased. The majority of the population is well housed and well clothed. New discoveries and technologies facilitate life.

Yet, there is also the other side of the coin—the darker side. The exercise of the freedom to profit overpowers other freedoms and values. The rights to make money and spend it without restriction are fundamental American principles with far-reaching implications. Their influence is evident in campaign contributions and lobbying activities that are so essential to the modern political process. Those practices and the inevitable repayment in the form of favorable legislation are tantamount to a government for sale. They undermine the democratic process and lead to economic inefficiency.

The clash between economic freedom and democracy is evident in local television and print news. The market-oriented media, for the most part, do not provide widely disseminated high-quality news because it is unprofitable. However, this choice is detrimental to the political process. Voters are left without the information necessary at election time and, sometimes, end up voting against their economic self-interest.

An unleashing of the profit motive has led to a materialistic society where the quest for personal gain overshadows religion, tradition, voluntarism, and patriotism. It is evident in the consumption culture and its promotion and in the Faustian bargains involving the exchange of personal freedom for debt. The profit motive intrudes on all areas of life including areas where many believe it does not belong. This can be seen in the commercialization of religious holidays, in the lies told to sell the product or get the deal done, and in the way people modify their principles to conform to profit opportunities.

The triumph of money is discernible in health care, education, and the justice system, contrary to common perceptions of the ideal society. It is evident in increased litigiousness and in the loss of trust between doctors and patients where physicians purchase expensive malpractice insurance and patients, suspicious of the profit motive of health maintenance organizations (HMOs), second-guess medical recommendations. It can be seen in concerns about the safety of food, medicine, and toys and in the clash between profits and privacy. Profit-making ventures are the norm; they have the ear of legislators and the sympathy of the courts. There are no comparable institutions to defend traditions taken for granted or to monitor the rate of change and uncertainty in one's life. Change is justified and praised in the name of modernity and progress. More generally, the onslaught of a fierce individualistic, profit-seeking outlook erodes notions of community and society.

In the economic realm, substantial government help is given to corporations, including subsidies, tax exemptions, and many other forms of economic and legal protection. Freedom to profit has led to bailouts of immense proportions involving troubled but politically influential corporations and their creditors. Yet government assistance to the less fortunate is deemed an affront to free market principles, as is protection from mass layoffs or financial predation. The free rein given to the profit motive plays its part in America's high gross domestic product (GDP) per person but without necessarily a corresponding high quality of life for the average person. Current consumption patterns, despite being inefficient and wasteful, are virtually unassailable. The nation's finest minds are squandered at times on activities that are individually rewarding but questionable, if not useless, from a societal point of view.

The social acceptance of unbridled greed and government acquiescence gives corporations license to subject employees and suppliers to more intense competition from domestic and foreign sources. Corporations' costs are reduced. However, for many individuals, quality of life is diminished through stagnant wages, curtailed employee benefits, increased job instability, and constant uncertainty. Greater risk is passed on to employees, suppliers, and customers. The motive behind some of these changes, all too often, is the reward structure of top managers. Forgotten is Joseph Schumpeter's (1962) warning that managers' seizing control from owners (an outcome of the individual pursuit of profits) undermines capitalism. Social and political changes are precipitated by many factors; yet, when the dust has settled and the final outcome has been established, the imprint of profit-seeking organizations is discernible, regardless of the source of change.

There has been a growing awareness that something is awry in America. An undercurrent of disquiet and anxiety has resulted from corporate downsizing, outsourcing, and the increased use of temporary workers. Together with the rising cost of health care and doubts about the viability of social security, these developments have brought home the realization that the middle-class paradise of the 1950s and 1960s is vanishing. Misgivings about the working of the "free market" system came as a result of the collapse of Enron, huge pay packages for chief executive officers (CEOs) regardless of performance, and above all, the recent financial bailouts. There is increased apprehension about the power over people's lives possessed by credit card, credit rating, and mortgage companies as well as other financial organizations. The above developments and other unsettling changes seem to intrude on Americans' lives with greater frequency and suggest that the economic system and the political-economic philosophy are not working the way they are supposed to, the way they are described.

1.2 Questions Asked

The most important questions posed in the book revolve primarily around the concepts of economic freedom, including free markets and individual economic freedom. Some of the issues examined are the following: Is economic freedom distributed equally? How do different economic freedoms interact? And does one group's freedom comes at the expense of another's? Arguably, the most important issue addressed is the cost of unrestricted economic freedom. Related questions deal with the impact of economic freedom on democracy and other values.

Given the presence of oligopoly markets and government assistance to large corporations, is it still appropriate to describe the economy as free market? Can a competitive free market economy survive in a laissez-faire environment without rules of competition? Finally, should there be concerns about the dangers of private economic power in addition to concerns about government power?

Questions dealing with democracy include the following: Why is the American political system amenable to the influence of money and economic power and what problems arise as a result? What are the reasons for Americans' acceptance of the political-economic system? Can a market-oriented media provide quality news and competition in the marketplace of ideas so crucial to a well-functioning democracy?

1.3 Topics Covered

From the time the nation was founded, a highly sought after freedom was the right to do business. Economic interests influenced the structure and logic of government. The economic sector's involvement in the political process would intensify with the advent of large corporations and politicians' growing need for money. This involvement has led to corporations acquiring political dominance to the detriment of democracy. Presently, both major parties defend corporate positions and privileges to the extent that the political-economic differences between the two major parties are negligible, certainly as they pertain to acquiescence to unelected corporate power.

America has adopted with few reservations the economic ideology of corporate capitalism. The system is seen as offering most, if not all, citizens an opportunity to compete and seek their fortune. The dangers to political freedom from economic power are minimized or else ignored as is its market-distorting political influence. Individual freedom to profit is, in principle, respected; yet corporations' freedom to profit is the predominant liberty. The latter freedom overrides all other principles and ideals. It certainly has precedence over Adam Smith's vision of free markets.

The American economy has experienced considerable success. It is noted for its flexibility, adaptability, and above all, the free rein given to the pursuit of profits. The acceptance of change and the introduction of new products and processes as well as the respect for business and entrepreneurs play a role in that success. However, economic success is also due to the unusual weight given to economic matters, including the willingness to uproot one's family and endure longer work hours with less protections and benefits than in most advanced industrialized nations. In the last two decades, downsizing, restructuring, outsourcing, and globalization have brought anxiety, instability, and dissatisfaction to employees. The financial events of 2008 strengthen suspicions that the free market economy is a mirage. Easy credit, intensive advertising, and laws that give preference to consumption all help promote a consumerist culture founded on indebtedness.

Examined also are the effects of economic freedom on lesser players positioned on the lowest rung of the ladder on both the production and consumption sides of the economy. On the production side are numerous small firms owned by entrepreneurs who epitomize the opportunities and benefits of economic freedom available to individuals pursuing the American dream. The findings suggest that entrepreneurial endeavors are consistent with the idea of individual economic freedom, although there are misconceptions. Particularly disadvantaged consumers are analyzed on the consumption side. Their plight represents some of the harsher outcomes of economic freedom, including the rights of firms to deceive, mislead, and practice usury.

The book reviews the factors responsible for the establishment of large corporations. Two competing hypotheses are discussed. The efficiency hypothesis proposes that the establishment of corporations was a free market response to potential efficiency gains in production, distribution, organization, and management. The power hypothesis suggests that, to avoid the market and its uncertainties, firms acquired market power to control supply and the power of large size to gain leverage in dealings with legislators, suppliers, rivals, customers, and employees. The issue is whether large corporations emerged as a genuine response to free market signals or as an attempt to destroy free markets and reduce other market participants' economic freedom.

Corporations are the dominant force in the U.S. economy. They produce a substantial share of the nation's output and enjoy considerable freedom and power. Contrary to prevailing arguments, such outcomes are not necessarily market-determined. Giant corporations engaged in economic planning and sometimes protected from the discipline of the market represent neither superior economic efficiency nor the essence of the free market. Power over competitors, suppliers, customers, and government and the potential profit opportunities from that power are better explanations for their size than efficiency. It is doubtful whether the stock market and takeover threats can monitor management efficiency effectively. Corporations have long ceased to be, if they ever were, a passive conduit for the transfer of income to stockholders. A nagging question raised long ago is still relevant: is the separation of ownership from control compatible with capitalism?

Political influence acquired and exercised by large corporations through their special access to government undermines democracy. In addition, when government intervenes in the economy at the behest of corporations, there is a cost to economic efficiency and a discarding of free market principles. Large corporations are granted government help in a variety of ways. Notwithstanding the laissez-faire rhetoric and the arguments on behalf of rewards for risk taking and initiative, government plays a major role in wealth creation and redistribution. The recent bailouts are an extreme example of how unprecedented government help ensues from unchecked economic freedom.

Media firms' freedom to profit clashes with the information needs of democracy. The former objective has a priority which, unfortunately, conflicts with the requirements of political freedom. The problem is that, at election time, voters often lack essential information. Rising market power in the media has worrisome implications for competition in the marketplace of ideas. Advertisers fund media products and programs and as such have considerable say in the selection of programs and their content, including the news, which does not bode well for either democracy or economic efficiency. Large media firms have been helped by government policies that they, in turn, influence.

Generally, competitive economies, with an emphasis on price competition, experience a more efficient allocation of resources and display a greater awareness of consumer requirements than noncompetitive economies. In addition, they benefit from greater freedom of opportunity as a result of a lack of barriers to resource mobility.[1] Adherence to free market principles in parts of the economy has contributed to U.S. economic success. Yet in more than a few industries, the freedom to gain market power triumphs over competitive free market principles. Despite widespread use of price signals to direct resources, in key industries the guidance of the invisible hand is replaced with private coordination and significant public intervention. Oligopoly power is present in major parts of the economy, and the entry of new domestic firms into established industries often has not injected meaningful price competition. Significant changes are more likely to be brought about by new technology and international competition than by internal competition or domestic entry. The conclusion, once again, is that the freedom to profit of corporations takes precedence; in this case, it has priority over the freedom of markets.

In the past 30 years, competition and its safeguarding have been neglected. Yet there are clear benefits, both economic and political, to maintaining a framework for the protection of competition. In addition, there is no guarantee that a laissez-faire environment, without rules of competition, will lead to competitive markets. Therefore, restrictions, such as antitrust laws, are necessary to prevent the suppression of both current and future competition.

America in many respects is a land of opportunity. The open job market, educational choices, business possibilities, and evidence of mobility support the argument. However, the nature of opportunity for many Americans has changed, and not for the better. Higher education has become increasingly the key to success, and high-paying blue-collar jobs are disappearing. Greater economic freedom exercised by corporations, including the abandonment of paternalistic obligations toward employees, means more limited economic opportunities and uncertainty for many. New attitudes regarding executive remuneration have played a part in effecting those changes. When individual opportunity clashes with the freedom of large organizations the former rarely triumphs.The outcome is that a way of life agreeable to many is disappearing.

American values have been transformed by commercial forces. A society based on family and communal ties gave way to a money society and its obligations. An emphasis on conspicuous consumption financed with credit has replaced saving and frugality. Increased freedom to profit is most likely responsible for those developments.

PART I

America

CHAPTER 2

We the People: Government and Politics

The U.S. political system is rooted in a curious mix of classical liberal ideals and a belief in popular rule combined with a mistrust of government. It is characterized by a two-party system that is, for the most part, nonideological and a conviction that the purpose of government is to improve the lives of its citizens—yet citizens are expected to be self-reliant. The U.S. embraces an egalitarianism measured in terms of opportunity rather than outcome. There is strong protection for private property and for freedom to pursue economic self-interest; a twentieth-century development is the tacit acceptance of corporate power not only in the economic sphere but also in politics.

Alexis de Tocqueville, the most famous observer of American democracy, admired the governance of small New England towns in the 1830s, especially their democratic nature. Tocqueville was of the opinion that, despite the representative nature of government—that is, no direct participatory democracy—the real power lay in the hands of the people.[1] Their opinions, interests, and prejudices had a strong influence on society and presumably on their elected representatives. Since Tocqueville's time, major economic changes, including the unleashing of the profit motive and, particularly, the rise of giant corporations, warrant a less sanguine assessment regarding the locus of power. Economic considerations influenced the structure of government at the nation's founding, and their influence on the political system remains undiminished. Large economic organizations through the introduction of legal, political, and judicial changes have become the conduit of power and have crossed the imaginery divide separating politics and economics.

In this chapter, key features of American government and politics are surveyed with special attention given to the interplay between economic and political freedoms. Noted are the supremacy of the economic sector over the political and its detrimental effect on democracy. It is claimed that corporate dominance is attained through the medium of money and preserved skillfully by disingenuous appeals to free markets, antigovernment sentiments, and even cultural values.

2.1 The Constitution and Economic Motives

America's most important political ideas are contained in documents dating back to the founding years of the Republic. The Declaration of Independence states that all men are created equal. American citizens are entitled to rights that include life, liberty, and the pursuit of happiness. A government established to secure those rights must have the consent of the people. Three words with tremendous significance to the American view of government are contained in the Preamble to the Constitution: "We, the People." A century later, in the Gettysburg Address, President Abraham Lincoln presented the essence of the American view on the ideal government: "a government of the people, by the people, for the people."

The U.S. Constitution is an impressive document. It serves as a model for people around the world seeking a unifying national foundation based on principles of liberty and justice. Together with the constitutional amendments, it contains a remarkable list of rights and freedoms guaranteed to Americans, including freedom of religion, free speech, a free press, free assembly, and the rights of accused in criminal cases. It also establishes the separation of powers between the different branches of government and a system of checks and balances by which each branch keeps an eye on the other branches. This particular feature is often seen as one of the more admirable and prodemocratic features of the U.S. system of government. However, as discussed below, its original purpose may have been somewhat different.

The U.S. Constitution is not entirely a work of abstract ideals. It has been proposed that it is also an economic document founded on the primacy of property rights. Charles Beard (1986) in *An Economic Interpretation of the Constitution of the United States*, his controversial book written almost a century ago, emphasizes the importance of economic interests in the design and ratification of the U.S. Constitution. More recently, statistical economic studies provide support for his hypothesis.[2] Beard points to the composition of delegates to the Constitutional Convention, the declarations they made on the need to defend property, and the creation of a strong national government at the expense of state governments. He also points to the different election rules for the Senate, the House of Representatives, and the president, and, especially, the checks and balances on the different branches of government. To Beard, this grand edifice was designed in part to protect private property from the potential tyranny of democratic majorities. James Madison, Alexander Hamilton, and Samuel Adams all discussed ideas related to the protection of property rights and recognized the economic divisions present in society. Their views, as well as those of other writers, on property rights and class antagonisms convinced Beard that the Constitution was based on more than just idealism.[3] More often than not, concerns about property rights paralleled the delegates' or their constituents' economic interests. He found that the vast majority of the delegates, to varying degrees, benefited economically from the new Constitution and therefore could not be considered as disinterested parties.[4] The proposed structure of government would protect property owners, in part by making it difficult for a majority to control all branches of government simultaneously. A combination of property qualifications, as well as ignorance and apathy, limited the number of voters to less than a quarter of the adult white males and this, argues Beard, helped property and commercial interests pass and ratify the Constitution.

The predominance of the economic motive was not a particularly new idea in late eighteenth-century America.[5] A key feature of the Federalist–Whig philosophy was the moral and practical priority of private property rights over government.[6] Public service and devotion to the public good were laudable goals, but when establishing the institutions of government, it was essential to take into account in a pragmatic way people's desire for power and property. Douglas Adair's (1957) finding regarding the influence of philosopher David Hume on the writers of the Constitution lends additional support to Beard's thesis. Hume emphasizes that, in establishing a constitution's checks and controls, people should be assumed to be motivated by self-interest, and the whole system of government should be founded on this premise.[7]

The writers of the Constitution, whether due to pressure from commercial interests, self-interest, or a desire to promote the national interest, established a system of government where property rights would be afforded protection from government. These rights facilitated economic development but checks and balances were not created to protect democracy because the U.S. government was established as a representative republic, not as a democracy with political equality.[8] The democratic aspects came later. Instead, a fundamental feature of the political system was the intent to thwart majority rule, in part to ensure the above rights, and in so doing to maintain the status quo.[9]

The United States is a federal republic consisting of 50 states. For several years both before and after the Declaration of Independence, the United States was governed by the Articles of Confederation, which gave more power to the states and less to the federal government. The U.S. Constitution reversed matters, but states retained a good deal of autonomy. States have their own legislative bodies, governors, courts, police, and education systems and compete with other states to attract industries and jobs. Yet an ongoing source of tension has been the uncertainty over which body of government has jurisdiction. This has weakened government's legitimacy[10] and has led to debates on issues such as capitalism versus democracy and economic versus political freedom. A split in the powers of government between state and federal jurisdictions has also strengthened the economic sector's control over the political domain. Corporations, when profitable, demand centralization and federal jurisdiction, yet when the need arises, they insist on the rule of state laws on grounds of democracy, autonomy, or some other noble goal.[11] The practice of choosing one's government according to need has also been extended to the global arena by multinational corporations.

2.2 The Political System

The idea of a democratic form of government is treated with reverence. It is taken for granted that this is a fundamental tenet of the political system although, as noted before, this was not part of the original design. Modern democracy, writes Schumpeter (1962), may simply mean that people have the opportunity of electing or rejecting their rulers in a competitive election. Contemporary democracies, including that of the United States, resemble classic democracy only roughly. Citizens vote for candidates to represent them, but afterwards, it is all in the hands of the elected representatives. Americans also have a direct vote for the president, the Electoral College aside. However, despite the homage to the concepts of the common good, the common will, and the utilitarian foundations of democracy,[12] the U.S. political system is not much different than other modern democracies in approximating the ideal—in some respects, it is possibly farther away.[13] The United States has made progress in extending the vote to most of its citizens and in eliminating some of the obvious forms of election fraud. However, in the United States as elsewhere, when it comes to the shaping and serving of ideas, the political agenda, and the persuasion, it usually comes from politicians or interest groups, including corporations, and not the public at large. Consequently, the views of many Americans are not represented effectively. Instead, they are instructed as to where their interests lie and what their values should be. John Kenneth Galbraith (1983) describes this as subversion of the democratic electoral process while giving voters the illusion of sovereignty.

A system of proportional representation is, with some exceptions, considered preferable to a two-party system such as exists in the United States even though it also is not the ideal version of democracy. In a proportional representation system, people can vote for a party that comes closer to representing their views because there is a greater choice of parties.[14] Therefore, voters are likely to identify more closely with either their party or their representatives and generally become more involved in the political process. In the United States, federal nominating elections are based on a plurality rule that, according to political scientists, is not particularly desirable.[15] In plurality two-party systems, other political factions are severely underrepresented because, usually, they lose in all districts.[16] Voters in such a system may refrain from voting for their preferred party or representative so as not to waste their vote given the slim chance for victory.[17] Despite criticism the two-party system, it is not without advantages, including having more stable governments.[18] It is also claimed that the centripetal forces of American politics tend to weed out or discourage extremism from both ends of the political spectrum. Looking at the history of the twentieth century and the horrors brought on by extremist views, this is certainly a favorable attribute.

Every citizen has the right to vote, but he or she has to register first, and U.S. registration laws are strict and may result in a reduction in number of voters.[19] Election Day is not a holiday in the United States. The information available to the public on political candidates comes primarily from the media—television, radio, and newspapers—and these sources vary widely in their objectivity.

Americans, relative to Europeans, tend to be apolitical or less interested in ideological issues. For the most part, American politics might be described as centrist, conditional on market-oriented economics. Several studies claim that the goal of political parties in the United States is to win elections, not to promote particular policies; those come afterwards.[20] The fact that there is relatively little ideology associated with the two-party system is not a recent occurrence; it was already noted in the nineteenth century by the English writer Bryce.[21] The old image of the two parties was that the Republicans represented big business and the rich (property owners) whereas the Democrats represented labor unions, the poor, and minorities. In a general sense, Republicans are associated with right-wing politics. This basically translates to conservative economic and social policies, including reducing taxes and social programs and support for a strong defense. Democrats, with some regional exceptions, usually promote more social and safety net policies, claim allegiance to the middle class, support unions and the rights of minorities, and favor a higher minimum wage. The two parties also differ on the extent of government intervention in the economy.[22] The fact that Democratic administrations have focused on unemployment while Republicans have been more concerned with inflation is seen as indicative of dissimilar economic objectives.[23]

Notwithstanding those differences, a key point, especially in recent decades, is that both parties tend to curry favor with corporate interests because of the need to obtain funding for election campaigns. Therefore, politicians are willing to support the economic and legal status of corporations and their managers, in addition to serving their business interests. Corporations are often provided with various tax breaks, generous subsidies, protection from foreign and even domestic competition, and exemptions from labor laws. Neither party favors government-run businesses or government ownership of business. Both parties accept corporate economic dominance and have no desire to change the economic system.

Representatives, certainly, take up parochial issues and support local constituents. However, the granting of favors seems to be skewed toward those who can contribute financially to reelection campaigns or have the resources to engage in lobbying. Large corporations certainly qualify. The outcome frequently is deterioration in national welfare because the gains to special interest groups are usually outweighed by the loss to the nation as a whole.[24] When politicians pursue political donations from corporations and provide them with various kinds of help, this is not usually reported in the local press or on local television and only infrequently on national news shows. The public is led to believe that such donations are trivial and a routine part of the democratic political process. The counterargument for not reporting is that the public is not particularly interested in knowing too much about this and perhaps does not need to know.

Thomas Frank (2005) argues that the Democratic Party turned its back on the economic concerns of the working classes to appease corporate backers and professionals. It continued pursuing liberal (modern) positions on social issues while yielding on economic issues. If true, then campaign contributions may have succeeded in weakening the Democratic Party's traditional economic focus and populist concerns, thereby ensuring that few questions are raised about corporate influence and power. However, there are alternative explanations. John Roemer (1998) discusses situations when voters encounter multidimensional issues, for example, economics and race, rather than just economics. A party devoted not only to helping the poor but also concerned about fighting racial discrimination may have to compromise to some extent on the economic issue to capture enough wealthy voters who are sympathetic to its antidiscrimination position. Roemer is of the opinion that the Democratic Party found itself in this situation in the 1980s. Other explanations point to the fact that the blurring of ideological differences between the two parties is in line with Downs' theory regarding the outcome in a two-party system.[25]

Regardless of the reason, with the Democratic Party relinquishing populist economic positions, the corporate sector is left without any significant domestic opposition and with no political force likely to question major aspects of its economic or political activities. Not everyone sees this as an unmitigated disaster. To the contrary, some writers see this as a triumph for liberal capitalism and a model for other nations.[26] Others suggest that the system is characterized by a multiplicity of interest groups without the supremacy of any one group.[27]

With no strong ideological differences, politics all too often is left to focus on personalities and values. Voters are frequently instructed to ignore economic policies that would affect their lives and instead to focus on charisma and how the candidate would act in a crisis. There is concern about the fact that the percentage of eligible voters actually voting appears to be declining. The percentage of eligible Americans voting in the 2000 presidential elections was about 56 percent, even though this was a tightly contested election where it was unclear who would win.[28] This is blamed on selfishness, cynicism, a lack of public spirit, poor education, or too much education, the deliberate trivialization of politics, and many other factors. What is rarely acknowledged is that when it is difficult to discern substantial differences in the positions of the two major parties on key issues, voter apathy becomes understandable. In addition, the political system is controlled by money and whoever is elected will offer access to contributors and lobbyists, who in turn will, undoubtedly, influence the politician. An awareness of this practice hardly induces people to rush out and vote.

The liberal-conservative divide is the commonly accepted categorization of ideological differences in the United States. It is a dichotomy that both depicts and supports the political-economic status quo and covers the spectrum of respectable and marginally respectable political views. Common to both liberals and conservatives, not unlike the Democratic and Republican divide, is the acceptance of corporate control, not only in the economic arena but also in the political one. The issue, apparently, is beyond debate; both parties are loyal to the "king." This is described as acceptance of "the rule of free markets" (or corporate capitalism, outside the United States), and because it is well known that the free market is the superior form of economic organization, only misguided radicals would complain.

The implications of this acquiescence, such as its impact on individual political and individual economic freedom, is generally ignored, as is the fact that such an arrangement is harmful to free markets, contrary to common belief. The conflicting obligations to protect capitalism and popular rule, corporate interests on the one hand and principles of justice and freedom on the other, tend to undermine government's legitimacy.[29] Freedom to profit, especially of giant firms, appears to have triumphed over democratic principles—or any other principles for that matter. As described throughout the book, this is evident in many laws and rules, such as, on election financing, lobbying, taxes, credit, banking, finance, labor, and international trade; it can also be seen in government policies on subsidies, tariffs, antitrust, stock markets, energy, transportation, and many other areas. With a freedom so absolute came a recklessness that almost brought down the U.S. financial system in 2008. It demonstrated in stark terms the cost of relinquishing responsibility and leaving rules and regulations to the discretion of those who stand to gain the most. This was certainly not the first time and probably not the last time. The willingness to protect corporations at taxpayer expense, evident in the bailout solution to the current crisis, was also apparent in the Saving and Loan crisis of the early 1990s.

2.3 Politics and Money

In modern American politics, large amounts of money are required for presidential and Congressional campaigns. According to the Center for Responsive Politics, the amount spent on presidential elections in 2008 was $1.759 billion. Candidates for the House of Representatives spent a total of $938 million, with an average of $1.39 million per candidate from the major two parties, and Senate candidates spent $429 million, with an average of $2.87 million per candidate from the two major parties. Politics requires substantial sums because of the need to advertise. Whether to promote oneself or to attack an opponent, political advertising is usually effective, and it is hard to win a statewide, let alone a national, election without it.

Money can and does influence candidates. Studies show that contributors seek to influence politicians on issues of concern to the contributor;[30] and other studies point to a relationship between contributors' interests and the committee assignments of the politicians they contribute to.[31] That is not to say that politicians are only influenced by campaign contributions.[32] They are also affected by their personal beliefs and opinions as well as constituents' political leanings. However, it would appear that these factors are often outweighed by concerns about donations.[33] The fight over soft money campaign contributions and political action committees (PAC) money reflect an underlying concern that U.S. elections are getting close to an outright buying of an election and that elections go to the highest bidder.

One result of a political system where money is so crucial and influential is that the public has come to look on politicians with suspicion. Politicians are often perceived as people who will say anything to get elected and on taking office will renege on their campaign promises, which, some argue cynically, is inevitable given the conflicting promises made. So politicians have to live with a certain amount of hypocrisy. They request and accept payments from interest groups while claiming to fight for their constituents, although the two are not always in conflict.

The problem, however, is not the perfidy of individual politicians. Personal ethics play a role, but the fault lies primarily with the system. If the politicians do not accept donations from interest groups, they lessen their chances of winning in two ways. First, they will have less money for campaigning. Second, they face a distinct possibility that the rebuffed interest group will fund their opponent. Given that most campaigns are not ideological, there is more leeway in accepting financial help from diverse sources. In the past, the general attitude toward the political system was to shrug one's shoulders or joke, "We have the best politicians money can buy." Today there is a greater unease about the situation. Yet while voters accept criticisms of politicians and the political system, they do not believe that it applies to their politician. The person representing their district is fine. The other politicians are the scoundrels. This attitude helps preserve the system.

To some, the use of money for such purposes is not only acceptable but even desirable because it brings politics closer to approximating market behavior[34]—the hallmark of efficiency—and outweighs concerns over equality and democracy. If people and interest groups are willing to spend money, does it not indicate the intensity of their feelings on the issues? Regardless, there is a clash between democratic elections and the economic freedom to spend one's money as one sees fit, including the right to purchase elections or candidates. It is hard to reconcile the present system with commonly held beliefs regarding democracy or popular rule, and it has already been noted that the economic gain to interest groups is often exceeded by the economic loss to the nation as a whole. Several European legislatures have tried to reduce the influence of money on politics and prevent parties from becoming dependent on corporations or wealthy individuals by limiting private funding.[35] Such a solution is unlikely to be accepted in the United States.

In the past, elections were restricted to the wealthier members of the community. Today, there are no property or asset requirements for election, yet money is still a crucial factor. People donate money for a variety of reasons; some donors expect a return and regard donations as investments. Even if donors do not expect a return, at the very least, they would not stand for deterioration in their financial fortunes as a result of policy changes.

So is there a substantial difference between the eighteenth century's legal wealth requirements for legislators and today's practical necessity of raising large sums for elections? The latter is more democratic and inclusive and represents more of a market-oriented solution; yet the influence of money remains intact with all the obligations to big donors and the predictable outcome.

2.4 The Image of Government

The idea of a benevolent paternalistic government is not popular in the United States. Henry David Thoreau's[36] quote "that government is best which governs least" has many supporters and is a widely disseminated point of view. There is good deal of antagonism toward government, particularly the federal government. In popular culture as well as in conservative publications. government is usually cast as incompetent. Economists specializing in the study of politics describe politicians and bureaucrats as seeking to maximize their personal rewards and expand the size of government,[37] to the detriment of the public at large.

The origins of the mistrust of government may have to do with the aforementioned split in governmental powers as well as different military and political events, such as the Civil War and its aftermath, the Vietnam War, and the events of Watergate. Some blame the media for encouraging suspicion of politicians and political institutions, while others blame the fights over desegregation, busing, and federal land issues in the western United States. Yet in addition to political, social, and historical reasons for the hostility, economic factors play a role in exacerbating resentment. Freedom from a foreign government was always a high priority but so was economic freedom from any government. Liberty also meant the right to pursue profit, free enterprise, and later on, establish enterprises of any size. In the twentieth century with the threat of Communism, government economic intervention during the New Deal, and the public's experiences with the Great Depression, it became more important to extol the virtues of the free market system and its main players while belittling the role of a government that might challenge corporate autonomy. Large corporations became more vociferous in their demands for protection from government interference and in the 1970s took concrete steps to protect their interests from government and critics. The media were, not surprisingly, supportive, and academics wishing to argue in this vein could obtain funds for their research.

It is interesting to note that the U.S. Post Office was for several decades a target of television comedy shows. Private sector corporations are only infrequently the target of comedy and usually only after a spectacular failure.

More generally, the private sector is considered worthy of greater respect, partly because it is not funded by taxpayers—hence, one should not meddle in its affairs—and partly because it is considered more efficient.

Considering the probusiness policies of most U.S. administrations and the corporate sector's predominance and easy access to government, it is surprising to see the oft-repeated, criticisms of government coming from corporations. This is even more puzzling given the generous financial help squeezed from government in one form or another, let alone the many laws, regulations, and policies that support large corporations. One possibility is that the government can be blamed for a myriad of problems over which it has limited control and which really are the responsibility of the economic sector and not, directly, government.[38] It has relatively little direct control over economic decision making—the domain of the private sector—yet it has to take the blame for economic failures. So government becomes a convenient lightening rod deflecting attention and criticism.[39] An additional objective is to ensure that taxes, if not lowered, then at least are not raised.

There is a certain amount of hypocrisy in the antigovernment positions of corporations and wealthy individuals because it is government that defends their property at home and overseas and provides them with benefits ranging from agricultural price supports to restrictions on imports.[40] The phenomenon of enriching oneself or one's organization from government contracts and then attributing the success to the wonders of the free market is not uncommon. Government spending, especially social spending aimed at society's less fortunate, stirs resentment and has a negative connotation. It is contrasted, in the public's mind, with images of self-reliant farmers, risk-taking entrepreneurs, and the typical citizen who works and pays taxes. Of course, as recent events demonstrate, when the individual or organizational need arises, views on the role of government can change quickly.

There is greater tolerance of income and wealth redistribution when it flows up, rather than down, the wealth pyramid. In 2008, a massive redistribution was undertaken with the support of both political parties. Huge sums of taxpayer money were given to managers, creditors, and owners of banks and insurance companies. The national interest was invoked, as it always is in these cases. Yet given the stated objective of enhancing credit availability to ameliorate the state of the economy, it was puzzling that the recipients were not required to lend out the money. The government came to the rescue of large economic organizations, and its actions, intentionally or otherwise, protected the status quo at a cost to efficiency and fairness, never mind the free market. Criticisms abounded, but the beneficiaries had enough defenders to lessen public hostility and allow the bailout to go forward. Both parties accepted the idea that large financial organizations must survive no matter how inefficient. Little if any ideological differences in the positions of the two major parties could be detected.

2.5 Politics and Culture

Thomas Frank (2005) notes, with some sarcasm, that "people getting their fundamental interests wrong, is what American political life is all about." Social scientists report that the phenomenon of people not necessarily voting for candidates or parties who would give them a greater share of the pie is common to democracies. Frank relates the experience of Kansas in the last decade where people with the lowest per capita income and residents of working-class districts often provided strong support to conservative factions of the Republican Party. Why would people vote for candidates favorable to wealth and large corporations but refuse to vote for candidates sympathetic to their economic circumstances and offering them more of a safety net and more money for their children's education?

One answer might simply be that voters lack information.[41] However, according to Frank, the answer lies in values, culture, and morality.[42] Voters were persuaded that cultural issues were more important than pocketbook or economic fairness issues. Anger over issues such as abortion, busing, elitism, Hollywood, political correctness, religious symbols in public places, and the teaching of evolution in public schools was used to obtain votes.[43] There may have been an element of disingenuousness here in that many of the cultural issues could not be won, and the real objective—besides anger arousal—was economic.[44] The end result, notes Frank, was that cultural issues gave conservative politicians the votes to implement their economic policies, including cuts in capital gains taxes, lower taxes for high income earners and corporations, no increase in minimum wages, and more corporate welfare. The social safety nets erected in the 1960s for the poor and in the 1930s for middle class were dismantled, and America moved toward greater income inequality.

The irony here is that the very movies, music, magazines, and television shows that arouse cultural anger are mostly products of corporate America and the profit motive.[45] Yet Hollywood, the liberal media, intellectuals, and academics are blamed for the undesirable culture. Corporate America is not criticized, and the economic system is rarely blamed for undermining values and beliefs. This myopia is not accidental, claims Frank. Vast amounts of money were spent on planning and organizing this campaign. To achieve the requisite indoctrination, money was granted to supportive universities, magazines were established, and think tanks and institutes did their part in providing funds for writers and commentators imbued with the right orthodoxy. Given the outcome, these efforts achieved their objective.

In conclusion, economic interests already played a major role in determining the structure of government at the founding of the nation. The economic sector's involvement in the political process would continue with the advent of large corporations and politicians' growing need for money. It is argued that money is so crucial that both major political parties accept donations from corporations and consequently defend corporate positions and privileges. The outcome is that political-economic differences between the two parties are almost nonexistent, and corporate control is accepted in both the economy and politics. The result is attributed to unrestricted economic freedom, a key feature of which is the freedom to profit by influencing the political system, and it often comes at the expense of democracy.

CHAPTER 3

Ideology and Myths

Examined in this chapter are some key features of the American political economy. The relationship between political and economic freedom is discussed, particularly contemporary tensions between democracy and large economic organizations. The concept of a free market is explored and how the common description that appears to rationalize corporate power in both politics and the economy differs from Adam Smith's original insight. Also reviewed is the laissez-faire revival of the past 30 years and, not unrelated, why Americans are amenable to corporate capitalism.

3.1 Economic and Political Freedom

The founders of the American Republic were heavily influenced by European liberal (classical) writers whose objective was either liberty or equality.[1] Democracy was only a means for attaining those goals[2] and, as noted above, liberal and republican, not democratic, ideas prevailed at the birth of the nation.[3] One of the most sought-after liberties was the freedom to do business, which in turn required freedom from government in the economic domain.[4] John Locke, whose ideas were especially influential, linked the preservation of property and preservation of life, thereby connecting economic and political freedoms. The nation's founders debated the relative roles of capitalism and democracy, with Alexander Hamilton favoring capitalism while James Madison and Thomas Jefferson opted for democratic principles.[5] To Jefferson, an ideal society would consist mostly of economically independent small farmers, thereby allowing for genuine political discourse and free elections. The same would not be true of factory workers fearful of losing their jobs.[6]

In the late nineteenth century, unfettered laissez-faire, fortified by the ideology of social Darwinism influenced the intellectual outlook of the nation, including the judiciary and the economics profession. It led to a weakening of regulation and a strengthening of business.[7] It was also used to defend increasing disparities in wealth and living standards. It was not a coincidence that these ideas gained ascendancy with the shift to a more industrial economy and the emergence of giant corporations. Here was a theory favorable to wealth and power even though, carried to its logical extreme, it could justify outcomes inimical to those interests.[8] Principles of economic freedom would dominate democratic principles, and governments of that era, for the most part, did not try to stem the tide.[9]

In the twentieth century, with the growing importance of large corporations in the economy, it became necessary to perform an intricate alchemy, equating in the public's mind corporate autonomy with individual economic freedom, free markets,[10] and even democracy. With the exception of the Great Depression when serious doubts surfaced, corporations' freedom to profit became an American tenet. It was impressed on the nation that protecting this liberty would safeguard all other freedoms. The corporation was depicted as a heroic figure from mythology repelling the invading hordes of bureaucrats and planners with little gratitude from the public. A related idea, promoted vigorously, was that government and its meddlesome operations are worlds apart from the noble enterprise of private sector corporations.[11]

A century ago, Max Weber disputed the existence of a direct relationship between capitalism, freedom, and democracy.[12] While there is evidence of a positive correlation between increasing economic freedom and rising per capita income the relationship between income growth and political freedom is less clear. Therefore, contrary to popular belief, it has not been established conclusively that higher income or greater economic growth leads to democracy.[13] Yet the idea that market systems are inextricably linked with democracy is popular among economists, although political scientists and sociologists are more skeptical.

Milton Friedman (1962) advances the argument that economic sanctions cannot be used against political opposition in an economy free of state control.[14] Therefore, he concludes that economic freedom is a requirement for attaining political freedom. Competitive capitalism promotes political freedom because it separates economic power from political power and in this way one offsets the other. Friedman writes that societies enjoying political freedom invariably have a market-oriented economic sector. In a free market, the consumer is protected from the seller because of the presence of other sellers. The seller's protection comes from the existence of numerous consumers. By the same token, the employee can choose among employers and vice versa. Importantly, all this happens through the invisible hand of the market without government intervention. Unlike politics, argues Friedman, markets provide considerable choice. Everyone can buy whatever he or she likes, and this has important political ramifications. Because an economic sector free of government cannot be used to coerce citizens, it also creates a check to political power somewhat analogous to the checks and balances within the American political system.[15] The above description represents an ideal in terms of the interaction between markets and politics. A key condition contained in the description is the word *competitive*. Without competition the economic efficiency arguments do not usually hold, and it is questionable whether the desirable political implications hold. What exactly would be considered sufficiently competitive is debatable. The economic theoretical conditions required for an optimal allocation of resources are rarely met in actual markets because they require perfect competition, a market structure that is almost nonexistent. (Friedman's notion of economic freedom is basically that economic activity be conducted by the private sector.)

An opposing argument is that capitalism brought about a political system labeled *democratic* but without genuine popular representation because its primary goal is to ensure the protection of commerce and property.[16] Charles Lindblom (1977) casts doubts on the correlation between democracy (polyarchy) and market economies. What democracy and market-oriented economies have in common is their tie to constitutional liberalism, which was designed to give individuals the freedom to profit through trade. Consequently, one would not expect democracy without such markets.[17] Many market economies are not democracies, but all democracies have market-oriented economies. Is it not conceivable, asks Lindblom, that some democracy, no matter how misguided, might want to extend popular control into the economic sphere and displace the market? He points out that this has not generally happened. Therefore, one might question whether modern Western democracies are genuinely democratic. Lindblom does not find this argument by itself sufficiently compelling. However, additional evidence does convince him that present-day democracies are designed to protect business and privilege and that the system of representative government may have been selected because it accommodates the market system not because it is genuinely democratic.

Business has special access to government and enormous influence exerted through both the normal channels of democracy and outside it. Additionally, businessmen have the necessary resources to dominate politics. Therefore, argues Lindblom, business control over government and politics helps explain the consistent adherence of democracy to markets as well as the primacy of the economic over the political domain. In support of this view, he cites the relatively few conflicts between business and government on issues, such as corporate reform, enforcement of antitrust laws, proposals for income redistribution, and planning. Lindblom's conclusion is that modern Western societies, including the United States, do not have a democracy based on genuine popular control. This is not to deny the enormous progress made in terms of government formation; yet in terms of attaining popular control, there is still a long way to go.[18]

A question arising from Lindblom's analysis is what economists call the *free rider problem*. It is expensive to gain control of politics, directly or indirectly. So how is it decided which company or industry pays for what? The railroads in the nineteenth century might have had an incentive to control politics and indoctrinate the public while footing the bill (or getting the taxpayer to do so). Do contemporary industries have a similar incentive for a broad-based control that benefits not just one firm or industry but many? This would seem to require a certain degree of coordination or collusion, but Lindblom rules this out. Instead, he suggests that the process or mechanism of business control over government has already been institutionalized: both established and widely accepted in society. These arrangements are protected by many laws, rules, and policies on matters, such as, elections, lobbying, corporations and managers' rights.

3.2 Free Markets

Although the term *free market* is not particularly controversial, there are disputes over its definition, application, and even origins. Free markets are generally characterized by decentralized and noncoercive economic decision making. Forces of supply and demand rather than government set prices. A key issue is the importance and type of competition necessary for free markets to exist. One argument is that competition is required for a free market and if it does not exist, government intervention is justified. Intervention is considered desirable on grounds of improving resource allocation and falls under the economic category of remedying a market failure. Antitrust laws and consumer information programs are examples of such intervention.[19] However, some laissez-faire proponents see antitrust laws as a violation of the requirement that no element of coercion be involved even if used to prevent anticompetitive practices. They are suspicious that government intervention may have ulterior motives and see the cure, in terms of loss of freedom, as worse than the disease.[20] Their argument is that a free market is consistent with any type of competition, including imperfect competition, as long as no coercion is used to restrict competition. Although competition is not considered essential, mobility of resources is generally accepted as integral to a free market.[21] However, it is debatable how prevalent are noncompetitive markets without barriers to the entry of new resources. The term *competitive free market* is used here. It refers to markets where noncoercion in economic decisions applies not only to government but also to the private sector because interference with the working of a market is as likely to arise from the private sector as from government.

Adam Smith is considered the most influential exponent of free market capitalism. He proposes that if economic decisions are left to individuals pursuing their own self-interest with a minimum of government intervention, this would lead to the best possible outcome for society. Therefore, the coordinating process of free market capitalism is self-interest or greed.[22] The idea is well known, well publicized and has been adopted to the extent that Smith has become a sort of patron saint to laissez-faire advocates.[23]

Yet, receiving far less attention are Smith's views on competition as a counterforce to greed—views that may have been in part anticapitalist or at least contrary to the interests of business classes of his era.[24] Self-interest, he argues, has to be kept in check by competition. Smith's great insight is that greed countered by competition would bring about the goods and services that consumers want and are willing to pay for at prices that provide producers a normal profit.[25] (Although for society to obtain all the benefits of the market requires the checks and balances of perfect competition.[26]) Without competition, the guidance of the invisible hand vanishes.[27] There is also one other dimension to Smith's model, albeit somewhat more abstract and also long forgotten, and that is the necessity of assessing the moral cost to society from sanctioning greed and wealth accumulation.[28]

Smith did not ignore the realities of power and politics inherent in the economic system. He understood that political influence could distort his economic vision. Businesses with political influence would do their utmost to avoid or suppress competition; they would obtain higher prices for their products and, in the process, make a mockery of the free market and preclude its benefits from society.[29] Smith hoped that conscientious politicians with the public good in mind would prevent economic interests from bypassing the market and the beneficial forces of competition.[30] He knew that it is all too easy to sabotage the free market and circumvent its competitive discipline.[31]

Smith's ideas have been strongly embraced, especially in the past three decades. However, as noted above, it is only the government nonintervention part of his idea that is hailed. This is in contrast to the more comprehensive acceptance of Smith's free market principles by an earlier generation of economic liberals (classical). It is debatable whether the current omission is based on genuine ideological belief or whether it represents expediency masquerading as ideology because, coincidentally or not, this view appears to rationalize corporate power in both the economic and political realms. Although it is presented as a free market view, it often results in striking departures from those principles.[32] At times, it embodies a Darwinian "anything goes" interpretation in both the economic and political spheres wherein the acquisition of political influence is considered an unavoidable cost of doing business in conformity with economic freedom. Such positions often parallel the interests of large economic organizations but are not consistent with Adam Smith's views on competition, and economic efficiency. Absolute freedom for giant corporations can disrupt or destroy markets if that is a profitable course of action.[33] Easy access to the political arena facilitates this option and, contrary to economic convention, there is no great wall separating the economic and political domains.

There are laissez-faire proponents who claim sympathy with Adam Smith's views but do not object to subsidies, tax breaks, bailouts, and other forms of government largesse granted to large corporations. Others favor the rule of money in politics, including corporate money. They see little problem with business lobbying or corporate political donations, never mind that these may eventually result in market distortions inefficiencies, and tilt the balance artificially in favor of big business. Laws and rules favoring corporations are not considered incompatible with free market principles. Some, oblivious to government's active role here, interpret them as an efficient outcome of free market operations. Hostility is displayed toward antitrust laws that place restrictions on the conduct of large corporations. The freedom of large economic organizations is favored unfailingly over competition and, consequently, individual economic freedom. "Lesser" objectives such as democracy, fair elections, and consumer welfare do not even merit consideration in this context.

The above ideas may represent a distinct ideological viewpoint but one that, in important respects, is incongruent with Adam Smith's ideas on free markets. The standing of corporations in America is aptly described by Robin Marris's (1970) observation that capitalism, despite the homage to individual liberty, insists on the liberty of the organization. The freedom of corporations comes first and has precedence over the freedom of individuals and markets.

3.3 Acceptance of the System

In the United States, at all socioeconomic levels, there is a firm belief in the economic system, economic growth, materialism, and the emphasis placed on economic success. Capitalism is far more palatable to Americans than to

Europeans because business success is unequivocally admired, and America has enjoyed affluence.[34] Locke's natural rights of man and the search for the good life are widely accepted. The common European derogatory term—*bourgeois*—is rarely used in the United States.[35] At a personal level, the incentive structure of the American economy is attractive to talented people who support the system as do business people relishing the prospect of a "winner take all" reward structure, regardless of their actual earnings.[36]

If today the dominance of large private corporations is taken for granted, in the early nineteenth century there was no public consensus that railroads should be privatized or unregulated. Later on different groups such as farmers and labor voiced their opposition to corporate power and the lack of regulation.[37] Contrary to later claims, public-private cooperation and even government ownership were quite common and accepted in America as was regulation.[38] Charles Perrow (2002) argues that the emergence of large corporations probably clashed with key aspects of American culture. It reflected neither American culture nor democratic politics, a point of view shared by Alfred Chandler (1977).[39] The public had to be indoctrinated with the idea that corporations represented America's finest traits, including free markets, individualism, and democracy. This was accomplished with the skillful use of modern media as well as help from academia.

In the twentieth century, Americans accepted more readily the alliance between big business and government and saw it as an inevitable cost of economic success. The fact that the U.S. population believes in market-oriented economics and the importance of economic growth more so than in any other democracy gives U.S. corporations an advantage over their foreign competitors. The old saying "What is good for GM is good for America" was obviously an exaggeration, but at the same time it was understood that the corporation's special position was essential for America's economic success. There was an implicit socioeconomic contract between Americans and big business: You had a steady job. You earned a decent wage. You did not tell the boss how to run the business. That is not to say that there were no frictions, for example, between business and labor; but the fights that did occur were usually about wages and working conditions, not about ideology. European corporations were disadvantaged in this regard. Several factors played a role here, including the existence in Europe of vestiges of aristocracy, politically oriented labor unions, and numerous political parties, not all of which were enamored with large corporations. To some extent, these factors counterbalanced corporate interests in Europe even though corporate ownership was often more concentrated. In addition, the American focus on individualism and social mobility prevented the formation of a popular working class party and labor unity.[40]

Another reason for the acceptance of the system is the belief that the United States, unlike many other societies, is basically a classless society. The inference drawn is that, in a classless society, there is equality of opportunity and therefore it is up to the individual to make the most of those opportunities. So ingrained is this point of view that those who have the most to gain from social safety net policies can be persuaded at times that such policies are inconsistent with free market ideals and self reliance, and therefore should be rejected.

A different explanation for the acceptance of the system is that America is still influenced by Calvinist values that have transcended religion and become part of America's core beliefs and values.[41] A person attaining great wealth is worthy of admiration. Their success is seen as representing not only hard work, business skills, and risk taking, but also a moral success. In fact, it is seen as a sign of favor from above and serves to legitimize both morally and socially the accumulation of wealth and an economic meritocracy.[42] Failure, writes Edward Luttwak (1999), is associated with divine disfavor, and losers find it hard to maintain their self-esteem. Because losers blame themselves, there is very little room for political candidates to rally the losers and represent their interests. People want to believe that they are part of the system and usually do not resent those who are more successful than they are; to the contrary, they see the winners as a source of inspiration, assuming they did not inherit wealth.[43]

Lindblom (1977), Galbraith (1985), and several other writers see a darker side to the populace's acceptance of the economic system, one that involves indoctrination. People's choices are molded to serve business interests rather than their own. Corporations spend large sums promoting their positions and protecting their privileges. More generally, the appearance of a genuine political debate is often an illusion.[44] Citizens are taught that business influence and control over government are natural parts of democracy as is its privileged position, a view reinforced both by academics and the media—two groups dependent on corporate funding.[45] The special position of business comes to be widely accepted. The public is also led to believe that an attack on the economic system is equivalent to an attack on democracy in that the two are almost identical.[46] Sports and capitalism are linked, and individuals seeking help from government are depicted as no different from athletes seeking to obtain an unfair advantage over their rivals. Lindblom (1977) states that key political-economic issues such as corporate autonomy, distribution of income and wealth, and business's special access to government are considered unsuitable for political or public debate. Therefore, there is little mention of these topics in the media. Public opinion is formed to ensure a favorable disposition toward the economic system, and many voters remain uninformed and at times vote against their economic self-interest.[47] Terms such as *free market capitalism* and *free choice* are used repeatedly in print and on the airwaves and may help mask the undemocratic nature of corporate control. The agrarian ideal of independent yeomen confident in the control they have over their lives is still promoted, despite the fact that the United States is no longer an agrarian society. The economic freedom of the farmer is then equated with the autonomy of the corporation.[48]

Galbraith (1985) describes how the issue of power in the economy and society is either dismissed or ignored. The ruse devised is to claim that power is subdued by the impersonal forces of the free market and guided to socially desirable outcomes. Therefore, it is not an issue. Economics, argues Galbraith, teaches the benefits of existing social arrangements, oblivious or hostile, to issues of power in the economy and politics. Economics neglects the part played by large corporations in molding social priorities and attitudes. Particularly clever, he argues, is the way corporations have come to impress on the public that their objectives regarding production, consumption, technology, and growth are identical to those of society at large and represent human and social progress. The public has come to accept corporate control in various areas without realizing that these are not isolated instances atypical of the system—they are the system. Notwithstanding the praise heaped on the idea of individualism, Galbraith sees this as a cover for protecting organizations, not individuals, because "it is not the buyer's right to buy that is protected but the seller's right to sell."[49]

A final explanation for acceptance of the system is the "bonanza" or "casino" factor. There is a common belief that in America, with good luck, one can become a multimillionaire. Hard work and business acumen are one way to accomplish this. Yet what stir the imagination are real or mythical stories about people becoming wealthy beyond their dreams almost overnight. Now one may dismiss this as harmless daydreaming, but the belief is strong, it is centuries old, and it is not restricted to the United States. In many parts of the world, it is believed that there is a better chance of becoming rich in the United States than elsewhere. Regardless whether there is evidence to substantiate this belief, it does give people hope and attracts immigrants from all corners of the world in search of their own El Dorado. It also generates support for a system that grants people this type of opportunity.

The above belief became interwoven with one of the most important and enduring symbols in American history—the myth of the frontier. The frontier represents the formative experience and the molding of the American national identity. Progress in the United States came to be identified with a westward expansion of territory and migration. Richard Slotkin (1992) notes that different forms of regeneration—spiritual, democratic, national, and even one's personal fortune—were associated with the frontier at different times in American history. Political movements such as the Populists and Progressives could find an affinity between their objectives and the myth of the frontier despite their conflicting economic and political goals.[50] Both movements saw a danger to the nation from the "closing of the frontier."

Frederick Jackson Turner's original argument had been that the success and growth of the American economy could be attributed to the extension of the frontier and the resultant gains in land and resources.[51] However, in later years, new sources for bonanza were found. There was, of course, the California gold rush of 1849, and what was characteristic of that and future bonanzas, according to Slotkin, was the opportunity for quick riches with minimal investment or effort. The nineteenth century industrialization was a bonanza of sorts, especially when combined with market power. It may also have been the precursor to future bonanzas in terms of its beneficiaries.[52] In the 1980s, there was a bonanza in financial capital.[53] A notable example was the Savings and Loans Bill, which was expected to energize the banking industry as well as real estate. Instead, it ended up costing taxpayers more than 150 billion dollars to bail out savings and loans institutions. For some, this turned out to be a bonanza based on socializing risk and privatizing gain. In the first decade of the new millennium "flipping" houses also had the trademark of a classic bonanza—little effort and quick and high returns—at least for a while. A related bonanza with huge costs to taxpayers was the high, and largely unregulated, leveraging undertaken by financial institutions. Combined with the selling of subprime mortgages, it resulted in the costliest bailout in American history with a massive redistribution of wealth from the public to financial corporations and their creditors.

3.4 The Laissez-Faire Revival

In the past 30 years under the guise of values, efficiency, and, above all, economic freedom, there has been a laissez-faire revival. It has resulted in tax cuts for the rich and organized, deregulation of financial institutions, strengthening of corporations, successful attacks on social policies, and, by and large, a turn away from the philosophy of the New Deal.

The Great Depression, with its devastating effect on the nation's economy and psyche, changed attitudes about laissez-faire, market solutions, and social Darwinism. The threat to individual freedom from business power was taken seriously, and some claimed that government could play the role of protector.[54] New laws, policies, and institutions were introduced and would prevail for the next 40 years. In the 1970s, the charge that Keynesian economic policies had been unsuccessful in dealing with stagflation reopened the door to laissez-faire. The 1980s and 1990s witnessed a forceful advocacy of laissez-faire ideas through networks of foundations, think tanks, societies, journals, and university chairs.[55] The studies produced praised economic elites, corporate takeovers, the right to use one's money as one sees fit, including for political donations, and, generally, laissez-faire policies. The campaign's purpose was to counter the influence of the New Deal and government intervention in the economy as well as undo a perceived liberal (modern) bias. It succeeded in bringing about an intellectual climate more favorable to wealth and corporations, while reducing government help to the poor. Government social and economic regulatory policies were retrenched and taxes, primarily for high-income earners, reduced. Individuals and communities were left unprotected from the threat of calamitous economic changes.[56] Kevin Phillips (2002) points to the fact that laissez-faire was a myth in both the Gilded Age and the 1980s. Its advocates in the 1980s did not hesitate to use the power of government to promote their economic objectives. The laissez-faire revival was helped by the stock market boom of the 1980s and especially the 1990s and the growing economy. It became easier to convince the public that markets and democracy were identical and that the acts of buying and selling were akin to voting in a democracy.[57] Markets, so went the argument, were the essence of democracy and reflected the people's will more so than corrupt politics that required compromise and hence limited one's choices. Thomas Frank (2000), who named this movement "market populism," notes its contradictions, especially the claim that it brought about economic fairness because its purpose was to do the opposite: to maintain or increase income and wealth inequality. Voters' anger and frustration, as noted above, were channeled to cultural issues and then used to achieve economic policies favorable to corporations and wealth.[58] A rhetorical trick that made the new laissez-faire palatable was the denial that economic factors played a role in social class.[59] Economic differences, corporate ownership, and corporate power had to be denied or ignored.[60]

Major economic changes such as globalization, deregulation, and privatization were helped by the laissez-faire movement.[61] Privatization and deregulation, and ultimately the shrinking of government, were seen as crucial for improved economic efficiency. It was argued that government social programs had mostly failed and had created a culture of dependency[62] America also had to improve its competitiveness to succeed in the global marketplace. In the late 1980s, U.S. economic prospects looked dim, especially in comparison with the success of Japan. Reducing taxes, chiefly marginal tax rates, would increase work effort and result in an expanding economy. Government should not shelter people from risk. People had to learn to adapt to changes that would probably increase in frequency throughout their lifetime. Government help was not only inefficient and badly executed, it also was morally wrong: "give a man a fish and you feed him for a day; teach a man to fish and you feed him for a lifetime." The United States was founded on the idea of free enterprise, initiative, and risk taking, not on building a social safety net and incentive-reducing pampering. Proponents of these arguments pointed to West European unemployment rates as evidence of the detrimental effects of overly generous unemployment compensation. The new laissez-faire targeted individuals for reduced government assistance, although similar reductions were rarely aimed at corporations. On the contrary, taxes paid by corporations as a percentage of total taxes declined while corporate subsidies increased. Hence, critics questioned the genuineness of the new laissez-faire.

Ideas based on mid-twentieth-century concerns about the threat of totalitarianism were adopted and repackaged in the service of corporate control. Corporations' freedom to profit was placed above all else. Galbraith (1985) argues that laissez-faire proponents, while claiming to shield entrepreneurs from the state, were ignoring the ever-closer alliance between corporations and government and its implication for freedom. A pattern emerged whereby conservatives denounced government in public while seeking its support in private.[63]

Advocates of laissez-faire, in the name of freedom, seek to weaken government's powers. Yet a weaker government is more easily manipulated by large corporations, and the economic and political power of large corporations is no less dangerous than the power held by big government. Why then the preference (de facto) for corporate rule? After all, government is at least elected. The standard retort is that corporations originate within and embody the free market. Yet a strong case can be made that not only did large corporations emerge as a result of various forms of government help, mostly antithetical to a free market, but also in many cases, these organizations can destroy free markets. William Roy (1997) writes that the late-nineteenth-century pools and cartels were established to shield their participants from the workings of an anarchic market. When these agreements failed to achieve the desired stability, mergers to create giant corporations (holding companies) seemed a preferable alternative to the free market.[64] The idea that government is needed to sustain, if not create, free markets is denied by some because it supposedly taints the market concept. In the laissez-faire scheme of things, corporations play a neutral or passive role—intermediaries between owners (stockholders) and resources other than the stockholders' capital.[65] Notwithstanding declarations of love for free markets, it is often the status quo that is being protected, specifically the unique status of powerful corporations, not the freedom of markets.

The elephant in the room is invisible to some; a singular focus on government's power blinds them to similar dangers arising from large private organizations. One wonders how economic freedom that benefits primarily the managers of large corporations (and to a much lesser extent their shareholders) can be the epitome of economic freedom let alone freedom.

In conclusion, Americans have adopted with few reservations the economic ideology of corporate capitalism. The system is seen as offering most, if not all, citizens an opportunity to compete and seek their fortune. The dangers to political freedom from economic power are minimized or ignored as is its market-distorting political influence. Individual freedom to profit is respected in the abstract, yet the prevailing but unheralded principle is corporations' freedom to profit. This freedom is paramount and overrides all other principles and ideals.

CHAPTER 4

The Economy

4.1 The Economic System

The United States is seen as the standard-bearer of laissez-faire economics, a capitalist society where the profit motive is given free rein and the pursuit of economic success is the top priority. A confluence of philosophies, such as Adam Smith's invisible hand, John Locke's emphasis on private property, and Thomas Jefferson's view of a limited government, serve as the intellectual underpinning. U.S. governments generally refrain from substituting bureaucratic decision making[1] for that of the market and eschew picking the industries of the future. It is accepted that government has no special insights in this matter, and efficiency dictates that markets determine the allocation of resources. The price mechanism, more so than in most nations and ignoring issues of corporate administrative coordination, guides the workings of the economy.

The American view is that crony capitalism lacking the discipline of the market is doomed to failure. Arm's-length dealing is seen as a critical component of successful capitalism; contacts and long-standing personal relationships should not be used as a substitute for impersonal market forces. The success of the U.S. economy during the 1990s convinced many that the United States was on the right path because it adhered sufficiently to that discipline. Galbraith's (1985) argument warning that there was an economic system consisting of several hundred miniplanned corporate economies behind the free market façade has been dismissed, and corporations' influence over government is generally ignored.

Although the U.S. economy is associated with free markets and risk-taking entrepreneurs, it is more accurately defined by its dominant economic organizations—large corporations—whose imprint on the economy and society is unmistakable. They employ millions of workers and are seen as desirable employers offering better wages and promotion opportunities. These hierarchical firms benefit from many laws and regulations designed to protect them. Galbraith (1985) argues that macroeconomic policy is undertaken to ensure a steady demand for their products. Their economic power allows them to extend their control to government and the political process. Despite their large market shares and influence augmenting size, the orthodoxy is that they are an integral part of a free market system.

4.2 An Overview of the Economy

The U.S. economy is the largest in the world with its 2007 GDP exceeding $13 trillion and its GDP per capita of $46,000 larger than that of most other nations.[2] Of course, the mean income does not necessarily convey the typical family's income, and per capita GDP is not synonymous with happiness. Nonetheless, the U.S. economy until 2008 had performed well for 25 years and, ignoring the 1930s, for most of the twentieth century. It has been regarded as a model of efficiency and admired for its dynamism and flexibility. Resources generally flow to where they can obtain the highest return, and unprofitable lines of business are discarded and their resources freed to move to more remunerative pursuits. It is relatively easy to set up businesses in all states. Importantly, not only is change tolerated, but it is also encouraged; innovators and entrepreneurs are held in high esteem. The United States is admired for the fast growth of high-tech companies such as Intel, Microsoft, and Google and the skillful use of information technology by Federal Express, Amazon, and eBay.[3] The rapid rise of those companies and their contributions to the economy represent advantages of economic freedom.

The United States has an impressive infrastructure designed to facilitate commerce. It consists of a fine national highway system, numerous airports, a reliable telephone network, and a mostly reliable electricity supply. It is also endowed with many natural resources. The percentage of arable land is relatively high, more than double that of Russia and quadruple that of Canada.[4] While at the beginning of the twentieth century it required one-third of the nation to provide food for the populace, today the share of Americans on the farm has dwindled to less than 3 percent. America produces and exports grains and large amounts of cotton, meat, and dairy products. Needless to say, U.S. supermarkets are well stocked with food. During the second half of the twentieth century, the economy shifted from manufacturing to a predominantly service economy. With this change and other factors, unionized workers as a percentage of the civilian labor force declined from 31.6 percent in 1950 to 11.5 percent in 2000.[5] Over the past 30 years, the U.S. economy has become more integrated into the world economy. Imports and exports have risen not only in absolute terms but also as a percentage of the GDP with imports usually exceeding exports.

4.3 Government Policies

Government has been molded to fulfill certain economic objectives, including safeguarding the common market aspects of the United States. A solid infrastructure is accompanied by a suitable legal infrastructure. The government provides subsidies, inducements, and tax concessions to businesses notwithstanding the belief in laissez-faire. The government is an important customer for many businesses and does its best to assist American firms overseas, including the opening of new markets to U.S. products. It provides substantial grants for basic research that serves as a foundation for commercial research. The evidence, for the most part, suggests that U.S. governments have fairly consistently subscribed to Calvin Coolidge's assertion that "the chief business of American people is business."

Following World War II, U.S. policy makers applied Keynesian policies based on management of aggregate demand to combat recessions and inflation. The fact that during those years the United States did not experience a recurrence of a thirties-type depression boosted the confidence of economists in such policies. Yet, to some, Keynesian economics is associated with redistribution policies, while to others its adoption has more to do with economic growth becoming the secular religion of the United States[6] and therefore too important to be left to the vagaries of the market.[7] Government management of aggregate demand is in the interest of mass consumption and its largest producers as well as politicians for whom economic prosperity facilitates reelection. However, Keynesian economics could not handle the stagflation of the 1970s, that is, the simultaneous occurrence of unemployment and inflation, with a resulting loss of faith in its ability to cure all economic ills. Although several alternative theories have been proposed, none has been widely accepted yet as a replacement for Keynesian economics.

Until very recently, in terms of economic policy, emphasis has shifted from fiscal to monetary policy conducted by the Federal Reserve Bank. With increasing rates of economic growth and the almost continuous rise in the stock market in the late 1990s, the Federal Reserve acquired an aura of infallibility. However, a series of events in the New Millennium, beginning with interest rate increases in 2000 and their aftermath, raised questions about the limits of current knowledge in controlling the economy. The Federal

Reserve persisted in downplaying the threat to the national economy from a housing bubble. It refused to intervene in the mortgage market despite highly questionable lending practices that eventually resulted in a severe decline in the housing market and the near collapse of the financial system. No less consequential was the Federal Reserve's fight to prevent regulation of derivatives by the Commodities Futures Trading Commission. "Markets know best" was the justification, although it happened to coincide with the interests of large financial entities.

Starting in the late 1970s, America entered a deregulatory phase. Industries that had been sheltered from vigorous competition, cost-saving efficiencies, and the need to innovate would encounter the discipline of the market proper—asserted proponents of deregulation. The regulated industries, for example, airlines and phone companies, had always been an anomaly marring the free market image. Although regulation had its defenders and sometimes even economic justification, many economists welcomed the advent of deregulation. There was the anticipation of new cost efficiencies that would culminate in boosting the GDP and living standards. The fact that the profit motive, in a broader sense than just cost cutting, had led to deregulation,[8] just as it had earlier brought about regulation, was sometimes ignored. Economic efficiency (and a rather narrow definition at that) was deemed a sufficient reason for deregulation; The turn to deregulation was alleged to be in line with markets and away from a managed economy.

Deregulation affected banking, brokerages, and insurance companies. Derivatives and hedge funds remained unregulated, and in the process, a shadow banking system in the trillions of dollars was created. The cautious but unfashionable few who proposed oversight were chided for their ignorance. After all, laissez-faire would enlarge the pie and enrich all. Few outside Wall Street realized that what was being legalized was highly leveraged gambling. Yet those who made profits got to keep them, and later, during the financial debacle, some of the losers were considered "too big to fail" and were rescued with taxpayer dollars. The collapse of the subprime mortgage and the derivatives markets resulted in a sharp and noticeable turn from the stated policy of non-intervention and freedom of markets. The justification offered was that it was done to prevent systemic financial collapse; however, it also resulted in the protection of assets of the powerful, the organized, and the wealthy.

Government collects a variety of taxes, including income, social security, and state and local taxes (primarily in the form of property taxes). A major economic choice confronting society is how the provision of goods and services should be divided between the public and private sectors or how much of their income people should hand over to the government for public services. In the United States, roughly 33 percent of GDP goes to government. The citizens of Sweden and Denmark, for example, have opted for considerably higher levels of public services and more of a social safety net. Approximately 50 percent of their GDP goes for public spending which, of course, means a much smaller amount is left for personal spending. Antipathy to taxes is universal and centuries old, and in the United States, it has been integrated into the culture. Understandably, there is great interest in how taxes are set and changed but, as Galbraith (1985) emphasizes, it is just as important for people to understand how their incomes are determined and how the prices they pay for goods and services are established. Yet the level of interest in those decisions rarely matches the attention paid to taxes.

The U.S. income tax system is progressive, or graduated, meaning that high-income earners have to pay a larger share of their earnings, both percentage-wise and in absolute dollar amounts.. However, numerous legal loopholes undo some of the redistribution goals of the income tax structure. For example, the top 400 income earners in 2000, whose average earned income exceeded $100 million, paid an average rate of 22.6 percent in federal income tax, equal to what a family of four pays on an annual income of $226,000.[9] Under both Presidents Reagan and George W. Bush, taxes were reduced for top earners and corporations, followed by demands for cuts in social benefits for the poor and middle class to make up for the shortfall.[10] The tax cuts, argues Paul Krugman (2003), were designed to bring about a fiscal crisis and a reduction in the social safety net and were accompanied by complaints about the excessive tax burden imposed on U.S. taxpayers. The tax cuts reduced substantially the marginal tax rate of top earners, the effective tax rate of corporate profits, the tax on dividend income, and the inheritance tax. Although they benefit primarily wealthy Americans, they were publicized as middle-class tax cuts.[11] In 1950, corporations paid 26.5 percent of the total U.S. federal tax burden; by 1990, they only paid 9.1 percent.[12] Similarly, in 1957, corporations paid 45 percent of local property tax revenues; by 1987, their contribution amounted to 16 percent.[13]

Throughout most of the twentieth century, arguments favoring tax cuts were presented in terms of choosing either greater efficiency or more fairness. In the past two decades, some hypotheses have been proposed that dispute the inevitable trade-off. (One argument is that inequality might be detrimental to growth[14] and another is that when capital markets are imperfect, there is no trade-off.[15]) America's best growth in a generation took place after the Clinton administration raised taxes.[16] There is also little evidence to support the trickle-down economic argument that higher tax rates on the rich would reduce economic growth significantly.[17]

Value-added or consumption taxes are popular among economists because they would encourage more saving. However, they would also require large structural changes in the tax system and its accompanying industry. Politicians fearing that a new tax system may not function smoothly and vested interests opposed to the change have prevented adoption of these taxes. The sanctity of consumption plays a role in the rejection of alternative tax systems.

4.4 Consumption

For American manufacturers to adopt mass-production techniques, mass consumption had to be created. A nation without either an entrenched culture or an aristocracy as an arbiter of taste was more receptive to mass-produced goods and to the enticements of its sellers. The freedom to pursue happiness was given a rather materialistic interpretation, and consumption was promoted as a vital component of happiness. The consumption habit is catching on in other countries, suggesting that there may be something in the human psyche that lends itself to such behavior and people can be persuaded to seek comfort in consumption. For large segments of the population, excess cash over the amount necessary for subsistence is a relatively new phenomenon in human history. The channels to which excess cash are diverted are astonishing, and more puzzling is the eagerness to use debt to satisfy this desire. So pervasive is the shopping culture in the United States that one might describe it as practiced with the fervor of a patriotic duty. The difference between what is a necessity and what is a luxury has been blurred. There have been lengthy debates on whether consumer sovereignty is an illusion and whether consumers are manipulated into believing that what they purchase is what they genuinely desire.

The wish to spend, as noted above, is substantially more powerful than the desire to save, despite the educational efforts of mutual funds. There is little hesitancy in paying high monthly fees on credit cards to maintain a standard of living that would be impossible otherwise. This often means borrowing money to pay for luxuries. The wish to keep up with the Joneses or with the standard of living portrayed on television is powerful indeed. The negative implications of competitive consumption, analogous to the arms race, have been noted.[18] There is, however, little public or political pressure to change things by curtailing consumer purchases. Far too many economic interests have a stake in current consumption patterns. Hence, government is also careful to minimize regulation of products. The justification offered is the principle of noninterference with consumer sovereignty. It is also claimed that any abrupt change could bring about shocks to the economy. Robert Frank (1999) points to our preference for conspicuous consumption, such as large homes, and luxury cars over inconspicuous consumption, such as clean air and water, uncongested traffic, time with friends and family, and public transportation. Frank claims that this has to do with the importance of relative standing in our society despite our focus on absolute rewards. When individual satisfaction is contingent on other people's spending habits, as in fact it is, Adam Smith's selfishness principle does not necessarily provide society with the optimal mix of goods and services. The extra income spent does not give people enduring increases in satisfaction, whereas spending on inconspicuous goods would have that effect.[19] However, notes Frank, people will not withdraw unilaterally from the conspicuous consumption race because that would affect their relative standing in society.

The ingenuity used to part American consumers from both surplus and essential cash is amazing. No stone is left unturned. Every trick, gimmick, and psychological ploy is used with little hesitation. The citizen as a consumer is considered fair game, and the difference between legal and illegal means is a rather gray area. Advertising and other forms of marketing are used extensively. The amount spent annually on advertising is about a quarter of a trillion dollars.[20] Advertising is the primary source of revenue for key segments of the media, and it would be difficult to argue that this relationship does not lead to media caution in reporting on its customers and their products. The deceptiveness of advertising also influences life and attitudes in the United States[21] and leads to a nation inured to hyperbole and trickery.

The Latin phrase *caveat emptor*—let the buyer beware—holds true here as anywhere else when buying products or services. Phony stock deals, questionable currency deals, fake auto repairs, and real estate swindles have become a staple of American folklore. Supposedly reputable phone companies were not above "slamming," which means that, without your permission, they provide you with phone service and bill you. Rental companies do not feel obligated to keep for you the promised car, and airlines can overbook and bump you, subject to some compensation. Is there no legal protection for consumers? There is some; however, it is not pervasive or strong, and even where it exists, insufficient resources are provided for enforcement. In many states, consumers are left unprotected from misleading insurance contracts, difficult to understand credit terms, and usurious loans because the perpetrators see to it that the government, in the name of free markets and individual economic freedoms, does not intervene. The justification offered is that nobody should have to protect you from your own foolishness. Additionally, according to the laissez-faire argument, reputable companies will lose business if they engage in deceptive practices; therefore, they will not do so. In short, the public is assured that unfettered markets will work to the consumer's advantage. Consumers on their part must act prudently and rationally; otherwise, all bets are off. Yet this is an incomplete picture, in part because it ignores the imbalance in resources and power between consumers who may seek redress and the offending companies and because of the utilization of government to protect dishonest and economically inefficient practices. A confusing mix of state and federal jurisdictions is skillfully applied by companies to evade legal responsibility. Paul Blumberg (1989) points to numerous acts of everyday deception, such as in buying, financing, and repairing a car, that the public has come to accept as inevitable. In the late 1980s, about one-third of the $65 billion spent annually by Americans on auto repairs was unnecessary, according to government estimates.[22] The freedom to profit through deceit is facilitated by consumers' lack of information.[23]

4.5 *Saving and Productivity*

Saving is important for both individuals and nations. Social Security is considered inadequate for funding retirees' needs, and hence a supplementary source of income is necessary. For economic investment the nation requires capital, usually from domestic saving. If this source is unavailable, the money has to come from overseas, otherwise investment declines. Yet there are no policies to encourage saving to increase productive capacity and ultimately standards of living. In the United States, there is a strong bias in favor of consumption as reflected in the tax code, laws, and subsidies. Even more to the point, consumption has become embedded in the culture with significant help from the media.

American personal savings rates have fallen sharply over the past 20 years. In 2005 they became negative for the first time since the Great Depression.[24] When one looks at net national saving, which also includes business and government saving, the picture does not improve much. Despite claims that comparative cross-country personal savings rates understate Americans' saving rate and acknowledging deficiencies in measurement, the basic conclusion remains unchanged. On a comparative basis, the prevailing attitude is that an unspent dollar is a missed opportunity. Even the formerly popular notion of saving for a rainy day is basically rejected as implying a defeatist or a pessimistic outlook on life. One interpretation is that Americans are discounting the future heavily. Yet this is puzzling in that the "eat, drink, and be merry because tomorrow we die" philosophy does not accord with the social or historical dogmas of the nation. So to what does one attribute this behavior? It could be a universal trait common to nations reaching a certain level of affluence. However, Madison Avenue exhorting people to spend bears some responsibility . Economic freedom, especially of mass producers, gave rise to radical social and cultural changes wherein the relative importance of saving and consumption was reversed. Little attention was paid to the fact that the changes also brought about more indebtedness and lessened individual economic independence.

U.S. productivity declined from the 1970s to the mid-1990s as investment in capital equipment slowed down while growth in hours worked accelerated.[25] America, argues Lester Thurow (1999), did not buy the tools necessary to improve productivity, and slower rates of growth in the capital to labor ratio inevitably led to slower growth in productivity. In addition, while in the 1950s and 1960s the median years of education per worker increased by 1.1 percent per year, in the 1990s, the rate of growth was only 0.5 percent per year.[26] Statistical data indicate that part of the decline lies in weak productivity growth in the service sector, although there was some improvement after 2000.[27] A disturbing phenomenon was that the component of productivity attributable to technology—an important contributor to U.S. productivity in the 1960s—almost disappeared. This is surprising given the explosion of innovations in information and communication technology. The higher rate of growth of U.S. output after 1995 is due primarily to capital inputs, particularly information technology (IT) investment.[28]

4.6 *Finance and Real Estate*

Relatively open capital markets, despite a patchwork of state and federal regulations, have been considered a contributory factor in the economic growth of the U.S. economy. Well-developed stock and bond markets have seen innovations extending their scope and ability to raise money for both new ventures and existing businesses. There are also some less desirable aspects, such as the fascination with the daily movements of the stock market and certain speculative activities based on easy credit and high leveraging. Several financial regulatory agencies exist, but they often act as facilitators for their charges rather than protectors of the public. The Federal Reserve's seemingly strenuous efforts in 2007 and 2008 to prop up the stock market and its massive intervention to rescue financial institutions of all ilk call into question some of the assertions about the efficiency of unchecked capital markets. The socialization of risk for large banks as well as investment and mortgage companies is clearly at odds with a free market philosophy. In fact, it raises questions if markets can ever be entirely free of government.[29] It has become apparent that a very thin line, if any at all, separates financial markets from government and politics.

Credit is a key lubricant of the economy, and here America has had an important advantage over economies with less-developed financial sectors. Credit is also a way of life in the United States.[30] There is the convenience of a credit card as a substitute for cash, although this is becoming prevalent elsewhere. Americans buy houses, cars, vacations, furniture, appliances, and jewelry on credit; similarly they finance operations and weddings. It is usually easy to obtain credit in the United States. It allows people to attain higher levels of consumption more quickly than they would otherwise. There is no need to save. If the consumer has a job, then the seller will give them the car or the house. They may have to pay usurious rates on the loan, but there is no need to delay gratification. Of course, how one repays the credit card companies is another issue. In 2004, 1.6 million Americans filed for bankruptcy. In 2005, bankruptcy laws were changed at the request of creditors who were of the opinion that bankruptcy was being used as a way to wipe out debt. Critics question the easily availability of credit and contend that it results in millions buying products and services that they cannot afford while promoting a consumer culture at the expense of saving.

For most of the first decade of the New Millennium, the United States experienced a thriving real estate market that employed more than a million people. The preference for all things new including houses, the high rate of labor mobility, and the availability of credit help boost this market as does the popular law that allows mortgage interest to be deducted from income tax. Some of that money might have been better invested in capital equipment to boost the nation's long-term prosperity. Quasigovernmental institutions provide mortgages for those who cannot obtain them elsewhere, and home ownership is promoted enthusiastically, including turning a blind eye to dubious financing schemes. A housing bubble, aided by an intentional policy of low interest rates, "Alice in Wonderland" lending policies, and the securitization of mortgages including subprime, began to burst in 2007. Many mortgage banks and construction companies shut down. The Federal Reserve throughout the second half of 2007 and in 2008 undertook a series of measures to avert collapse of financial markets by increasing liquidity. This included the bailout of an investment firm's creditors as well as the issuers of credit insurance. The administration demanded and received Congressional authorization to bail out the mortgage giants Fannie Mae and Freddie Mac. Later on, a U.S. Treasury plan to provide financial institutions with 0.7 trillion dollars was passed by Congress with few checks and regulations. The laissez-faire ideology got lost in the panic. Principles were jettisoned in the rush to protect the economy or the status quo. Financial organizations' freedom to fail was severely restricted as were the workings of the market. The economy started to slow down, the unemployment rate began to rise, and the government's budget moved further into deficit.

4.7 Health Care

Unlike many advanced industrialized nations, the United States does not have a national health-care system (although there are currently attempts to move the nation in that direction). Health services are produced and bought in a predominantly market-oriented system. Employers, mostly, purchase health insurance for their employees, although the latter's share of the cost has been rising. The U.S. government provides health insurance for the elderly (Medicare) and the poor (Medicaid). The health system is said to reflect a combination of diverse interests that include those of the elderly, the poor, the sick, private nonprofit and for profit insurance companies, the federal government, large employers, physicians, hospitals, and drug companies. In 2003, health-care expenditures amounted to $5670 per person or a total sum of $1.68 trillion. The latter sum equaled 15.3 percent of the GDP.[31] By comparison, in 1960, health expenditures amounted to only 5.1 percent of GDP. In most other advanced industrialized democracies, medical expenditures as a share of GDP have also risen but not as fast. Also noteworthy is the fact that in 2008, approximately 45 million Americans had no health insurance. One can find in the United States highly advanced treatment for some diseases and state-of-the-art medical technology, but the United States does not fare well in terms of population health-care indicators[32] despite the large expenditures. U.S. economists and health experts are of the opinion that the market fails to deliver satisfactory health services. Two major problems are present here. The first is an economic problem; the health-care industry suffers from market failures. For example, consumers lack knowledge and are unable to determine, for the most part, whether a medical procedure is necessary. A second problem is a social or moral issue, and it is more striking than in other sectors of the economy. The issue is whether medical care should be provided to those who cannot pay.

4.8 Manufacturing

Despite the decline in the relative importance of manufacturing, the United States is still a major producer of many products. In industries, such as, aerospace, electronics, food processing, petroleum, autos, and chemicals. America has some of the world's largest and best-known corporations, such as General Electric, IBM, Microsoft, Coca Cola, and Exxon-Mobil.[33] The United States exports electrical and electronic equipment as well as various types of transportation equipment. Interestingly, it also imports large amounts of the same type of goods.

Two major industries, auto and steel, have suffered substantial inroads from foreign competitors over the past 30 years. Employment has declined by hundreds of thousands of workers in each industry. Those jobs were among the highest paid jobs in manufacturing and afforded their holders a comfortable middle-class life. Needless to say, as a result of the job losses, the region where these industries are primarily located, which includes parts of Michigan, Ohio, and Western Pennsylvania, has been hurt economically and socially.[34]

The fortunes of the American economy appeared for many years to be tied to the auto industry. Inventiveness in auto production in the first decade of the twentieth century was followed by Ford's mass-production techniques in the 1910s that led to increasingly cheaper versions of the Model T. The labor battles of the 1930s, the postwar World War II boom in sales, and General Motor's success were all hallmarks of American business history. The introduction of planned obsolescence changed consumption patterns. The reduced number of firms, the competition from Japan followed by downsizing and globalization, as well as ad hoc government protection symbolized the decline of the industrial Midwest and U.S. manufacturing.

More generally, many industrial firms have had to switch to more specialized, knowledge-intensive production while labor-intensive operations were shipped overseas, further reducing the number of industrial workers.[35] The U.S. government aided in this process with special laws and subsidies.[36] American corporations tried conglomeration and diversification and then sought a solution in global production.[37] Auto companies hoped that global cars would reduce their production costs, particularly labor costs, while satisfying developing nations' demand for domestic production. However, the inventory and quality control costs of a global car proved prohibitive.[38] To further cut costs, U.S. corporations adopted inventory control and procurement methods that placed pressure on their domestic suppliers.[39] More independent small businesses essentially became subsidiaries of large corporations, used at times to evade regulations protecting workers.[40]

In the 1990s, there came sweeping changes in organization and structure due in part to computerization and new pressures to meet financial expectations. Some changes were attributed to the adoption of flexible manufacturing systems and a shift away from mass production.[41] Layers of middle management were dismissed. For those who remained, whether in management or on the shop floor, loyalty and trust often went by the wayside.[42]

Corporate employees came to dread the next wave of reorganization whether it was from downsizing, merger, or outsourcing. The nature of work and its importance to one's sense of worth changed; it became much harder to associate one's identity with a workplace.[43] For those laid off, the chances of finding equally remunerative work were slim. All too often, the alternative to unemployment was a service sector job paying slightly above the minimum wage and without health insurance or other benefits.

4.9 Economic Waste

The amount of waste generated by American society used to surprise overseas visitors. Some examples include the planned obsolescence of automobiles, the discarding of appliances, and the many new gadgets that prove to be commercially unsuccessful. The rapid exit of many new firms after having proven to be uncompetitive also involves waste. There is the demolition of sound buildings to make room for new and presumably more profitable businesses. A different but more serious waste is the unsentimental discarding of workers during economic downturns or reorganizations.

For better or worse, most of the above examples, including the freedom to lay off workers, are seen as signs of an innovative and flexible market system. It is claimed that the freedom to lay off workers quickly with little, if any, advance notice contributes to a low national unemployment rate. In comparison with other nations, such as France, U.S. employers are not afraid to hire workers knowing they can easily be dismissed should the need arise. However, sometimes the human and social costs may exceed the private gains. Economists are learning that calculating properly the cost of unemployment is not as simple as once thought, especially when there are psychological costs, irreparable damage to families, and an impact on communities.

Some of America's most capable people—its top labor resources—are attracted to the legal profession, investment banking, and, in the late 1990s, dot-com businesses. Freedom of choice is evident in the response to signals about financial rewards. Yet while the private gain is being maximized, society may have been better off if the investment banker had chosen to be a teacher or an engineer instead. The teacher or engineer's salary may not fully reflect his or her benefit to society. Price signals coming from markets where the top people earn extremely large sums may result in too many entrants with unrealistic expectations and too few entrants into more traditional labor markets, thus leading to a possible reduction in national welfare.[44]

Unrestricted economic freedom has led to large amounts being spent on legal fees, both in absolute terms and as a percentage of the GDP. Similarly, a growing percentage of the GDP is devoted to health care, more so than in many other industrialized nations. Yet the care provided is hardly a model of efficiency, quality, or availability. The greater U.S. labor mobility is seen as representing economic efficiency, but it also entails the expense of frequent moves to new locations. Large amounts are spent to fight and protect against crime, in addition to the cost and damage of crime itself.[45] Numerous deceptive commercial schemes, legal and illegal, are devised, often based on asymmetry of information between seller and buyer. They result in a waste of resources and are excused as an unavoidable cost of economic freedom. A tolerance of business failures, as noted before, not only encourages risk taking but also leads to a waste of resources. The merger wave ongoing for more than two decades has created turmoil in the lives of many employees and their families. Yet despite claims of cost-cutting benefits or other economic efficiencies, the net benefits may be scant. The reason for amalgamation is often the financial benefits to top corporate officers and the merger specialists involved. Once again a discrepancy may arise between societal and private benefits.

In conclusion, the American economy, characterized by large corporations, has experienced considerable success. It is noted for its flexibility, dynamism, and above all, the free rein given to the pursuit of profits. The acceptance of change and the introduction of new products and processes as well as the respect for business and entrepreneurs play a role in that success. However, economic success is also due to the primacy given to economic matters, including the willingness to uproot one's family, have both spouses work, and endure longer work hours with less protections and benefits than in most advanced industrialized nations. In the past two decades, downsizing, restructuring, outsourcing, and globalization have brought anxiety, instability, and dissatisfaction to employees at nearly all levels. Easy credit, intensive advertising, laws, and subsidies that give preference to consumption all help promote a consumption culture and individual indebtedness. The financial events of 2008 suggest that the cost of unrestricted economic freedom has been underestimated and that the free market is somewhat of an illusion.

CHAPTER 5

The Secondary Economy

The previous chapter surveyed key features of the U.S. economy. In the following chapters, the focus will be on large corporations. In this chapter, attention is drawn to the effects of economic freedom on lesser players in the economy. Specifically, two groups are examined, one each on the production and consumption sides. What these seemingly unrelated groups have in common is that they are both positioned on the lowest rung of the ladder in their particular sector. On the production side are small firms, particularly entrepreneurs, who epitomize the opportunities and benefits of economic freedom available to *individuals*. Entrepreneurs are an integral part of business folklore—prime examples of the quest for the American dream. In addition they are of interest because often they operate in a competitive environment resembling a free market, more so than their large counterparts. The secondary tier on the consumption side has received far less attention. Here the focus is on individual consumers who are particularly disadvantaged and therefore labeled secondary consumers. Secondary consumer status is also an outcome of economic freedom except that the freedom in question turns out to be not so much that of consumers' freedom to purchase but firms' freedom to profit. The findings suggest that entrepreneurial endeavors accord with the idea of individual economic freedom and its opportunities, although there are misconceptions, whereas secondary consumers represent some of the harsher outcomes of economic freedom.

5.1 Secondary Producers

On the production side of the economy, a primary tier of firms consists of hundreds of giant economic organizations, each with tens of thousands of employees and considerable resources. A secondary tier contains several million small firms with far fewer employees and assets.[1] In comparison with their smaller counterparts, the largest corporations have not only economic advantages but also important legal and political advantages that magnify the economic ones. They also receive all sorts of help from the government that are not usually available to small firms, at least not to the same extent. It is claimed that America's largest corporations find the free market system too volatile to serve as their principal guiding mechanism and therefore replace the market mechanism with administrative coordination.[2] In comparison, small second-tier firms frequently operate under conditions that approximate a free market.

Michael Piore and Charles Sabel (1984) see the origins of the two-tier system in the oligopoly structure of manufacturing and its requirement for long, stable production runs, particularly in capital-intensive industries. The resulting division of labor is such that large firms service the nonchanging base of demand and the fluctuating component is left to smaller, possibly more flexible, producers. Second-tier firms are praised as being the primary generators of employment in United States[3] as well as contributing to productivity, innovation, and growth.[4] However, several studies have challenged the assertion that small firms hire proportionally more workers.[5] While it is claimed that mass producers lost some of their advantages, several trends in the past 30 years have worked against smaller companies. Modernization in the 1970s, pressure on suppliers from large corporations, the switch to the just-in-time system, and global outsourcing all led to large firms reducing the number of their suppliers and subcontractors.[6] Another trend, throughout the second half of the twentieth century, involved the entry of large corporations and national chains into retail and service businesses that were once the domain of individual entrepreneurs and small local firms.

Corresponding to the two-tier split among firms are differences among their workers. The employees of first-tier firms usually work full time whereas their counterparts in the free(r) market segment of the economy are often seasonal or part-time workers brought in to deal with the fluctuating component of demand.[7] First-tier workers fare better with more stable employment, more opportunities for promotion, and relatively higher pay.[8] Large-firm employees earned on average 39 percent more than their counterparts in small firms; tenure in large firms was on average 8.5 years versus 4.4 years in small firms.[9] First-tier jobs have their drawbacks in that they are often repetitive and offer little autonomy, but second-tier employees usually are the first to be laid off in an economic downturn. The latter employees have not only lower pay but fewer, if any, benefits, particularly, health care.[10] At large firms, 68.7 percent of employees were covered by pension plans and 78.4 percent had health insurance compared to 13.2 percent and 30 percent, respectively, at small firms.[11] Even after adjusting for differences in education and occupation, the gap in rewards remains large. However, in the past 15 years, job insecurity has increased across the board, essentially bringing more employees into the second tier. With the advent of import competition, hundreds of thousands of first-tier workers lost their jobs in industries such as steel and autos. It has also been argued that the two tiers are segmented along racial and ethnic lines.[12] One statistic in favor of small firms is that work satisfaction appears greater in both small plants and firms than in larger production units.[13]

If at one extreme we have large and fairly stable corporations that often survive for generations, at the opposite extreme we have more precarious individually owned enterprises. These two types of business operate in very different environments. The typical new enterprise lives a short life characterized by instability and low returns, followed by a rather quick exit. Between 2004 and 2005, 0.77 million new, predominantly small, businesses were founded; yet 0.68 million firms, again mostly small, exited.[14] Despite their uncertain life, these businesses and their owners are held in high regard. They are seen as pioneers in an important process that may eventually lead to a successful firm providing jobs and growth and symbolizing an economy consisting of numerous independent agents.

America has had for decades a reputation as an entrepreneurial society with its citizens constantly alert to profit opportunities. There is pride in the traits presumably possessed by entrepreneurs, such as initiative, risk taking, and a fierce determination to succeed. There are many stories, true and apocryphal, about famous businessmen who failed initially but persevered and eventually became enormously wealthy. The folklore is that the real failure lies not in being unsuccessful but in never having tried. Another common view is that opening a business is the road to riches, and with sufficient ambition and hard work one is bound to succeed. Freedom to profit does exist. Markets and industries are open to all regardless of size.

However, the popular depiction of contemporary America as an entrepreneurial society may be exaggerated or outdated. International comparisons suggest that Americans are no more entrepreneurial than people in other nations.[15] Data from the Organisation for Economic Co-operation and Development (OECD) show that in 2002 only 7.2 percent of the U.S. population was self-employed.[16] One might question whether agriculture and farming should be included in such comparisons. Some studies distinguish self-employment in poorer nations, which may fall under the category of "necessity entrepreneurship,"[17] from self-employment in nations where there are viable alternatives. However, even if the comparison is restricted to advanced industrialized nations, the United States does not top the list.[18]

A more favorable statistic is the rate of new businesses[19] where, if adjustments are made for agriculture, the United States would be among the top industrialized nations. More generally, the fact that the United States does not have the highest ratio of entrepreneurs can be explained by the fact that entrepreneurship increases inversely with a nation's wealth and directly with the rate of unemployment. As countries get wealthier and real wages rise, the opportunity cost of running one's own business goes up.[20] In addition, a move from an agrarian to a manufacturing society results in a smaller proportion of self-employed people.[21]

Suggestions that the United States is in the midst of an entrepreneurial era are also dismissed because, regardless of the measure used, entrepreneurship has not increased over the past 20 years.[22] The total number of self-employed persons in the United States in 1994 was less than in the late 1940s, a trend attributable to a decline in small farming and rising incorporations.[23] Contrary to another widely held view, Scott Shane (2008) asserts that few entrepreneurial endeavors actually lead to great companies, innovations, increases in employment, or economic growth. Even the common depiction of the entrepreneurial personality appears to be at odds with reality because, in terms of risk tolerance, social confidence, networking, and other factors, there is little difference between entrepreneurs and employed Americans.[24] Despite greater risk for privately held companies, including their low survival rates (34 percent or less over 10 years), the wide distribution in equity returns, and the idiosyncratic risk of a single private firm, their average return to equity is similar to that of public companies.[25] This suggests that entrepreneurs are either motivated by nonmonetary objectives and are willing to accept a surprisingly low rate of return for the degree of risk, or they suffer from excessive optimism. Another finding leading to a similar conclusion is that entrepreneurs enter and stay in business despite a median earnings differential in favor of their *employed* counterparts of 35 percent for individuals in business for 10 years.[26] Indeed several studies suggest that making money is perhaps secondary to objectives, such as the desire to be independent and be one's own boss. There is also the possibility that entrepreneurs are seeking to hit the jackpot, to have a shot at "winning big" despite the small odds,[27] and despite being risk averse.

Nascent firms financed by venture capital are a notable exception to the above somewhat gloomy description of entrepreneurship. Some of the best-known success stories of the past twenty years originate from this group. Unfortunately, these businesses are hardly typical, because venture capital is available to less than 2 percent of small businesses,[28] but it is their success that inspires many to emulate them by opening a business. Most new entrepreneurs use either the owner's savings or personal debt to finance their business although, it is claimed, financial resources are not a barrier to starting a business for most individuals.[29] Other than for the 5 percent wealthiest households, there is no clear relationship between wealth and entrepreneurial endeavors.[30] Other studies, however, point to a correlation between the probability of a *successful* start-up and capital availability.[31]

Despite the economic explanations, it is surprising to learn that America is not the most entrepreneurial society. Perhaps it is just easier in the United States to open a business: less red tape, more financing options, greater moral support, more admiration for success, and more tolerance of failure.[32] The willingness to try a new business is ingrained in the culture. It has already been noted that change is more acceptable in the United States than in most places, and this serves to encourage an entrepreneurial culture. Closing down a business, starting a new one, changing jobs, changing place of residence, and adapting to business dictates are more the American way. More generally in a hospitable business climate, where economic considerations are paramount, entrepreneurial endeavors are bound to be pursued. It could be that conventional measures do not capture all aspects of entrepreneurship and that the United States might fare better on tests that measure the number of employees who switch to entrepreneurship or the number of different ventures attempted per person.

The statistical evidence, including the high failure rate, high opportunity cost, and relatively low average returns, suggests that, at least in some industries, too many people try to become entrepreneurs. Despite the freedom to enter (some) markets, the freedom to profit, and the freedom to fail, the entrepreneurial process is not necessarily efficient. The investments undertaken have, on average, a low probability of success; and even among the survivors, a sizable number may not meet standard criteria for profitability. Perhaps from a national perspective the brilliant success of a few justifies the waste resulting from the many failed attempts. The aforementioned start-ups financed by venture capital have had a beneficial impact on the economy. According to Shane the 2,180 publicly traded companies that received venture capital from 1972 to 2000 accounted for 20 percent of all public companies in United States and 11 percent of their sales, and they provided jobs, economic growth, and innovations.

Individual economic freedom to start a business does exist and has led to some spectacular successes, most recently in the high-tech area. However, starting a business is an opportunity fraught with risk often undertaken in highly competitive markets, as evident from the failure rates.

Notwithstanding the difficulties involved and the hard work and sacrifice, many avail themselves of this opportunity and see it as a way to attain their American dream. The explanations offered for this choice are based on factors that include a desire for independence, a belief in one's ability to beat the odds, and a desire for a shot at the big prize.

5.2 Secondary Consumers

Individuals are usually at a disadvantage in terms of buying and selling when a large corporation stands on the other side of the trade. This is true of individuals' main asset—their labor—and holds when consumers obtain a mortgage, a credit card, and banking services and purchase cars, computers, and medicine. However, the current focus is on people who are in a particularly inferior or vulnerable position as consumers and therefore are more likely to be preyed on and taken advantage of. Those consumers are labeled here as secondary consumers. Income, obviously, is a dividing factor, rich families can afford more and better quality goods and services and also protect themselves better. Yet there is more to this division in that additional factors are involved especially, information. Location, age, ethnicity, mobility, and credit worthiness play a role here and result in very different consumption environments.

In the primary economy, consumers have more choices, better-quality goods and services, and often, more competitive prices. They also have more safeguards against being preyed on and cheated. Members of the secondary economy are more likely to encounter deceitful and predatory practices. Practices common to the secondary economy include charging very high interest rates, amounting at times to usury; concealing fees, often in incomprehensible fine print; and setting outrageous prices not justified on cost grounds. In addition to outlandish interest rates and fees, some businesses try to ensnare their customers into perpetual debt, thereby exacerbating their financial plight. In recent years, government policies, in the name of economic freedom, have helped expand membership in the secondary economy. But the freedom extended is not individual consumer freedom; it is the right to profit from questionable business practices (an element of unrestricted economic freedom). The primary-secondary division is evident in banking, financial services, autos, real estate, appliances, furniture, and food stores.

Financial services offered in the secondary economy include payday loans, check-cashing services, subprime mortgages, loans for autos, and rent-to-own appliances and furniture. Those with no recourse to conventional checking accounts and no savings for an emergency are the most likely candidates for the alternative financial industry.[33] Frequently they are poorer, less educated, and members of a minority group.[34] Payday lenders also target the elderly and the disabled who receive social security and other government benefits.[35] Although lenders are prohibited from receiving Social Security checks directly or from seizing those benefits to pay for debts, they find ways to circumvent the law. Several studies suggest a racial component to subprime mortgage lending, with a larger percentage of such loans given to African Americans than to whites with similar income levels.[36] Credit history is not always taken into account in such studies. However, one nationwide study by Manny Fernandez (2007) that did account for credit history found that African Americans and Hispanics were 30 percent more likely than whites to be charged higher interest rates. Similar findings have been obtained in studies on consumers of alternative financial services[37] and purchasers of cars on credit.[38] Active duty military personnel were far more likely than civilians to borrow from payday lenders until Congress prohibited such loans in 2007.[39] Michael Stegman (2007) suggests that mainstream banks have not entered the high-cost, short-term credit business because they have found similar and equally profitable activities, including charging regular customers a slew of high fees for overdrawn checking accounts (which is really a short-term loan) and bounced checks—practices made easier by the fact that neither usury laws nor truth in lending laws apply here.

Lack of information is a key characteristic of consumers in the secondary economy, especially in the market for financial services. In 2007, newspapers across the nation complained that borrowers with good credit ended up, unnecessarily, with risky subprime mortgages. They were subjected at times to aggressive and misleading promotions that concealed the total costs of the loan.[40] Brokers had incentives to engage in deception regarding the true nature of the loans. Deceitful practices facilitated by lack of information are hardly confined to mortgages. They also can be found in loans for the purchase of cars,[41] in the rent-to-own industry where consumers may end up paying two to three times the retail price,[42] and in excessive fees charged by some tax preparers for rapid refunds and earned income tax credits.[43] Blumberg (1989) describes how the elderly in New York City are overcharged by pharmacies, especially in neighborhoods with a high concentration of elderly people where lack of mobility may also be a factor.

In the United States, the use of credit cards is almost obligatory. Although the extent of competition in the industry is debated, customers often pay substantially more than they expect and much higher interest rates than they pay on cars or mortgages.[44] The majority of states do not limit credit card interest rates. In addition a hands-off attitude on the part of regulators and policy makers encourages misleading practices.

Payday loans are made for 7 to 30 days and do not require a credit check.[45] These lenders have experienced significant growth. Payday loan volume rose to about $48 billion in 2007 from about $13.8 billion in 1999,[46] and the number of payday lenders grew from a few hundred in 1990 to 25,000 in 2002, which is not surprising given profits twice as high as those on standard pawn shop loans.[47] The interest rate charged can reach 1,000%. Also troublesome is that payday loans frequently are rolled over to the next time period, thereby maintaining a nonending cycle of debt.[48] Banks ceasing to make small, unsecured consumer loans may have accelerated the growth of payday lending.[49] Payday lenders cooperated with banks to evade state usury laws until the Federal Deposit Insurance Corporation (FDIC) placed restrictions in 2005 on repeat borrowing by a single lender.[50]

The recent decline in the U.S. housing sector started with the now infamous subprime mortgage loans. Borrowers with weak credit were granted adjustable interest rate loans that often came with no interest or a low "teaser" rate for two to three years before turning into unaffordable high rates. In many instances, little or no proof of income was required for a loan. Whether the borrower could afford the house was deemed superfluous as were credit checks (conventional wisdom was that house prices could not fall). Such loans were not restricted to the poor, the uneducated, and the credit impaired; middle-class borrowers with good credit were also persuaded to use them. The amount of money people could borrow as a percentage of the home's value increased steadily.[51] In 2008, when housing prices started to decline, numerous borrowers ended up owing more than their house was worth. The chicanery did not end with a misleading loan. Lenders found ways to profit from excessive document preparation fees, appraisals, and recording fees.[52] The securitization of subprime mortgages with questionable ratings and the lack of concern on the part of mortgage issuers on whether or not the loan would be repaid paved the way for the subprime, and later global, financial crisis. In line with prevailing attitudes, financial regulators offered platitudes about the merits of free markets, efficiency, and financial innovations while denouncing the evils of government intervention—that is, until they had to bail out their charge,—the financial industry,—at taxpayer expense.

In many cities, competition is insufficient to reduce what are essentially usurious rates in financial services sold in the secondary economy. Given the high profit margins, it is puzzling that entry of new firms does not result in more reasonable rates. Howard Karger (2005) believes that because most of the customers have weak credit, their options are limited, which allows lenders to set high rates. An alternative explanation for why competition fails to reduce interest rates might be that if one firm chooses to educate potential customers about hidden fees and outrageous rates charged by their competitors, the more knowledgeable customers might use their knowledge to gain better deals from competitors;[53] therefore, disseminating such information may prove unprofitable for one firm.[54] However, it is unclear whether this explanation applies to the alternative financial services industry.

Several writers have drawn attention to the government's role in compounding the plight of consumers in the secondary economy. Glenn Simpson (2007) describes how the subprime industry, with generous political donations and lobbying efforts and with the help of a bond rating company, succeeded in preventing efforts to minimize abuses. These included the frequent refinancing of mortgage loans in Georgia, New Jersey, and several other states. In addition, in 2003, the Office of the Comptroller of the Currency issued regulatory orders asserting the supremacy of the National Bank Act over any state laws. It sought to prevent states from applying their own consumer protection laws against national banks,[55] thereby rendering states powerless and their citizens defenseless from predatory financial practices.[56] Similarly, the payday checking industry was able to overcome objections to its presence in several states and from 2000 to 2005 gained access to 15 additional states.[57]

Consumers turning to credit counseling agencies seldom realize the conflict of interest involved. These agencies often work for the benefit of credit card issuers that seek to prevent consumers from declaring bankruptcy and stopping payments.[58] The Bankruptcy Abuse Prevention and Consumer Protection Act of 2005 forces those in trouble to seek counseling from such agencies. There was no outcry over the resulting loss of individual economic freedom, the patronizing attitude, and the increased government intervention in the marketplace. Firms' freedom to profit won out over the economic freedom of individuals and markets.

In recent years, many federal regulations were amended to protect makers of unsafe food, drugs, and other dangerous products from consumer lawsuits. In other instances, the federal government argued for federal sovereignty to accomplish the same objective.[59] The highly touted private legal route for seeking redress (that is, without the need for government intervention through regulation) from commercial wrongs was being denied further tilting economic freedom in favor of corporations. The 2003 Medicare law prevented states from correcting abuses against the sick and the elderly despite the objections of the National Association of Insurance Commissioners.[60]

The aforementioned examples by no means exhaust the list of differences between the primary and secondary consumer sectors. One could add the differences in the quality and even health of food sold in supermarkets and groceries, which vary by affluence, location, and information; the quality of health care; and the quality of public education. The situations described above suggest an economy wherein some of its most vulnerable citizens can be targeted for commercial abuse. Such outcomes violate ethical standards and common notions of fairness. Yet when they are based on either lack of information or market power, they also represent inefficient economic outcomes. From an economic point of view, they are considered market failures where government intervention could be used to improve efficiency in the allocation of resources. Therefore, it is difficult to justify the refusal to intervene. Instead, the purchase of political influence ensures that unrestricted freedom to profit prevails, including the freedom to engage in predatory practices, prevent correction of market failures and stop states from protecting their citizens. Some, oblivious to government's role here, let alone the economic sector's influence over government, describe this as a free market solution.

A genuine demand for services such as payday loans exists, but it is doubtful whether these services could be provided only on such onerous terms. Economic freedom does offer secondary consumers options that might not have existed otherwise. However, its unchecked harmful features, including the right to deceive, mislead, and practice (legal) usury, reduce consumers' freedom and diminish society's welfare.

PART II

Corporations

CHAPTER 6

The Rise of Large Corporations

Economic freedom enables large corporations to exert considerable influence over the nation. However, before exploring this influence, it might be useful to examine how large corporations emerged. More specifically, what factors led to the establishment of giant hierarchical corporations with in-house transactions and administrative coordination? Two alternative views are discussed. The efficiency hypothesis proposes that the establishment of corporations was a free market response to potential cost-saving and efficiency gains in production, distribution, organization, and management. The power hypothesis suggests that, to avoid the market and its uncertainties, and control supply, firms acquired market power. They also sought the power of large size to gain leverage in dealings with financiers, legislators, suppliers, rivals, customers, and employees. In terms of the current framework, the issue is whether large corporations came about as a genuine response to free market efficiency signals or as an attempt to destroy free markets and reduce other market participants' economic freedom. The latter was accomplished primarily by taking advantage of unrestricted freedom to profit through the use of political influence.

Debates about the origin or purpose of large corporations are hardly new. Teddy Roosevelt and the Progressives viewed big business as a natural, hence inevitable, development of modern industrialization and consequently argued for a public policy focused on corporate conduct, not on size or wealth. Woodrow Wilson countered that the trusts reflected a man-made scheme to acquire economic power and restrict competition.[1] Those presidential viewpoints encapsulate the debate.

6.1 Efficiency Hypothesis

The efficiency explanation is associated with business historian Alfred Chandler (1977) who claims that the nineteenth-century organizational revolution originated from a desire for economic efficiency. This was made possible by advances in technology, new sources of energy, faster means of transportation and communication, and growing market size. New forms of production permitted economies of scale, which led to mass production. The source of these economies was speed, such as speed of throughput of materials in production. New and faster means of transportation and communication enabled mass distribution and mass marketing. An administrative hierarchy, staffed by professional managers rather than owners, supervised the new organization. Corporations that successfully implemented the new mass-production techniques and organizational methods enjoyed considerably lower costs.[2]

Large corporations built their own marketing and distribution networks, thereby internalizing several phases of operations and replacing the invisible hand of the market with administrative coordination.[3] Internalization, according to Chandler, led to lower transaction costs, including lower information costs, a more intensive use of facilities and personnel, a steadier cash flow, and prompter payment. Mergers led to a consolidation of production, centralization of administration, and the establishment of marketing and purchasing organizations. Chandler insists that mergers undertaken for financial gain, or to control competition, were profitable only in the short run. Without efficiency gains, the merged firms were unlikely to survive. Chandler concludes that the corporate revolution was immensely successful and a contributing factor to American economic progress.

Oliver Williamson (1981) offers another efficiency explanation for the corporation based on organizational changes intended to economize on transaction costs. He does not believe that the desire for monopoly profits and technology can explain the choice between internal coordination and markets, although these factors played a role. In his opinion, most firms did not possess the structural characteristics, such as high concentration and barriers to entry, to engage in strategic behavior. According to Williamson, only transaction costs can explain satisfactorily the organizational innovations that led to the modern corporation. Transactions costs include the myriad costs involved in negotiations, the writing of contracts, the execution and monitoring of contracts, and the resolution of disagreements. Firms, as noted by Ronald Coase (1937), have to decide whether it is cheaper to avoid or minimize these costs by producing internally or else go with market transactions. This analysis, writes Williamson, is influenced by the presence of bounded rationality (for example, limited computational ability) and the threat of opportunistic behavior, which require modifications to the economic assumption of rationality and point to difficulties with contracts. The extent of asset specificity and forward integration plays a crucial role in determining whether internal organization has an advantage over market transactions. In the face of complicated contractual problems related to asset specificity, the railroads selected administrative coordination and hierarchies over markets, which, argues Williamson, accords with a transactions costs explanation. He also points to the different rates of forward integration from manufacturing into distribution among industries as additional support for the transaction cost hypothesis.

6.2 Power Hypothesis

Market power, as well as power derived from large absolute size, is a nonefficiency explanation for the establishment of corporations. Although mass production had the potential for large savings, a large stable market was required to sell standardized products and cover expensive sunk cost investments in equipment.[4] Such large stable markets, explain Michael Piore and Charles Sabel (1984), had to be created, and this was the purpose of the modern corporation. In addition, mass production was practiced successfully long before the rise of giant corporations. In the late nineteenth century, various cartel-like schemes were attempted unsuccessfully. Their failure led to horizontal mergers (and sometimes vertical mergers) and the emergence of modern corporations with a commanding market share to ensure stable production.[5] Firms did not merge or grow bigger to achieve economies of scale or acquire the requisite technology; they already had that, especially in the continuous process industries. Yet to benefit from economies of scale, they had to control the market, reduce instability, and therein lay the advantage of market power[6] and a departure from free markets.

William Roy (1997) and Charles Perrow (2002) also argue that power rather than efficiency was the goal of large corporations. Government granted corporations rights, privileges, and exemptions that gave these organizations considerable power. Legal rulings and legislation on privatization, incorporation, exemption from public accountability, the legal status of an individual, limited liability, and the right to purchase the stock of other corporations all contributed to the rise of corporations. In fact, argues Roy, the corporation was essentially a form of privilege, and if the legal changes were simply a response to economic needs, then why the wide variations among the states? Large industrial corporations with tremendous legal and financial resources were increasingly able to dictate the terms of interaction with governments, workers, customers, and even investors.[7] This power gave them access to additional economic resources and resulted in government sanctioning and enforcing their economic relationships and institutional forms. It is little wonder that the establishment of large corporations was seen as an attractive proposition.

The railroads became private corporations while holding on to previously granted government privileges (limited liability, permanent existence, and the separation of ownership and control) yet ridding themselves of their previous accountability.[8] Political power and economic power, secret kick-backs, and financial power played their part in the success of large railroads.[9] Perrow asserts that the railroads molded the American corporate structure and, in a sense, bequeathed them their powerful rights, private status, and minimal regulation.[10] These rights and exemptions afforded them substantial leverage in negotiating with states and communities desperate to have rail service. They could demand favorable terms for construction and service and receive public grants, tax exemptions, eminent domain, and the right to set rates as well as substantial grants of land.[11] Efficiency and market considerations had little to do with the private status of the railroads. They were probably far less efficient for their first 50 years than state-owned railroads in Europe, and it was the federal government's susceptibility to corporate influence that led to private railroads.[12]

Corruption, argues Perrow, was a crucial element in the emergence of railroad corporations and, later, industrial corporations. Corruption in the financing, construction, and operation of the railroads was not incidental or just a matter of a few individual transgressions, it had distinct organizational roots and certainly benefited railroad corporations. The possibility of reaping substantial gains from various fraudulent schemes had its own economic logic and overwhelmed more traditional and socially beneficial economic considerations.[13] Corruption played a key role in creating a favorable environment for enacting laws and statutes for the benefit of corporations, which would provide them with considerable power and wealth. Railroads gave stocks and money to legislators and judges and unduly pressured members of railroad commissions. Future corporations probably would not have had as many rights, privileges, and exemptions from public scrutiny were it not for the railroads. The efficiencies that were generated by railroad corporations were not in the allocation of resources, but in the raising of capital and in the creation of large systems.[14]

Although European investors considered American railroads risky, those investors were not averse to state bonds issued to finance railroads. This method of financing the early railroads set a precedent and cemented the links between government and corporate finance.[15] Corporations and financial institutions had a very strong mutually reinforcing impact on each other's development.[16] Financial institutions influenced the use of bonds rather than stocks. Bonds provided greater security to foreign lenders, and domestic borrowers found that they could expand their business through bonds and still retain control.[17]

When other businesses imitated the railroads' organization, it was not because of their economic efficiency but to benefit from financial advantages exclusive to corporate organizations, including opportunities to raise capital from investment banks, the ability to sell securities, profit from speculation, the possibility of growth through merger, and financial manipulation.[18] Suppliers of capital in the late nineteenth century often preferred large firms with market power[19] as well as incorporation and the separation of ownership from management.[20] The implication is that the corporation's origins had little to do with productive or organizational efficiency of the firm itself.

6.3 *Analysis*

Notwithstanding the turn to administrative coordination and imperfect competition, Chandler sees the rise of corporations as essentially a free market success story. The convergence of different efficiencies and technological advances, shaped by forces of demand, resulted in large economic organizations. Successful corporations adopted managerial, organizational, and production changes. Yet, point out Piore and Sabel, specialization of mass production does not necessarily imply efficiency. In the early days of the automobile, aircraft, and computer industries, there were many competing technologies, and usually it was economic power that determined the winning technology, not efficiency. In addition, a firm can possess survival skills and prosper for reasons that have little to do with operating or production efficiencies. The reasons could include, among others, political connections, outright corruption, financial ties, and illegal business practices. Such factors should not be confused with economic efficiency where a firm survives because it has, for example, a lower average cost of production than its rivals[21] and society benefits from savings in resources. The need to resort to bribery, predatory pricing,[22] intimidation tactics, patent warfare, and substantial investments to bring about legal changes raises questions about the efficiency explanation. Chandler's methodological approach involves an examination of the common characteristic of successful firms, not a test of refutable hypotheses. The support for efficiency is based on case studies and theoretical support, not statistical testing.

In the last years of the nineteenth century as well as the first four years of the twentieth century, the United States went through a merger wave that involved more than 15 percent of all manufacturing.[23] From an economic viewpoint, the distinguishing feature of this merger wave, which set it apart from later consolidations, was the creation of firms dominant in their particular industry. As a result, nearly 71 industries that were either oligopolistic or near competitive became near monopolies.[24] This transformation has had a strong and lasting impact on modern American business to this day.[25] Two nonefficiency motives attributed to this merger wave were monopoly power, especially in horizontal mergers, and speculative profits.[26] At times, there was an intermingling of the two motives, such as when promoters spread false rumors about anticipated monopoly power that enabled them to make quick profits from selling the stock to gullible investors.[27] However, there is little evidence to support an efficiency argument

Power over government was facilitated by the need of communities and states for railroads and economic development, by corruption, and by the ability of financial institutions to influence government. Promoters like J. P. Morgan and financial institutions in general benefited from promoting and selling the stocks and bonds of corporations as well as engaging in stock speculation. The power of the new corporations, as noted above, included many government-granted rights which, in turn, enabled not only the acquisition of a dominant market share but also the reinforcing power of large size in both the financial and political spheres.

At different times in the nineteenth century, either power or organizational efficiency might have been the motive for corporations, and sometimes both combined. Yet from the evidence presented, it would appear that profit-enhancing opportunities derived from market power and leverage that comes from large absolute size played a key role. It made sense to incorporate if a firm could obtain government subsidies by incorporating; if changes in the law offered newly incorporated firms better returns and guarantees of control, limited liability, less public accountability and therefore more flexibility; and perhaps even reduced costs. It also would make sense to incorporate or merge if by merging with smaller firms the corporation gained larger profits through the elimination of competition without running afoul of antitrust laws (after 1890) and if postmerger the corporation became large enough to extract concessions from suppliers, bankers, customers, and workers.

If organizational and managerial changes reduced costs, it certainly would have been advisable to implement them. However, whether organizational changes were in and of themselves the motivation for incorporation and the rise of giant corporations is debatable. Were nineteenth-century financiers willing to risk large sums of money based on the promise of organizational efficiency and administrative coordination? The possibilities for market dominance and/or the power derived from large absolute size would seem more compelling reasons for them to part with their money.

In conclusion, market power and the influence and leverage obtained from large absolute size most likely were important determinants in the rise of large corporations established at the end of the nineteenth century. For the most part, the desire to acquire greater freedom to profit, particularly through use of political and legal influence, was a primary motivating factor. Therefore the emergence of giant corporations had more elements of a multidimensional Darwinian struggle than characteristics of free market economic efficiency.

CHAPTER 7

Large Corporations and Economic Power

Corporations dominate the American landscape. Nearly 50 percent of working Americans are in the employ of corporations with 1,000 or more employees.[1] In 2005, the five largest U.S. corporations had revenues of more than a trillion dollars and employed more than 2.5 million employees.[2] The 50 largest corporate employers had an average employment of 231,000 and each one of these companies employed more than 100,000 people.[3] These numbers give some idea about the significance of giant corporations to the economy. In addition, in the past century corporations have become the organization of choice for raising capital for large investment projects.[4] The purchase of corporate stocks and bonds has become a popular means of investment for millions of households. Corporations' importance, power, and influence go well beyond economics. They play a major role in politics, media, culture, entertainment, medicine, dietary habits, and society in general. They determine labor practices, such as the two-wage-earner family, the acceptability of a seminomadic existence for their executives, and laid-off workers. They, although not alone, instill the tradition of the primacy of a job above all other priorities. Yet despite their size and influence, they draw relatively little attention or allow attention to be drawn from a mostly corporate-owned media—they fly below the radar. Most newspapers and television news rarely discuss or mention their powerful position in the economy and society. In recent years, they have been instrumental in reshaping the global economy and with it global politics and culture.

There are enormous disparities in size among several million corporations. Although several dozen corporations employ hundreds of thousands of workers each, the vast majority of corporations employ fewer than 500 people. The virtues of small firms and their contributions to the American economy are frequently praised by politicians and government officials; however, their impact and influence is negligible in comparison with that of the largest corporations. There are laws favoring small firms but, again, their larger counterparts fare better in dealings with the different branches of government. Of course, firms do not necessarily stay small; they sometimes grow and fulfill their dream of becoming large. Examples include Microsoft, Apple, and Wal-Mart. The focus in this chapter is on the largest firms, their power, and how their operations depart from free market principles.

7.1 Planning

The U.S. economy was successful throughout most of the twentieth century. Given the commanding presence of large corporations, it is often assumed that a correlation exists between U.S. economic success and the organizational form of its production units.[5] Yet the operations of large corporations depart from the free market ideal. An economy characterized by mammoth hierarchical corporations with a multitude of in-house economic activities appears inconsistent with free markets and the principle of arm's-length dealings. Such an economy resembles more closely the workings of a managed economy with planning. This fact is often overlooked when the benefits of free markets are associated with the corporate sector of the U.S. economy.

Several hundred giant corporations are entrusted as though by default—and some bold enough would say by the market—with the task of planning economic activity in the United States. This includes the choice of goods and services to be produced and the selection of the inputs used in their production. Despite the monumental responsibility for allocating vast amounts of resources, the corporations are only accountable to their shareholders, if at all.[6] The overall health of the economy is seen, politically and morally, as government's responsibility and not corporations. Various labels have been applied, especially by critics, to an economic system distinguished by large corporations. These include corporate capitalism, managerial capitalism,[7] corporate economy,[8] and private socialism.[9] Notwithstanding planning's connotation with collectivism, many embrace the system, praise its presumed efficiency, and go out of their way to deny any links with planning.

To Galbraith (1985), the essence of corporate planning involves minimizing the market's influence, especially the bargaining power of firms from which the large corporation buys and firms to which it sells. The threat of eliminating a market helps the large corporation control it.[10] Galbraith explains that the need to subordinate the market to planning comes from the dictates of advanced technology for reliability and certainty. Although Galbraith is insightful on the planning aspects of the system and its contradiction with free markets, the justification he provides is less compelling because there is little empirical evidence to support it.

A different viewpoint is that large hierarchical corporations represent a private response to market failure. Chandler (1977) writes that corporations' administrative efficiency had to be greater than that of the invisible hand of the market or else they would not have survived. Corporations grew in size horizontally and especially vertically and by so doing their in-house operations could supersede the market. So, according to Chandler, on the supply side, the coordination of production and distribution, including the allocation of capital and labor, has been taken over by corporate management. Other scholars suggest that on the demand side, too, corporate control has superseded the market.[11] The result is that large corporations and their managers have become the predominant force in the economy.

Chandler sees the managerial revolution as the main reason for the efficiency of corporations and consequently the economic success of the United States. But if one accepts this explanation for corporate success, a thorny question arises. If corporate managers could replace the market successfully in the planning or coordination of production and distribution, then perhaps they could do the same for the entire economy?[12] So here, as noted by Thomas Frank (2000), we run into several ideological dilemmas. Could an economy, where the visible hand of corporate management has to a large extent replaced the market, still be considered a free market? If so, where does one draw the line? When does an economy become defined as a bureaucratically planned economy and not free market? Is it simply a question of whom the planners work for—whether the state or privately owned enterprise? Is it the percentage of the economy involved in any one plan that makes the difference? Is it the extent of interaction among the different planners? Perhaps it depends on the efficiency of the plan.

J. Bradford De Long (1997) examines the issue in the context of the economic failure of the Soviet Union. He describes the U.S. economy as a corporate economy characterized by managerial planning and coordination. However, he notes that, despite the substantial amount of in-house economic activity, corporations are not immune from the discipline of the market and this, he sees, as the redeeming feature of the system. De Long reviews several explanations offered for the success of U.S. corporations in contrast with the failure of Soviet organizations.

The first explanation, along the lines of Ronald Coase (1937), is that inefficient corporations are weeded out by the competitive process. Unprofitable firms can be taken over by larger and more efficient firms or else broken up into several parts. With the threat of a takeover or bankruptcy hanging over their heads, corporation chiefs are forced to strive for efficiency. Indeed the United States relies on the stock market and takeover threats to monitor management more so than most other advanced industrialized nations.[13] Yet, empirical studies suggest that inefficient management is not necessarily under the gun because of takeover threats and possible restructuring.[14] Randall Morck, Andrei Shleifer, and Robert Vishny (1988) find that hostile takeover targets are more likely to be firms in *industries* with weak performance than *firms* with weak performance. There is also not much evidence to support the argument of takeovers leading to efficiency gains. In addition, takeover threats can have undesirable consequences, especially when managers attempt to protect their position or else stand to gain personally from a (friendly) takeover. The acquiring company's executives may also have considerations that do not necessarily accord with shareholders' welfare or with efficiency.[15]

Although takeover threats apply to some firms, if a large corporation can muster sufficient political support, it can defeat takeover attempts and even stave off bankruptcy—sometimes with government help. In addition, in more than a few industries meaningful competition is nonexistent, and the resulting market power or arrangements with rivals allow inefficient firms to survive for lengthy periods. Then of course there is the point already alluded to: that survival is not synonymous with *economic* efficiency.

A second explanation refers to economies of scale and coordination. The former is discussed below. As for the latter, the argument is that an economy that is flexible enough to allow switching from a market mechanism to administrative planning and vice versa is preferable to strict adherence to one regime. The assumption is that, in some production situations, an organizational hierarchy is more efficient than the market. It is claimed that corporations' size and the extent to which in-house operations replace the market are related to the cost of information required for efficient coordination, as well as other transactions costs. Private nonmarket means of organization are justified when a competitive equilibrium does not exist and there is no price at which supply equals demand. Possible examples include cases of substantial economies of scale in production, and increasing returns to scale in the development of new products for related markets ("core competencies"). A nonmarket coordination solution may also be required in cases of externalities and excessive search costs among others.[16] Yet, the transaction costs approach requires restrictive assumptions and its cost minimization objective is at odds with more conventional goals attributed to firms.[17] In addition, strategic motives and consequences are not accounted for in explaining firm structure.[18]

A third argument is that modern corporations are efficient because they are well governed and provide the right incentives for efficiency. Although corporate CEOs have substantial economic authority, De Long suggests that the image of the omnipotent CEO having effectively commandeered the corporation is exaggerated. There is the force of peer pressure from fellow CEOs; more importantly, dissatisfied shareholders can sell their shares, and the subsequent decline in share prices may attract corporate raiders. The market therefore functions effectively in replacing or warning incompetent CEOs. The counterargument is that this is more applicable to smaller corporations. Many giant corporations have "protective shields" consisting of politicians, state laws, employees, suppliers, investment banks, brokerage houses, and mutual funds. Sometimes top executives are offered attractive compensation packages to leave, and it is to their advantage to permit a takeover, which may or may not be in the shareholders' interests. In addition, especially in the past decade, the principal-agent theory has not worked quite the way it was intended. Incentives, presumably designed to enhance efficiency or protect shareholders, have led to an excessive focus on short-term financial goals, occasionally to the detriment of the company, its employees, and shareholders. Corporations' freedom to profit has become increasingly top managers' right to profit.

It is debatable whether corporate planning and corporate structure represent optimal efficiency. It is quite likely that alternative organizational forms could be devised that are no less efficient. Does it have to be specifically a large organization characterized by minimal government control, limited liability laws, with rights of individuals, access to politicians, and many forms of government protection including, sometimes, protection from bankruptcy? It is doubtful that an organization so narrowly defined happens to be the ultimate in economic efficiency.

However, this is not to suggest that the road to economic progress lies in some form of planned economy—quite the opposite. The answer more likely lies in decentralized decision making with genuinely competitive markets and firms blocked from and disengaged from politics. Therefore it is unlikely that powerful bureaucratic centers, undertaking economic planning while insisting that their operations are the quintessence of the free market, represent superior economic efficiency. They represent a departure from free markets despite torrents of claims to the contrary. Perhaps no evidence is more damaging to claims of a free market environment than corporations' relationship with government. In fact, argues Galbraith, corporations are interwoven so tightly with the state that one might infer that in important respects they are one and the same. In other nations, matters may be worse because large corporations are frequently controlled by just a few families.[19] However, those nations are not quite as loud in claiming to champion free markets.

7.2 Power

In the first half of the nineteenth century, Tocqueville warned prophetically of potential dangers arising from a manufacturing aristocracy, particularly to democracy. In the second half of the nineteenth century, giant corporations were resisted because of concerns about their power and its threat to democracy and the nation's entrepreneurial tradition. Opposition came from small businesses and commercial farmers. Their arguments, based on traditional economic beliefs, were well received but essentially futile in that the corporations continued to grow.[20] Again, during the Great Depression, the power of large economic organizations was a topic of debate.

Corporations did not neglect the battle for "hearts and minds". Roy (1997) notes how corporations started in the 1850s to use the individualism theme of their opponents who objected to incorporation and state charters. Adam Smith's anti-monopoly sayings were turned in order to defend market power.[21] In the 1970s in order to promote corporate objectives a large number of institutions were established, including think tanks, litigation centers, publications and lobbying agencies.[22] In the 1990s the terminology of democracy, and even the labor movement, with some changes, were adopted to enhance the social legitimacy of corporations.[23]

Today, the power of large corporations is taken for granted.[24] Economists are usually keen on minimizing government's role in the economy and warn of the dangers inherent in government control. However, the reverse possibility that key players in the economic sector control government receives less attention, in part, because it is considered outside the domain of economics proper. Analysis of the links between corporate size, political influence, and protection from rivalry and failure has not been a popular undertaking among economists.

According to Galbraith (1985), the modern giant corporation is an autonomous economic fortress, sheltered and secure from many of the uncertainties and vicissitudes that most businesses have to cope with. Corporations can obtain capital from retained earnings and therefore do not have to worry about bank officers looking over their shoulder and questioning their decisions. Giant firms, in many respects, are protected from the discipline of the market or have a degree of control over it, be it in purchasing inputs including labor or in the sale of their products. Through the use of advertising, the corporation can influence or determine the products that consumers will purchase. The corporation has little to fear from government in that its independence is considered a sacred right and, in addition, government sometimes is its best or even only customer.[25]

Why is the corporation worthy of autonomy, including protection from rivals, consumers, government, and shareholders? As previously noted, according to Galbraith, the answer has to do with planning and when it comes to planning, bigger is better. A more frequently cited economic justification for nonintervention by government is pricing efficiency. However, this overlooks the fact that corporate decision makers often supersede the market and set prices at odds with allocative efficiency.

Galbraith notes how large corporations have been adept at persuading the public that their objectives are identical with those of society. Yet it is corporations that establish society's goals as they mold social attitudes to specific corporate needs. Consequently, the nation has come to accept economic growth and production, increased conspicuous consumption, and unquestioning faith in the goodness of technological change (thereby justifying government subsidies for research and development (R&D) to corporations) as its top priorities.[26] In addition, government services not deemed essential to corporations are relegated to secondary status. Galbraith points to the obvious conflict between the needs of the "technostructure" and individual's free will. In terms of the present framework, this means that the economic freedom of large organizations clashes with and wins out over the economic and even civil freedoms of individuals. The ability to shape the goals and direction of a nation represents formidable power.

Large corporations seek control over government to protect market power.[27] This raises the question of whether there are "efficiencies" in this type of activity. Do their size and resources give them the political clout to shield themselves from economic competition and extend their lives? Perrow (2002) notes their power to externalize costs and require government to pay for them, thus suggesting another motive for large size. Several studies have found a positive relationship between firm size and corporate income tax avoidance.[28]

More generally, large corporations benefit most from what is described here as "unrestricted economic freedom". The term refers to freedom to profit not only through market activities but also through actions designed either to circumvent or suppress the market, resulting in a misallocation of resources. This can be accomplished through private efforts, government help, and, notably, a combination of the two. An example of the latter would be a firm either inducing or taking advantage of market failure while ensuring no government correction.[29] The 2008 bailout of large financial corporations is an outcome of unrestricted economic freedom.

Regardless of trends in corporate power, their existing power is already considerable. Some examples, more illustrative than comprehensive, include the following lengthy list: the aforementioned government bailouts, reductions in effective corporate taxation over the past 40 years, special tax exemptions, subsidies for research and development, the political lobbying system, the Pension Benefit Guarantee Corporation being used to avoid pension liabilities and pressure employees, companies shipping the bulk of their employment overseas and still qualifying for tax credits, laxity in antitrust enforcement, farm support programs defined by acreage and not income, nonmedia companies controlling television, the 2005 bill that prohibited government agencies from bargaining for cheaper medicine, the defeat of the national health care bill in 1994,[30] the power of credit agencies over the lives of Americans, privacy laws or rather lack thereof, and strategic lawsuits against public participation, or SLAPP,—initiated at times by corporations to silence opposition to their projects or activities.[31]

7.3 Size and Efficiency

As noted previously, there is a debate about the reasons for the emergence of large corporations, whether it was efficiencies in operations or the desire for profit enhancing power. Galbraith (1985) suggests that, for effective planning, a larger firm can better handle uncertainty than a smaller firm.[32] Congress and federal courts accepted the argument that bigness is related to efficiency.[33] Yet many empirical studies have been unable to find evidence of economies of scale in production large enough to account for the size of modern giant corporations, although there is some support for marketing economies.

Galbraith and Schumpeter's ideas on the need for large size corporations to conduct vital research and development (R&D) work have received little in the way of empirical support.[34] Neither the requirements of undertaking risks nor the need for large capital expenditures would appear to justify large size. The federal government subsidizes research extensively, and a lot of research can be exploited on small scale.[35] In addition, the probability of success in research is not as low as is commonly believed.[36] There are also concerns about the lack of creativity in bureaucratically managed R&D departments. In a large corporation, decisions must filter through a whole chain of command, which causes a bias away from imaginative innovations. Managers in large firms may be risk averse and refrain from difficult R&D projects.[37] Although there may be some advantage of size in the commercialization of inventions,[38] David Jewkes, David Sawers, and Richard Stillerman's (1958) study on the important inventions of the first half of the twentieth century found that more than half of these were invented by individuals working either completely independently or independently in academia. With some exceptions, empirical findings generally show that larger firm size does not necessarily result in greater R&D efforts or output;[39] and some evidence suggests that innovative activity per employee in small firms exceeds that of large firms.[40] In addition, from society's perspective, large corporations have been known to use patent warfare to impede competitors' research efforts.

Regardless of whether large sized firms were justified, it is claimed that beginning in the 1960s or 1970s informational and coordination problems arising from size and hierarchical organization started to affect adversely large mass producers. In addition, new technology permitted smaller minimum efficient scale production, and on the consumption side a trend away from standardized products further aggravated the plight of mass producers as did increased foreign competition. However, while some large corporations did decentralize operations, others shielded themselves through mergers, multinationalization and government protection.[41]

7.4 Separation of Ownership from Control

The separation between ownership and control, noted by Adolf Berle and Gardiner Means (1932), refers to the fact that the owners of the corporation (shareholders) are different from the managers who operate it supposedly on their behalf. The separation received legal backing when the courts adopted a natural entity theory and decided that corporations should be run by managers, thereby diminishing the rights of shareholders.[42] Much has been written on the incentive structure established to ensure that managers perform in accordance with shareholders ' wishes. It was assumed that stockholders or their representatives would create safeguards, along the lines of the principal-agent theory, to align managers' interests with those of shareholders. Yet recent events suggest that these incentives do not always have their intended effect, and large pay increases bestowed on corporate bosses have challenged these assumptions.[43] Concerns have been voiced regarding the dilution of earnings and stockholder equity as a result of stock option plans for top managers. Krugman (2002b) notes that, contrary to conventional wisdom, the cost to shareholders and even society at large of executive discretion in matters of remuneration may be far in excess of the actual compensation. Investments were made that were designed primarily to boost executive pay—not stockholder return or the welfare of the company.

The concern is that the correlation between job performance and reward is decreasing. Executives with a less-than-brilliant record of performance appear to reward themselves, with the consent of their board of directors, high sums.[44] In good times, that is, when the stock price rises, pay packages increase substantially; yet when the stock price falls and shareholders suffer, there is often no corresponding fall in the top executives' compensation. Disconnecting the link between job performance and reward is a blow to economic efficiency and suggests compensation sheltered from market discipline. Entrepreneurs are rewarded for risk taking, but managers do not bear the same risks. That is not to say that they do not engage in risky investments. In fact, when the money at their disposal is not their own, they may tend to undertake riskier investments.[45] There is also the suggestion that the separation of ownership from control may have resulted in a move away from interfirm competition for market control and monopoly rents to struggles among competing management groups for control of firms with market power.[46]

That the shareholders have very little say in the running of the modern corporation, including executive compensation, has been discounted as of little practical significance. Berle and Means's concern that the corporations' top echelon may appropriate the firm for their own benefit was dismissed out of hand. Yet events of the past 20 years suggest that such concerns are not trivial. There is a fundamental challenge to the institution of private property. If stockowners cannot control their property, that is, the companies they own, at least to the extent of having their employees work for their benefit, then a situation arises bordering on the confiscation of property. No harsher criticism is offered on this issue than that of Schumpeter (1962) to whom this represents as an attack on the very foundations of capitalism—private property. The retort—that shareholders can always sell their shares and that the practice is of long standing—does not resolve the ownership issue. Private property, along with markets, is a key feature of capitalism and may have given it an advantage over socialism in terms of economic efficiency. Yet in this context, the concept has been diluted if not distorted by the separation of ownership from control. Schumpeter envisions dire political and moral consequences detrimental to the survival of capitalism. The loss of the ability to do as one pleases with one's property, as well as the loss of the will to fight for what has become only remotely one's property, could hardly bolster capitalism. The disregard for property rights in the operation of modern corporations and capital markets is in conflict with both American political principles and capitalism itself. Once again, the economic freedom of organizations triumphs over that of individuals, including the right to property.

7.5 *Turnover Rates*

A different way to examine the issue of corporate power is to look at mobility among the largest firms. After all, even if giant corporations have substantial economic and political power but membership in the top tier of corporations keeps changing, then the potential dangers to the democratic process and even to the economy's efficiency may be lessened.[47] At the very least, the process would seem more egalitarian and inclusive because the identity of the power holders keeps changing.

Economists have approached the issue by examining turnover among the very largest corporations and find evidence of turnover over the course of the twentieth century.[48] Norman Collins and Lee Preston's (1961) study shows declining rates of turnover in the first half of the century. F.M. Scherer and David Ross (1990) extend Collins and Preston's study up to 1987 and find a strong increase in turnover rate for the last decade of their study. Thurow (1999) offers favorable turnover evidence from a comparative perspective. If 8 of the 25 biggest companies in America in 1998 were either small or nonexistent in 1960, then in Western Europe, all the top 25 biggest corporations in 1998 were already large in 1960, thereby suggesting greater turnover in the United States. However, an important question is this: what happened to the firms that did depart? Some exited because of changes in demand and technology. Dennis Mueller (1986) finds considerable turnover among the largest 1,000 U.S. manufacturing firms from 1950 to 1972. However, upon examining the reasons for exit he discovers that merger was the most frequent cause of disappearance. Only a few firms exited because of bankruptcy. The importance of mergers as a cause of exit is also reported in other studies.[49] Although business mobility is a desirable finding in the present context, it is unclear whether a lessening of economic or political influence can be inferred from such long-term mobility, especially when mergers play a key role in the disappearance of large firms.

7.6 *Combined Power*

Economists stress the need to differentiate between firms with a large market share and firms of large absolute size. Most studies have focused on the former issue. Yet, given the resources of giant corporations, their impact on the national economy, their authority over millions of employees and the increasing links between money and politics, there is concern about their combined power. Aggregate concentration refers to the combined share of the largest firms in the economy, or in a particular sector, as measured by assets, employees, value added, or some other measure. Some scholars suggest a connection between aggregate concentration and market power in individual markets.[50] Galbraith (1985) argues that big size is a manifestation of economic power and is skeptical of his co-professionals attempts to treat large size and large market share differently to defend the former. Additional arguments point to diversification and vertical integration as factors that can strengthen market power.[51]

In 2002, the largest 100 manufacturing firms (a tiny fraction of the total number of firms) produced 33.7 percent of all manufacturing's value added. According to Marris and Mueller (1980), the share of manufacturing assets owned by the 200 largest U.S. manufacturing corporations (with a changing composition) rose from the beginning of the twentieth century by an average of 0.5 percentage point per year. The authors also point to a strong increase in aggregate concentration in the financial sector, which according to Frederic Pryor (2001), continued strongly in the 1980s and 1990s. The evidence on changes in overall aggregate concentration for the top 100 firms from the 1960s to the 1980s is less clear,[52] and Lawrence White (2002) finds that for the 1980s and 1990s, despite the merger wave and for reasons not entirely clear, overall aggregate concentration did not rise. Even though the rise in aggregate concentration may have ceased, the numbers suggest that a small number of very large firms control vast amounts of resources; as such, they are bound to have a major impact on the economy and on the nation.

Marris and Mueller suggest that, if giant firms emerge due to internal growth strategies, this may have positive implications for the economy. However, if the growth is the result of socially unproductive investment—and mergers may fall into that category—then it could have a negative effect on social welfare. Walter Adams and James Brock (1986) also warn of another threat resulting from increased aggregate concentration brought about by conglomerate mergers. As control becomes located in fewer firms, the increased contact among these firms may lead to reduced competitiveness and result in cartel-like arrangements across markets and industries.

7.7 Labor

In the late nineteenth century with the rise of large corporations, Americans experienced major economic and social changes. One of the most significant changes was that Americans increasingly became wage earners. While in 1820 less than a quarter of the labor force worked for wages and salaries, by 1900, it was 50 percent, and by the end of the twentieth century, it was more than 90 percent.[53] As a result, the cherished independence of work that had given the nation a defining quality and had become part of its ideology almost vanished.[54] In fact, to this day, the change has not been entirely acknowledged. The legend of American workers as independent yeomen persists even as the switch away from manufacturing to services continues.

In the new organizations, there was little room for differences of opinion. These were strictly hierarchical organizations run by professional managers and at odds with notions of independent workers.[55] William Whyte (2002), a perceptive observer of corporate life in the mid-twentieth century, notes that corporate employees had to adapt basically to a collective life. They had to learn to conform, suppress their individuality, and become willing team members. There was a stark contrast between the strict conformity of the corporate working environment and the widely promulgated image of corporate employees as self-sufficient individualists following their inner voice. The collective aspect of corporate work was rarely discussed as such, which is not surprising given its negative connotation, especially in the 1950s.

There was an implicit understanding in the twentieth century that if one worked hard and played by the rules, then one would do well, which was considered an acceptable bargain. American workers tolerated the Taylorist-style scientific management in both factories and offices. For decades they accepted the status quo in the belief that they had a chance to achieve the American dream. Labor relations between corporations and their production workers were far from harmonious and in fact necessitated a higher ratio of managers to workers than existed in Germany or Japan.[56] Yet factory workers for the most part did not join radical trade unions. As long as jobs were available and access to a middle-class existence was possible, there was support for the corporate economic system.

If ever there was a social contract between employees and their corporate employers, then beginning in the late 1980s or early 1990s the perception materialized that the contract had been nullified. Large corporations were still providing better pay, better benefits, and greater opportunities than their smaller counterparts; but distressing developments were taking place. These included downsizing intended to make the companies more attractive to financial markets, the threat of jobs being outsourced overseas or to lower-paying domestic contractors, a rise in the number of temporary jobs without health and retirement benefits, and an increasing loss of privacy and rights.[57] The traditional well-paying manufacturing jobs as well as good service jobs that did not require a college education became scarcer. Regardless of the reason for the job cuts, the relationship between corporations and their employees began to change.

Job stability for U.S. workers was already lower than among the United States' main industrial competitors[58] but in the 1980s, job stability in the overall economy declined further.[59] Older and better-educated workers were more likely than before to lose their jobs.[60] In the 1990s, job stability furthered declined for workers on the job for at least a few years, including manufacturing, managerial, and professional workers,[61] although workers with relatively short tenure appeared to have gained somewhat in job stability.[62] Henry Farber (2005) examines job losses from 1981 to 2004 and finds that reemployed workers, even in full-time jobs, suffered a significant decline in earnings regardless of their level of education. He notes that for the 2001 to 2003 period, the decline in earnings was much larger than before for reemployed workers with more than a high school education. Additional statistics from this period paint a gloomy picture in that 35 percent of job losers had not found another job two years later, and those who did find full-time jobs earned on average 13 percent less than before.[63] Farber concludes that while labor flexibility adds to the economy's efficiency, workers bear an excessive share of the burden.

With the deterioration in job security, seniority, and pensions, it became clear to many that their work environment had changed, and not for the better. The technologically induced decimation of the ranks of middle management, pensions stocked with company equity, and the contrasting fortunes of top executives protected by "golden parachutes" led to some disillusionment. In earlier generations, employees had been known to enter the corporation with the zeal of a religious order. Being a corporate employee gave one a sense of identity and belonging—it was more than just a workplace.[64] Now there was a realization that free agency had arrived. The system was changing rapidly—partly in response to globalization and the fast pace of technological change and partly in response to the dictates of financial markets. The prospects of a job for life with one employer seemed more remote.

New jobs did materialize for most of the laid-off workers; unfortunately, the jobs were often inferior in terms of pay and benefits. Low-paying jobs in the service sector, with wages not much above the minimum wage and with minimal benefits, were labeled derogatorily "McJobs." Families with two full-time workers struggling to pay for a middle-class life became more common. A fundamental economic dilemma—the choice between efficiency and avoiding layoffs—caught the nation's attention. It was portrayed in movies—for example, "Other People's Money" and "Wall Street"—as a conflict between economic and social considerations. Should employees be treated differently from other inputs? In both movies, workers are threatened with layoffs—the company in question may survive as a business entity but more money can be made from the liquidation of its assets. With downsizing, outsourcing, and converting full-time jobs into temporary ones, there were heightened fears of job loss, and these were the good times with a booming economy and low national unemployment rates. Despite the changes in the workplace, many corporate employees continued to prosper, but many others faced reduced opportunities, greater uncertainty, and a diminished standard of living when laid off.

7.8 Social Responsibility

Ideally a firm should not be large enough to affect the regional or national economy. Yet, large corporations employing tens or hundreds of thousands of workers have a significant economic impact regionally and sometimes even nationally. Regrettably, that impact is usually dismissed as of little significance. Given that corporations' primary goal is profit maximization or some comparable objective, government, not corporations, is seen as responsible for smoothing the transition for those laid-off. The assistance provided is less generous than in many other advanced industrialized nations. Yet, when considering the power and influence of the economic sector over government, it is difficult to absolve corporations entirely from responsibility. A small part of the problem is the lack of knowledge on how to calculate the cost of unemployment other than the loss in earnings. The disruption to lives, families, and communities is as yet unquantifiable. A bigger part of the problem, however, is the lack of will to interfere with what is defended, at times erroneously, as a purely market mechanism. This is not surprising in light of the low priority afforded the issue by the economic sector's key players.

More generally, there is a conflict between corporations' primary economic responsibility of maximizing profits and demands for greater social responsibility. A common criticism is that when giant corporations focus exclusively on profits and shrug off social responsibility, their activities may impose large social costs on the nation. Blumberg (1989) asks how could moral people knowingly sell dangerous cars, conceal the dangers of asbestos, or sell unsafe drugs and chemicals in third world countries. As suggested throughout the book, the answer can be found in the elevation of the freedom to profit above all else. Blumberg also points to a lack of personal responsibility when one feels like an insignificant cog in a giant firm just following orders and far removed from witnessing the damage wrought by one's actions or decisions. Both advocates of laissez-faire and those favoring a more paternalistic government would delegate the responsibility for curbing or minimizing social costs to the government. If the economic sector and government were indeed completely separate entities with equal power, the argument for greater government responsibility would have more validity.

Corporations are the dominant force in the U.S. economy and enjoy considerable freedom and power. Yet, their unrestricted freedom to profit through either market or nonmarket channels conflicts with and often overwhelms individual freedom to profit, opportunities, and quality of life. Contrary to prevailing arguments, such outcomes are not necessarily market-determined. Giant corporations are often shielded from the discipline of the market and their operations, in fact, can be detrimental to free markets.

CHAPTER 8

Heads We Win, Tails You Lose: Large Corporations and Government

Two long-standing American political-economic principles are the sanctity of private property and the freedom to pursue pecuniary gain. The latter freedom has led to a third, albeit tacit, principle: the acceptance of corporate power in both the economic and political realms. The political system is not without its admirable features, but the failure to come to grips with the impact of economic power on government and politicians is a major weakness. The political influence of large corporations—the dominant player in the American economy—is ignored or else treated as a natural outcome of a competitive free market with all the inherent efficiencies. It is not a topic of political debate, it is rarely discussed in the media, and it draws little attention in academia. Yet this influence has disturbing implications for the political rights and freedoms established by the Founding Fathers as well as for the economic welfare of the nation. The writers of the constitution could not have envisioned the major role giant business organizations would play.[1] They could not have foreseen that their grand design would allow economic forces to go from a defense of property to a control of government.

The conflict between corporations' freedom to seek profits through political influence and democratic principles is highlighted in this chapter. The argument is that large U.S. corporations' special access to government and their influence over the political process undermines democracy. In addition, when government intervenes in the economy at the behest of corporations, there is a cost to economic efficiency and a violation of free market principles.

8.1 Government and Economic Power

Typically in a capitalist society, the economy is left primarily to the working of the market. Yet by giving up its right to control the economy, the government, from a historical perspective, is relinquishing considerable authority and effecting a major change in the balance of power between the political and economic domains.[2] The U.S. economic sector probably enjoys greater protection from government encroachment than the reverse. Government interference in the affairs of a private company is regarded as an egregious breach of jurisdiction and an affront to market efficiency. This is somewhat ironic because, as noted above, a distinctive characteristic of many giant corporations is the abandonment of the market mechanism for in-house operations and internal decision making.[3]

There are no checks and balances on access to government comparable to the checks on the power of the separate branches of government.[4] The only entity capable of checking corporate power has steadily given up its power, thereby enabling economic power to find a path to political influence and further weakening government. The process for acquiring such influence has been sanctioned and formalized so much so that it is now perceived as an integral part of the political process.[5] Government agencies often serve as lobbyists for private interests, bestowing on them a competitive advantage and in the process creating an undesirable dimension of competition.[6]

As noted by Lindblom (1977), business has special access to government because of government's concern about the economy and its keen awareness of the resources available to big business to influence politics and accomplish its objectives. Consequently, large corporations are in a unique position that allows them to bypass the normal channels of the democratic process.[7] Exemplifying the close links between government and business is the revolving door phenomenon, that is, officials easily switching jobs from one sector to the other, as well as corporate involvement in advising government on matters such as trade, energy, transportation, and foreign policy.

If private companies, especially large corporations, can make money from a business run by a public institution, the public institution's business is often doomed regardless of the relative social benefits of the public and private operations. Land on which private homes stand can be seized under eminent domain laws in which the public interest is broadly defined.[8] Corporations are noted for their ability to externalize costs and have government pay for expensive projects, thus exempting themselves and their customers from the expense involved.[9] In fact, according to Galbraith (1985), the idea that big government emerged at the expense of the private sector is fiction; large corporations need big government for maintaining aggregate demand, training personnel, providing subsidies for R&D, and building highways and airports.

The two major political parties cultivate corporate support and therefore back the economic and legal status of big corporations, including the prerogatives of top management. Even politicians from the Democratic Party usually avoid anti-big-business positions and accept corporate dominance in the economy. These politicians want to be seen as pragmatic, as having the good of the economy at heart, and therefore refrain from attacking big business. Either in their minds or in their constituents minds, this is regarded as sound economic policy—firmly grounded in free market principles. Then of course the ability of corporations to donate money for political campaigns is not an insignificant factor.

8.2 Where Does the Power Come From?

The role of money in politics has been discussed previously, so here the focus is on corporations' role in this process. The total amount of money spent in 2000 for federal elections was about $3.0 billion;[10] for all elections, it was about $3.9 billion.[11] An upper-limit estimate on business political donations is $1.1 billion,[12] with most of the money coming from corporations.[13] The pragmatic nature of corporate donations can be seen from the fact that in 2002 corporations gave 83 percent of their political donations to incumbents and only 4 percent to challengers. The motive behind campaign contributions is the desire to influence politicians' votes on specific issues and to receive special consideration.[14] This is evident in the relationship between the economic interests of the contributors and the committee assignments of the recipient politician.[15]

The amounts of money spent on U.S. elections are large by comparison with other nations (although there is an argument that more money would be donated if campaign contributions represented investments.)[16] However, there are also more indirect and less public avenues for influencing legislators. Money spent on lobbying is generally considered more important for interest groups than campaign contributions,[17] and business spent about $1.3 billion on lobbying in 2000.[18] Therefore, campaign contributions, while important, do not tell the whole story regarding money and political influence.

The U.S. political system, as is true of many other aspects of U.S. society, is more amenable to money and more tolerant of its influence than corresponding institutions in other industrialized democracies.[19] Several West European nations have limits on political donations and/or campaign spending by both source and amount. Despite these laws and regulations, they have experienced problems and scandals with election financing,[20] and it would be difficult to claim that Europeans have the perfect solution to election financing. Yet, whether by coincidence or design, money and corporations play a more pronounced role in both the U.S. electoral system and political process.[21]

If a person or corporation is seeking favorable legislation, it is probably easier, or at least more direct, to control an individual than a party. Hence, the American system, which focuses on candidates rather than parties, would tend to favor corporate influence or any other type of moneyed influence. The need to pay for political advertising bolsters the position of those with the means to defray such costs.[22] Additional features favorable to the influence of money include the winner-take-all election system, the two-party political system, the nonideological nature of American politics, the decentralization of government and uncertainty over state and federal jurisdiction, the separation of powers,[23] unlimited campaign expenditures, PAC money rules, the high cost of elections, and lobbyists' access to government.

Conditions conducive to the influence of money, combined with the acceptance of corporations' power, favor corporate political influence. In addition, fundamental differences in constitutional, philosophical, and judicial attitudes between the United States and other democracies further strengthen this influence. For example, European and Canadian courts are willing to accept arguments about "equality of participation" or a level playing field to preserve the integrity of the election system despite the apparent conflict with the principle of free speech.[24] In the unlikely event that arguments to limit donations or spending were accepted by U.S. courts, this would weaken the influence of money and therefore that of corporations.

8.3 Government Help

Until recently, given the identification of the United States with free markets, risk taking, and self-reliance, one could be forgiven for assuming that government has little involvement with business. Indeed, states are prohibited from interfering in interstate commerce, and with some notable exceptions, the federal government maintains a relatively hands-off attitude compared to most other industrialized nations. Yet government assistance to large corporations is far from inconsequential and is provided in a variety of ways. These include shielding market power from competition; passing laws and regulations favoring large corporations; providing tax exemptions, subsidies, and grants; socializing cost and risk; and, not least, government as a generous and ever-forgiving customer.

Corporations are dependent on government for legislating laws that define the rules of the game among themselves and in their dealings with employees and customers. In fact, the modern industrial corporation's very existence, more so than other forms of ownership, is a creation of the law, argues Roy (1997). The rise of corporations was facilitated by changes made to the legal system. This included laws limiting shareholder liability, the granting of unlimited life, the right to own stocks in other companies, and exempting managers from direct accountability to owners.[25] In the nineteenth century, state regulation of corporations was justified based on the entity idea. When the entity idea became an obstacle to expansion, corporations turned to the aggregate theory (to do away with state regulations) and later, for similar reasons, to the natural entity theory.[26]

In the 1880s, federal and state courts became increasingly probusiness after decades of selective appointment of judges.[27] Numerous legal rulings in favor of corporations were the result, including some innovative interpretations of the law, particularly regarding property rights. States' rights to take over private property and turn it over to commercial interests for development were increased, and the concept of eminent domain was broadened.[28] The Supreme Court declared that corporations were entitled to the rights and protection of a legal person. The authority of juries was diminished and that of judges increased. According to some scholars, changes to the legal system resulting from cooperation between judges and corporations constituted a legal revolution.[29] They certainly strengthened the position of corporations. More recent developments, such as the judicial focus on economic efficiency, have had a similar effect.

State and local governments compete for investments that promise new jobs or growth by offering incentives and inducements to corporations. Incentives can take the form of subsidies, tax exemptions for the company and its executives, appropriation of public or private land, exemptions from environmental and labor laws, absorption of the cost of training workers, and construction of access roads and other infrastructure. The U.S. government provides generous funding for industrial R&D, mostly to large corporations. In 1996, 4 firms received 37 percent of all federal R&D money contracted to industry, and 20 companies received 80 percent of that money.[30] Over the past 40 years, the effective tax rate on corporations' profits has declined by about 50 percent.[31] As noted before, from 1950 to 1990 corporations' share of federal taxes and property taxes fell considerably. Throughout the twentieth century, projects too costly for the private sector were sometimes financed with public money.

One of the best examples of government assistance is the help given to the railroad industry in the nineteenth century. Railroads received about

$100 million in subsidies and approximately 200 million acres of land.[32] After the Civil War, the federal government set up regulatory commissions to supervise the railroads to prevent cutthroat competition and price discrimination. The magnitude of government help raises doubts whether the railroads represent a truly private sector success story.[33]

The auto industry was able to persuade government to restrict auto imports in the 1980s. The steel industry received considerable import protection in the late 1970s and1980s through the imposition of quota systems and without being required to either modernize or enhance global competitiveness.[34] Other examples of industries receiving government help in the twentieth century include aviation, electrical power, radio and television firms receiving electromagnetic spectrum virtually free, the semiconductor industry, and biotechnology.[35] The 2005 bill prohibiting government agencies from bargaining for cheaper medicine benefitted the pharmaceutical industry. In agriculture, subsidies intended to help poor farmers have gone disproportionately to large agribusiness corporations. The ease in adoption of genetically modified food in the United States, with little public input, is cited as an example of corporate influence over the political process.[36] In recent years, the financial industry has been able to legitimize usurious interest rates and other questionable practices in different states. When, as noted above, states attempted to protect their citizens from predatory actions of mortgage lenders, the federal government claimed preemption of federal law, thus protecting corporate lenders.[37] Similarly, the 2003 Medicare Law did not permit states to protect consumers from abuse by private Medicare insurance plans.[38] Corporations can ship the bulk of their employment overseas and still qualify for tax credits. With the possible exception of price-fixing cases, antitrust enforcement has been less than aggressive in the past three decades.

The U.S. government continues with a generous program of corporate assistance known colloquially as corporate welfare. According to one estimate, in 2000, taxpayers were subsidizing U.S. businesses to the tune of almost $125 billion, which included tax breaks and direct subsidies.[39] In 1997, the federal government paid $1.4 billion in sugar price supports, of which 40 percent went to the largest 1 percent of sugar farms.[40] Oil, gas, and mining companies received $1.37 billion in 1998; pharmaceutical companies that set up offices in Puerto Rico received $3.0 billion; corn-based ethanol refiners received $0.5 billion; and timber companies almost $1.0 billion.[41]

This kind of financial assistance is of questionable economic value and clashes with free market principles. Not all government help is wrong; in some cases, there is an economic justification. This is true when the overall benefits from a product or service exceed the private benefits to the firm. Unfortunately, economic calculations of this type are rarely made; more often than not, politics is the reason for government assistance.

8.4 Government to the Rescue

The above examples do not exhaust the list of government help to corporations. From the 1970s on, America witnessed several large government bailouts including those of Penn Central, Lockheed, Chrysler, Continental Illinois, savings and loan institutions, and even a hedge fund—LTCM. In the most publicized case, the Carter administration provided Chrysler with loan guarantees that prevented it from collapsing. A popular argument at that time was that Chrysler had been denied its right to fail. The rescue of giant corporations presents government with two unattractive choices: either bail out the threatened firm, contrary to market principles (since bankruptcy, by transferring resources to more productive uses, can enhance economic efficiency), or allow failure, job losses, and damage to communities.[42] Who is entitled to such help and what is the underlying economic rationale has never been clear. The national interest is often invoked. In the case of savings and loan institutions, the argument was that thousands of jobs would be saved. A similar claim was made in the recent auto industry bailout.

In the LTCM case, it was argued that help was necessary to avoid financial chaos, nationally or even internationally. The Federal Reserve generated a rescue plan and intervened despite a private sector offer to buy out LTCM. (Management fared better under the Federal Reserve's plan,[43] and had it not been for the Federal Reserve, LTCM most likely would have accepted the private sector offer.[44]) The Federal Reserve's jurisdiction in the case has been questioned,[45] especially since it departed from its authorized role as a lender of last resort.[46]

In 2008, America entered an era of unprecedented government intervention to rescue financial corporations that had enjoyed unrestricted freedom to profit. Few risks were considered too large, higher leverage was permitted, and deceit was tolerated. Yet by late 2008, to protect failing financial giants, roughly $10,000 was being requisitioned (indirectly) from every person in the United States because the survival of these firms was deemed crucial to the economy. Officials alluded to the national interest and to catastrophic consequences should these behemoths be allowed to fail, socialization for large companies was a must, no matter how distasteful.

Earlier in the year, the creditors and credit insurers of an investment bank—Bear Stearns—were rescued. The Federal Reserve Bank loaned

$30 billion to JP Morgan to help buy out Bear Stearns Corporation. The loans were secured by somewhat questionable assets belonging to Bear Stearns, and taxpayers could face losses. The Federal Reserve argued that the financial system was in danger of collapse, and hence the Fed's actions were necessary. It has been pointed out that financial markets at that time did not display signs of an imminent collapse,[47] and others have questioned whether the Fed intervention, on behalf of an investment bank, was in conformity with the FDIC Act.[48] Two quasigovernment entities, Fannie Mae and Freddie Mac, had a change in status accompanied by grants of $100 billion each. More generally, the government stood ready to shield large investors from risky investments in subprime mortgages and derivatives just as it had earlier rescued savings and loan institutions and foreign currency investors. In September 2008, a large insurance company, AIG, was granted an $85 billion loan from taxpayers (that was later doubled).

In October, the U.S. Treasury submitted a plan to rescue banks and other financial institutions at a cost to taxpayers of $700 billion. The justification for such a massive redistribution was that it would solve the financial crisis and its key problem—the lack of credit—thereby sparing the nation from a severe economic decline. The Treasury secretary demanded and received from Congress carte blanche in this matter, and regulatory reforms were to be postponed to a later date. The plan appeared to be neither efficient nor fair. It contained an implicit assumption that, to increase credit availability and boost the economy, the institutions that brought the economy to the brink of disaster had to be saved at taxpayer expense. No alternative plans were presented, presumably because none were available. Yet it is hard to accept that, on a continuum of possible solutions for injecting liquidity into the economy, no plan could accomplish these goals without rewarding financial managers in direct proportion to their failed investments. From auctions for government funds to the extreme of creating new banks, there would seem to be several ways to enhance credit availability without rewarding excessive risk taking. What was rarely mentioned was that the government plan preserved the status quo within the financial sector—the special position of giant corporations and, for the most part, their managers and insurers. Public funds were used to protect existing wealth and power as well as a failed organizational structure from the discipline of the market. Despite official pronouncements about increased liquidity being the goal, the banks receiving money in 2008 were not required to lend the money, and they did not.

The Treasury plan conflicted with free market principles. Politicians, officials, and leaders famous for extolling the virtues of free markets and laissez-faire and known for preaching self-reliance and the importance of people adapting to the dictates of the market were ready to interfere with the market mechanism on behalf of private sector companies. They were now demanding that former colleagues, supplicants, and donors be bailed out at taxpayer expense. The free market homilies were shelved temporarily. Taxpayer money was being commandeered to rescue speculating CEOs who made fortunes in earlier years and got to keep their profits; but the rest of America was coerced into paying for their gamble. The rescue of financial institutions, including those involved in deceitful subprime mortgages and charging usurious interest rates, became the nation's top concern. Forgotten was the 2005 bankruptcy law characterized by its lack of compassion for individuals who fail financially and usually not because of extravagance but because of a job loss or a serious illness. The law was toughened, in part, to teach fiscal responsibility. Perhaps, due to the perceived emergency nature of the rescue, there was no time to consider such issues, but more likely, they were regarded as irrelevant. An early twentieth century saying had been transformed into "what is good for large financial institutions is good for America."

In none of the bailout cases, past and present, has a working rule been provided that could be applied to future companies. Assistance was at the discretion of those in charge. This may seem a reasonable and sensible approach in many nations but not in the United States. Bailouts usually are seen as arbitrary rulings with a motive of their own and at odds with "the rule of law rather than the rule of men." If a rule does seem to materialize from these events, it is that the federal government and its central bank are justified in protecting markets. Unfortunately, as was evident in 2008, this still gives government officials considerable latitude in deciding when and whom to protect.

A fundamental cause of the current crisis is not being addressed:—business's unrestricted economic freedom involving access to politicians and government, which led to the calamitous freewheeling financial environment. Politicians from both major parties endorsed the 2008 bailout. Whether or not past donations from the financial industry played a role is unknown. However, if they did, then several hundred million dollars in donations cost Americans a thousand times more. The rescue plan may prevent a nationwide collapse of financial markets and perhaps even help save the economy, but it certainly reduces economic efficiency, moves the economy away from a market-oriented system, violates standards of fairness, and weakens further the democratic political process.

There are serious economic issues here regarding production efficiency, the allocation of resources, capital market efficiency, and moral hazard. (Why be prudent when playing with house money?) Also, there is a commonly ignored issue:—the economic repercussions of the relationship between economic size and political influence. It would appear that within the private sector, there is a special category of firms sheltered from the vicissitudes of the market. With guarantees of access to the public trough, the firm's concerns about solvency or competition are lessened, as are the concerns of financial markets. The results include nonmarket-induced differences in risk and access to capital. To some, the acceptance of giant economic organizations is a primary cause of such problems; firms are allowed to grow to a size where their failure simply cannot be tolerated, notwithstanding inefficiency and mismanagement.[49] This is known as the "too big to fail" argument. An additional twist is that bankruptcy does not necessarily mean a complete shutdown of the firm, but rather it may be an ownership issue,[50] in which case the bailout, especially with taxpayer money, is even more questionable. To compound matters, in the recent crisis, authorities resorted to the creation of even larger financial institutions (with taxpayer help) through mergers with smaller failing institutions. The new companies are virtually assured of being regarded as "too big to fail" and, for all practical purposes, will be treated as public organizations except in the rewards of their executives and in descriptions of the economic system. Once again, they can engage in risky undertakings secure in the knowledge that the U.S. government will have no choice but to bail them out should they fail.

8.5 Influential Industries

In the nineteenth century, railroads often dominated federal and state politics. The importance of state legislatures went beyond local control. Through the legislatures, the railroads could control the U.S. Senate because its members were chosen by state legislatures. The increased importance of the Senate took place at the same time that the corporations were rising, and this was no coincidence.[51] The railroad's control widened from the Senate to the federal courts and other institutions; they had become a major player in politics. The elimination of some laws and the enactment of others facilitated corporate accumulation of power and wealth. The federal government's authority was weakened.[52] To Perrow (2002), these changes represented the starting point for an organizational revolution where, regrettably, corruption played an important role. The railroads gave bribes and gifts to congressmen and cabinet members.[53] Corruption also led to social costs such as pollution and accidents, because laws could be ignored.[54]

The extent and effectiveness of government help to the railroads has been debated. Such help may have been negligible in some regions such as the midwest in the 1850s,[55] but it was very important in the crossing of the Appalachians, in the antebellum South, and in the financing of the first transcontinental railroad.[56] Government played an instrumental role in financing railroads. Carter Goodrich (1970) estimates that, prior to the Civil War, government's share of investment in railroads amounted to 25 to 30 percent of the total. Federal and state grants eventually gave the railroads over 9 percent of the U.S. continental land. The railroads were also able to extract considerable sums from local governments. They insisted on the right to set rates, routes, standards of construction, and operation and even to determine the terms of public financial assistance and eminent domain. The rights and privileges granted to the railroads, including the right to merge, limited liability, and a weakening of public regulation, were to have long-range implications for corporate power in many industries.[57] Political control and judicial control were important factors in the rise of the railroads and later in the rise of corporations.[58]

A major question is whether the social benefits resulting from the construction of railroads justified government help. Economic historians Robert Fogel (1964) and Albert Fishlow (1965) have questioned the popular argument that railroads provided considerable stimulus to American industrialization. Fishlow also claims that government's railroad investments were ill chosen.[59] Although there are dissenting opinions, the economic case for government investment and other forms of help to railroads does not appear to have been clear-cut.[60]

A twentieth-century parallel with the railroads' political power has been the auto industry's influence over public policy. The industry has relied on an army of lobbyists, public relations experts, a trade association, and national business groups to lobby government.[61] Auto executives have served in the cabinet and held other important federal positions. Particularly helpful to the industry has been the fact that autos are produced in many states. Federal and state legislators were informed in no uncertain terms where the auto industry's interests lie. The industry's importance to the national economy in the twentieth century gave it tremendous advantages. One could see the industry's influence in taxpayer-subsidized highway construction, limits on auto imports in the 1980s, public schools funding driver education,[62] delays in requiring boosts in auto fuel economy, and the fact that public transportation did not receive the kind of support it receives in other industrialized nations. Despite energy crises, pollution concerns, and safety issues, government has neither questioned the role of the automobile in society nor adopted policies that would endanger its position.[63] In fact, the auto industry selected the relevant issues addressed by government.[64] This power has led to an acceptance of significant social costs, including pollution, highway deaths, oil consumption, a declining manufacturing base, and even the work experience of many Americans.[65] The introduction of "voluntary" export quotas on Japanese auto manufacturers in the 1980s also involved substantial costs. According to William Cline (1986), the quotas raised prices by about $370 per domestic car and by more than $900 per Japanese car. The overall annual cost to consumers from this protection was estimated at $4.5 billion.

One might point to the significant inroads made by imports in the U.S. auto market despite government protection for domestic vehicles. In fact, in late 2008, U.S. automakers were on the verge of bankruptcy and appealed for help. (Interestingly, while the financial industry was being granted mind-boggling sums of public money, there was a more begrudging and parsimonious attitude in helping the auto industry indicative of the changing fortunes and influence of the two industries in the twenty-first century.) Nonetheless, it is conceivable that, without government help, changes would have occurred sooner with substantial savings to taxpayers and consumers. Alternatively, the industry might also have made the necessary adjustments to meet foreign competition effectively and without incurring such large job losses. In addition, and contrary to official statements about giving the auto industry breathing room to improve, there was little if any productivity improvement from the 1960s to the 1980s.[66]

The railroad and auto industries played a key role in setting the course for the nation's economic development. Yet the relentless drive for political influence had an adverse impact on the political process, and the ensuing help damaged economic efficiency. The extensive economic aid received due to political influence clashes with depictions of America as a model free market.

8.6 Withholding and Misleading Information

The relationship between big business and government has played a major part in shaping politics and the economy. Throughout the second half of the twentieth century, Americans accepted the close alliance between the two domains as an unavoidable cost of prosperity. Barring an Enron-type scandal, the alliance is rarely discussed; it is taken for granted as—a natural by-product of the interplay between democracy and economic freedom. The less-savory aspects of this relationship, involving the mundane exchange of political favors for donations, are not widely reported. The same is true of lucrative contracts involving billions of dollars, political appointments requested by corporations, and deals between the media and politicians.

Business groups often set the agenda for elected representatives and can influence the outcome of political debates. A notable example is the spending by insurance companies to defeat the 1994 health-care bill. Particularly interesting is the ability of interest groups to influence political debates surreptitiously. It was once thought that economic regulation of public utilities was enacted for the benefit of the public. In the second half of the twentieth century, economists came to the realization that businesses themselves sought such regulation and for a sound reason:—it was a profitable course of action. Historians report similar findings of policies designed to facilitate business controls but presented as democratic reforms (for example, in meatpacking, drugs, and forest conservation) that were reforms in name only.[67] Corporations were able to obtain favorable legislation under the guise of serving the public interest with bills whose intended purpose was opposite to what their title suggested.[68]

Several authors argue that business indoctrination is responsible for Americans' acceptance of the economic system.[69] The point had to be driven home that corporations' special position is vital to America's economic success and that business influence over government is consistent with democracy. Academics and the media, two groups dependent on corporate and government funding, reinforce these views.[70] Inculcated in the public's mind is the belief that corporations represent America's most desirable traits, including free markets, individualism, and democracy.[71] Similarly popularized is the idea that an economic system characterized by oligopolies and giant firms is synonymous with Adam Smith's vision of a competitive free market.

Indoctrination is often aimed at schools and colleges. Use is made of all forms of media, including radio, television, movies, newspapers, and magazines. The result is that the basic political-economic institutions are taken for granted. Discussions on important but sensitive political-economic issues such as corporate autonomy, tougher antitrust laws, and income distribution rarely arise.[72] A dangerous development for democracy is what Ben Bagdikian (2000) refers to as the media's promotion of the idea that politics is unimportant and, consequently, attempts to organize social change are doomed to failure.

Whereas a century ago there were vociferous complaints about corporate control over government, by the second half of the twentieth century the public's attention had been redirected to the threat to individual freedom from an overly powerful government.[73] Considerable investments have been made to protect economic power and its influence over government. This has been accomplished, in part, through the dissemination of information depicting existing political-economic arrangements as in conformity with democracy and free markets. Economic freedom to profit permits corporate control of the media and hence the shaping of public perceptions regarding political and economic power. Notwithstanding the many advances in communication technology, including the Internet, misinformation and lack of information facilitate the weakening of democracy and the lessening of individual freedoms.

8.7 Political and Economic Risks

It is highly debatable whether democracy is compatible with great concentrations of economic power. Economic power makes its presence felt in politics even if it escapes publicity. There may be as yet no definitive work providing irrefutable evidence on the subject; however, a considerable amount of evidence and common sense leads to the conjecture that concentrated economic power does not stay aloof and beyond the political fray.[74] The danger to democracy from undue corporate influence was noted by several U.S. presidents (Jefferson, Jackson, Van Buren, Cleveland, and Eisenhower), either in office or prior to taking office.[75]

Government economic intervention resulting from the influence and power of large corporations distorts the market mechanism and produces inefficiencies. Corporations demand government protection from actual and potential competitors, domestic and foreign. By suppressing competition, they entrench their position within their industry, and in the process, eliminate an essential element of free markets. The resulting inefficiencies go beyond what economists call static inefficiency or resource misallocation. Protection from competition can also endanger dynamic efficiency, which allows new firms and new technologies to emerge and challenge or replace the old. With government support, existing firms can suppress new technologies and prevent the entry of new rivals. Because technological innovation is deemed essential for the growth of the economy and for raising living standards, obstacles to this process are considered a no-less-serious threat to the economy than the misallocation resulting from monopoly-type pricing.

Influence over government stemming from economic power results in laws, rules, and policies that are at odds with the workings of a genuine free market. The economic gain to interest groups is often exceeded by the economic loss to the nation as a whole. Mancur Olson (1982) argues that the favors received by interest groups in various countries may in fact account for differences in economic growth among nations. Long-entrenched interest groups receive more protection for a longer period, thus causing a misallocation of resources and obstructing growth and increases in living standards.

The modern corporation's objective is to maximize profits or, more generally, to succeed economically. Yet, as noted above, giant corporations have a large impact on the regional and sometimes even the national economy. The possible divergence between the private and public interest can be a cause for concern. The current globalization trend and the declining allegiance of multinational corporations to any one nation bring this issue into sharper focus. Yet there is no mechanism in the United States for public intervention other than an ad hoc type to ensure the survival of the corporation or to provide public assistance to laid-off workers. Decisions affecting the national economy are left almost entirely to the discretion of the corporation. This is considered satisfactory because a market solution is said to be involved.

Large corporations have considerable influence over the political domain, and as a result, they are granted substantial freedom to profit, including a variety of forms of government help. All too often these corporate advantages come at a cost to individual economic freedom and free markets. The recent bailouts are examples of greater freedom followed by unprecedented government help. Political influence reduces economic welfare but, more ominously, it undermines the democratic process. The lesson is that private economic power can be as harmful to society as excessive government power.

CHAPTER 9

Media and Freedom to Profit

Large corporations dominate the economic and political landscape. Helping cement their commanding position in both domains is a favorably disposed media. The media mold the views and opinions of Americans. They present the economic system favorably and describe it as an indispensable counterpart to the democratic political process. The media also play an important role in the sale of products and services through advertising and in the promotion of a consumption culture. The present chapter highlights the clash between a profit-seeking media and the informational needs of democracy and questions whether reduced public involvement in media markets is justified economically and politically.

9.1 The Media and Power

The media consist of hundreds of local television stations, thousands of radio stations, a few national newspapers, and numerous local papers. There is an impressive variety of magazines and just about every profession, craft, industry, occupation, hobby, interest, and leisure has a magazine. Similarly, with the advent of cable television, viewers have numerous choices, including stations specializing in news, sports, food, pets, history, travel, home repairs, finance, religion, entertainment, and different types of movies. The choices are indeed amazing. Yet when it comes to the media's most important social function—to provide information essential to the functioning of a democracy, such as information voters need on social, political, and economic issues—there is less reason to celebrate. Notwithstanding all the advances in telecommunication technology, video and audio, satellites, and Internet communications, the news in terms of selection, analysis and perspective provided cannot be said to exhibit commensurate progress. A crucial media dilemma in American society is the conflict between market constraints—namely, profit maximization—and the requirements of democracy for information. Market incentives and freedom to profit as discussed below do not necessarily yield high-quality, widely disseminated news coverage.

The U.S. media are primarily corporate owned, including several large multinational companies, with considerable influence over politics and government.[1] They certainly affect legislation dealing with their own industry, such as rules of competition, ownership, and labor laws. The largest media firms have received subsidies and governmental help in the form of monopoly licenses for television and radio frequencies, monopoly cable television, and satellite television systems.[2] Their sway over politicians arises from the fact that the media decides whether or not to present the activities, policies, and personalities of politicians to the public. Therefore, politicians court reporters by providing access and information, and they try to please media owners with favorable legislation.[3] In part, the media's power is derived from the fact that, on many issues, the public relies on the media for information.[4]

The power of media owners is not limited to political issues, and it goes beyond the news. They can and do influence social and even religious issues.[5] Media corporations determine the entertainment that tens of millions of Americans view nightly. More important yet, they practically socialize each generation through their program selection and the virtual creation of youth cultures.[6] The lack of news diversity and the threat to democracy are of little concern to the population at large. However, there is resentment of the media's cultural power. It is seen as a dangerous influence in that it weakens or even negates learning coming from more traditional sources, such as family and school.[7]

9.2 Profitable News and Democracy

News in the United States is divided into local and national news. Local news consists primarily of reports on local crimes, local government, sports, weather, and human interest stories. National news is provided by six networks and their subsidiaries, although some require subscription to cable television. Networks other than the round-the-clock news companies provide a 30-minute evening news show. The networks also present news magazine shows where they dwell on a specific issue for a longer period than the two minutes allotted to stories on the evening news. Those shows, which have in the past decade become increasingly popular with the networks due to their low cost of production, include *60 Minutes, 48 Hours, Dateline*, and *Nightline*. Due to geography, size, and the importance of state and local government decisions on people's lives, U.S. newspapers are primarily local in scope, although many are owned by national chains. Two influential national newspapers are the *New York Times* and the *Wall Street Journal*.

On the face of it, it would seem that America, as befitting a democracy, has a rich choice of news sources to provide its citizens with the information necessary at election time. Due to advances in technology as well as professional coverage, viewers could watch live battle scenes from halfway around the world in their living rooms during the Iraq war in 2003. Extensive and quick coverage is usually provided for most international and certainly domestic crises whether they are fires, floods, or riots; and it is acknowledged that the media generally provide accurate reporting of public events.

However, critics question the selection of news stories and what is omitted or ignored.[8] The prevailing rule for decades has been to minimize coverage of controversial issues that may offend advertisers, which are—the media's primary source of revenue. Attacks in the media on fellow corporations, especially large ones, are rare, except for cases involving major environmental disasters or failure. Newspapers and television stations are not eager to serve as consumer advocates. One has to subscribe to a specialized magazine such as *Consumer Reports* to learn about defective products, questionable services, and deceptive commercials. A criticism of local news broadcasts is that, more often than not, there is little to inform the viewer on political and social issues other than official statements.

James Fallows (1996) states that a proper press is vital to a democracy because it gives meaning to the news and provides the "agreed upon facts" used in public discussions and political debates. Yet substantive differences in the positions of political candidates have typically been ignored. Instead, voters' attention is drawn to personalities and values. The media, rather than increasing voter information and by so doing strengthening the democratic process, assist in diluting political and economic differences.

There is an emphasis in the United States on what is known as "objective" news, without analysis or guidance to let the viewer know where the story stands in the scheme of things and its overall significance.[9] Bagdikian points out that, even on *60 Minutes*, a highly regarded television news magazine show, less than 20 percent of the stories covered could be described as having "long-term national significance." Most television news focuses on what is current, what is happening at the moment, but it offers little in the way of perspective. Bruce Owen (1974) describes it as a medium without memory. Viewers see daily events that are rarely connected with past events or other events or put into any meaningful framework. There is also little follow-up after the original event is shown. There may be sound business reasons for this approach, but it does suggest a potentially dangerous disparity between the offerings of a market-oriented media and the information requirements of a democracy.

Another complaint is that news focuses on, magnifies, and even promotes discord. Fallows points to a dismaying modern journalistic creed: "no conflict no news." This is especially true in the political arena and is done to such an extent that it undermines reality and misrepresents the working of the democratic process. The focus on the adversarial and confrontational has several costs, not the least of which are the omitted stories, the underreporting on politics and business where agreements have been reached and progress achieved.[10] The social and professional strictures deemed the standard for journalism and for a properly functioning democracy have been discarded[11] and, as in other spheres of life, free rein has been given to the profit motive. Yet, according to Fallows, the hostile tone of press briefings and political coverage coexists with the media's willingness to give politicians a free pass on many issues of substance. Highly sought-after journalists may be inclined to pull their punches when investigating groups or people who pay for their speeches or sponsor their talk shows. Politicians may provide information to reporters in return for favorable public visibility.[12] This may be normal business, no different from what happens daily in many commercial transactions. But it is different because the cost or the loss is not just to a private party—competitors or consumers—but to democracy. Underscoring the danger is the question posed by Fallows: what happens to the politician who, for whatever reason, refuses to play this media exchange game? The precarious financial situation of newspapers around the country may further endanger the independence of the press. In 2009, the Washington Post considered, but eventually cancelled, a "salon" where lobbyists could meet administration officials, members of Congress and the newspaper's own editorial staff and reporters for fees ranging from $25,000 to $250,000.[13] Fallows points out that, in 1994, major newspapers presented many more stories on the Whitewater scandal than on the Clinton healthcare proposal that, if passed, would have represented a major social policy change. Instead of providing information on the merits of the proposal and its impact on people, the press treated it as just another political contest and in so doing affected the outcome of the debate. The current form of political reporting, which seeks the thrilling and the contentious, distorts political reality. It does not increase the public's knowledge on the issues reported and leads the public to believe that politics is just another game.[14]

An additional function of journalism is that of a watchdog over government activities—the fourth-estate function—which again is vital to democracy. Views differ on how well the press handles this role. Owen warns that for the press to function effectively as a watchdog over government the profit motive is usually the best incentive and superior in this regard to moral responsibility. However, others disagree and argue that the media fail to accomplish this task effectively and, in fact, have pushed politicians toward demagoguery and the adoption of the expedient over more difficult choices.[15] Bagdikian is skeptical whether the press can serve effectively as a watchdog because media corporations favor accommodation rather than confrontation with government and hence are not well equipped to handle this function. It appears that the market does not provide the media with sufficient incentives to carry out the watchdog function effectively.

The Watergate scandal with its monumental political and constitutional implications was seen as American journalism's finest hour. Democracy prevailed despite the attempt to undermine it. However, with regard to the media, one has to remember that hundreds of newspapers, television networks, and radio stations were either uninterested or unwilling to conduct an in-depth investigation of the break-in into the Democratic Party's headquarters prior to a presidential election. Part of the media was afraid to incur the wrath of the White House or else offend readers or sponsors, such was the political climate. So with the exception of a relatively small number of journalists, the media as a whole, contrary to popular image, did not emerge from the story as a knight in shining armor galloping to the defense of democracy.[16]

Market-induced changes in the newsroom appear to have intensified. Thomas Frank (2000) points to the dismantling of the wall separating the editorial and advertising sections. He cites the case of the *Los Angeles Times* where the news was to be assigned to reporters by coeditors, including one from the business department of the paper. To Ken Sanes (2000), news has been commodified and adapted to the needs of marketing in a way that makes it no different from any other product marketed. While American politics are based on thousands of towns, television news markets are based on a couple of hundred locations. This discrepancy raises issues of information distribution and its likely impact on the political process.

Critics contend that the market system, generally, does not produce high-quality journalism. Yet there is little evidence to suggest that viewers or readers demand a drastically different type of news except perhaps in the abstract, although Galbraith's skepticism about consumer sovereignty does come to mind. There are pressures on the supply side to minimize costs because quality journalism, with overseas reporters and in-depth domestic investigations, is an expensive proposition. However, many businesses have developed a profitable demand for a variety of products, and Robert Entman (1989) asks why news organizations have not cultivated a similar demand for quality news. He sees political tensions and pressures as a possible explanation. There could also be the fear of offending advertisers. An alternative explanation is the free rider problem where it does not pay for one news organization to change readers' or viewers' preferences, because it cannot reap all the rewards from its investment.

Nevertheless, a viable democracy requires informed citizens; so is there a solution? If consumers do not want sophisticated news and in-depth analysis, should such news be pushed on them? And, if provided, should public funds be used? Entman suggests that national news organizations be run by the major political parties and subsidized by the government. This would enhance political awareness and lead to greater participation in the democratic process. However, such a solution is unlikely to be acceptable in America. One party already has far more media ownership support, and usually funding, than its rivals and hence would object to public funding. Although this idea, in the context of American political and commercial reality, seems utopian, it should be kept in mind that all sorts of products and services receive government funding. Owen argues that, from a constitutional point of view, the right of free speech is different from, and does not extend to, diversity of opinion. Consequently, despite a concern about a monopoly in the marketplace of ideas, he argues against government-supported television channels to introduce additional viewpoints.

Criticisms of the news should be kept in perspective in the sense that they are based on comparisons with news provided in other democracies and not in totalitarian nations. Yet, an interesting question is whether there is a fundamental difference between news that is one-sided and under tight political censorship and news that is flawed and limited as a result of the profit dictates of media companies and advertisers.

9.3 Media and Ideology

Profit maximization is not necessarily inconsistent with ideologically motivated reporting. Media companies catering to the sentiments of their readers, viewers, and advertisers may still be following a profitable path. In the past, a media outlet as a pulpit for the dissemination of the owner's views, subject perhaps to a minimum profit constraint, was not uncommon. There may also be joint profit maximization considerations based on the combined profitability of the media outlet and other business interests of the owner.

There are democratic nations with right wing, left wing, centrist, and religious newspapers providing a range of views on economic, political, and social issues. In the United States, a more limited ideological range is offered.

The media basically reinforce an ideological status quo whether unintentionally or by design, and if the latter, either because of conviction or because it is profitable. The market system and large corporations are essentially taboo as a topic of debate, argues Bagdikian. He writes that American journalists are expected to adopt centrist positions, avoid anticorporate ideas, and remain silent on major social issues. They are expected to dwell on the positive and ignore the negative, celebrate the achievements of the market system, its undeniable wealth, the rags-to-riches stories, and the rewards for a sound work ethic. The other side of the economic story, the less pleasant side, is usually not considered fit for print or broadcast. There is no great demand for such stories, they do not boost consumer spending, and hence they are considered undesirable by advertisers and may antagonize fellow corporations that are either customers or potential customers.

The economic system is considered a sensitive topic, which is somewhat surprising in a nation that prides itself on freedom of the press and has confidence in its system. The flippant answer as to why this is so is that the prevailing system is the correct system and hence no debate is necessary. Alternative reasons are offered for the do-not-rock-the-boat approach, including suggestions that it is a legacy of the cold war and a desire to protect the economic status quo. It may also reflect the ideological views of the journalists, editors, or owners. The majority of readers and viewers are hardly holding their breath in anticipation of debates on the merits of corporate capitalism, suggesting that demand is small at best. And then, of course, there is the perpetual fear of offending advertisers and, to a lesser extent, readers or viewers. There may be concern that such debates may harm media companies in terms of leading to policies that reduce profits and raise owners' and top managers' tax liabilities. Even if the owners do not share this view, reporters may be apprehensive about offending them.

A claim made in the 1970s and 1980s, and to some extent in recent years, is that the American media is dominated by left wing or liberal ideology. In comparison with left-wing West European newspapers, the allegations seem far-fetched because there are no major newspapers in the United States that could be described as left wing. The liberal label, in the past, applied to a small number of newspapers and newscasters and had to do with domestic dissatisfaction with the Vietnam War, 1960s legislation on race relations, President Johnson's war on poverty, and support for a social safety net. The media generally supported conservative positions, but it was not unanimous. Entman points to the fact that most researchers have not found evidence to support the charge of a liberal bias in the press. Fallows cites media coverage of President Clinton as a challenge to claims of a liberal bias. Such charges exaggerate the degree of independence given to reporters and more importantly ignore the profit motive and the influential presence of large media corporations.

Owen writes that editors and owners have some latitude in projecting their biases because editorial selections may have very little impact on profits. However, Bagdikian doubts that editorial boards are really independent of their chain owners and cites the predominantly uniform political endorsements of newspaper chains.[17] When politics directly affects a newspaper or television station's own interests, one is likely to find little diversity of opinion. Few newspapers condemned the Federal Communication Commission's (FCC) decision to eliminate the Fairness Doctrine.[18]

The fact that the better news organizations adhere to rules of objective reporting would seem, on the face of it, to minimize bias; but, on closer examination, the implications of this approach are hardly reassuring. Objective reporting, as practiced, entails a reliance on the opinions and perceptions of authority figures, such as government officials, to authenticate all events.[19] Then there is the issue of analyzing or explaining the meaning of events without which the news is almost meaningless. According to Edwin Baker (2002), objective reporting parallels the interests of advertisers in that it is relatively inoffensive and hence minimizes the threat to sales of advertised products from potentially offended media customers. Finally, how do rules of objectivity apply in deciding what news to include and what to omit? This issue requires the rendering of judgment on the part of someone in the news organization. Bagdikian suggests that this approach results in a focus on politically safe stories that the authorities can safely confirm and has led to failures in reporting on sensitive political and social issues. Bagdikian notes that in the 1950s, Senator Joseph McCarthy was initially accepted enthusiastically as a certifying authority.

Entman sees cost minimization as one of the key reasons for the dependence of reporters on political elites for news stories. Other reasons relate to "cultural legitimacy" of elites and possibly reporters' shared outlook and common status.[20] The social cost of this arrangement is the undermining of media independence because, notes Entman, those news suppliers obviously have a stake in what is reported. They would like to advance policies they favor; thus, the information provided is tainted.

The reluctance to offend advertisers, owners, or fellow corporations has led to conformist news. Freedom to profit does not protect the news from bias, yet it is important to remember that neutral or completely objective news is nonexistent. The same problem always remains: how to decide on the appropriate stories, the right amount of coverage, and the interpretation or context when provided. The media outlets in other Western nations have their own biases, but the public had more choice of viewpoints. (In recent years an American style media has emerged in several West European nations with increasing corporate ownership along with complaints of bias) Yet, in the United States, there is probably greater acceptance of biases resulting from the profit motive.

There was a time when it was thought the answer to diversity as well as the desire for news untainted by advertising considerations was public television. However, the public television experiment in the United States has met, not surprisingly, with a good deal of criticism. Owen notes that public television does not correct deficiencies because the shows presented are not necessarily those that would meet the test of the market, but private networks refuse to produce them. Links with government alarm those concerned about freedom of speech, although similar concerns about advertisers as censors are more muted. In addition, a common criticism is that public television is regarded as elitist and hence not catering to the general public.[21]

The relevance of some themes discussed in this section came to light following the financial collapse and the recession of 2008. In the postmortem, questions were raised as to why there had been no warning from the media, especially the business media. Magazines and television stations specializing in this area were for years mostly uncritical just as they had been silent about the dangers of the dot-com bubble a decade earlier.[22] They went along, perhaps in the belief that high leveraging, liar loans, financial deregulation, and inaction by regulatory agencies were integral to a vibrant free market system. It is also possible that they did not fully understand the risks incurred by the financial sector and the nation[23] any more than did nonexperts. However, the aforementioned factors such as reliance on government and corporate officials' statements and reluctance to antagonize corporations (including their own) probably played a part. Financial journalists are reluctant to attack the Wall Street firms they report on, not unlike political reporters whom hesitate to criticize the politicians they meet frequently and from whom they may receive information.[24]

9.4 *Economic Characteristics*

Government has not been unfriendly to media corporations; quite the opposite. The structure and composition of several media markets is largely an outcome of government policies including subsidies, rights to scarce frequency, and favorable regulations.[25] Regulatory agencies over the years have made critical decisions regarding media companies and technologies, such as those affecting the rivalries between AM and FM radio[26] and VHF and cable television. The FCC tended to protect existing modes of broadcasting over new ones and in so doing impeded competition. In the 1990s, with the emergence of new technologies and opportunities, media giants sought and received more freedom to profit. Various restrictions on ownership concentration, cross-media ownership, newspaper mergers, and partnerships with competitors have been removed. The Communication Act of 1995 and the Telecommunications Act of 1996 were strongly influenced by media companies[27] and by the argument that competitive free markets would ensue from deregulation. Yet deregulation and competition are not synonymous.[28] The Telecommunications Act of 1996 allowed one company to own television stations reaching up to 35 percent of the nation's viewers.[29] It removed all limits on the national ownership of radio stations and permitted a single firm to own up to eight stations in the largest communities. Since then a small number of firms control most radio markets.[30] In 2003 the FCC attempted unsuccessfully to loosen further ownership restrictions.

The case for media deregulation on grounds of economic efficiency is far from clear in that the industry is subject to several types of market failure—where government intervention may improve resource allocation. Radio and television shows, despite being provided by private companies, are basically public goods. Radio listeners and television (noncable) viewers cannot be excluded, and there is nonrivalry of viewership (that is, if one person watches more television, it does not diminish another viewer's television choices). If the marginal cost of an extra viewer is zero, then economic efficiency calls for a zero price. Yet producing television programs costs money, and the costs have to be recouped. Under the current system, advertisers pay and therefore select the programs and their quality. In that sense, advertisers serve as an imperfect proxy for viewer demand. However, because their objectives are quite different from those of viewers,[31] the existing solution, despite its market determination, does not necessarily provide people with the television they want. Cable television represents an improvement in responding to consumer demand, but it also does not provide an optimal solution because viewers who are unable or unwilling to pay the fee are excluded despite their low marginal cost.

Market failure also results from the fact that prices charged by the media usually fail to include the benefits and costs to third parties; consequently, there is either underproduction or overproduction, respectively.[32] This is true of information essential to democracy that is not provided because it is unprofitable, such as the positions of candidates at election time. The media can influence viewers' and readers' opinions and how they vote, all of which has an effect on other people's lives. In such cases, notes Baker, people are affected positively by the extent to which others have experienced informative media or alternately suffer adverse effects from others being exposed to misleading or erroneous information. In a similar vein, he suggests that media products for education, information, or culture are underproduced while content aimed at mainstream tastes is overproduced.

Media markets are also characterized by imperfect competition, which may also introduce inefficiencies. Consumers do not get the quantity and quality they want and would be willing to pay for. In the past, a few networks dominated television and supplied local stations with most of their programs—an outcome attributed to government grants of scarce spectrum frequency and the economies involved in sharing program costs over large audiences.[33] Cable television has injected more variety and diversity in offerings as well as providing competition to the networks. However, the cable industry itself is dominated by a few large firms and since 1995, the basic rate for cable subscription rose by three times the rate of inflation.[34]

Magazine ownership is also concentrated, and a few companies own the most popular magazines. Many local newspapers are monopolies, and increasing numbers are owned by large chains. It is claimed that economies of scale also characterize the newspaper business and lead to monopolies. Baker argues that, given the uniformity in reporting among papers, there is little reason for consumers to buy more expensive competing papers, which, in turn, reinforces the monopoly trend.[35] In recent years, competition from cable news and the Internet appears to have adversely affected newspaper readership and revenues.

Finally, as mentioned above, many media outlets are reluctant to provide consumer information if it involves criticism of established producers. The result is market failure because consumers end up making purchasing decisions on the basis of incomplete or faulty information, which also leads to a misallocation of resources.

Baker notes that because of market failures, media regulation cannot be rejected automatically as elitist or paternalistic in that regulation is often aimed at correcting these failures.[36] If successful, such policies could improve both resource allocation and the political process. Although the FCC has at times obstructed competition and delayed new technologies, resulting in social costs, if deregulation leads to the suppression of competition by private firms, it will not represent much of a gain to society.

9.5 Advertising and Information

The primary source of revenue for most media outlets, whether they are newspapers, television stations, or radio stations, is advertising. Media companies take great care in editing news so as not to offend their sponsors. This results in tension between independent programming, particularly news shows, and the wish to accommodate, or at least not alienate, advertisers. To Owen, the negative side of advertising is that it forces the media to respond to incentives different from those of consumers, and he blames advertising for creating the popular myth that television is free. However, he also sees a positive side in that certain shows and programs would not be produced were it not for the revenues received from advertising.

In recent years, a deliberate blurring of the difference between advertising and the news itself has become more common. It is not always clear what is genuine news and what is product promotion. On radio shows, broadcasters endorse products in a way that makes it difficult to tell where the news ends and the advertisement begins. Attempts are often made to conceal the promotional aspects of infomercials, which are 30-minute paid television advertising programs devoted to promoting a product. The muddling of information is inconsistent with economic efficiency and does not lead to an informed public.

Richard Brown (2005) notes how media imagery, opinion surveys, and impression management are used to create facts and have become sources of legitimacy. Robert McChesney (2008) attributes the rise of the public relations (PR) industry to the lack of context in uniform reporting, thereby allowing PR agents to shape the news to corporate requirements. He suggests that a sizable portion of the news is based on information obtained from public relation sources and, in addition, there are significant links between advertising agencies and PR firms.

The companies paying for ads want distinct groups of viewers, especially young viewers with money to spend. Usually, regardless of the artistic merits of a show and sometimes even the size of the viewing audience, if a show does not attract sufficient numbers of viewers from desirable groups, it is cancelled. A similar factor is evident in the sale of magazines where advertisers are concerned that people with the "right income" are reading the magazine. This results in some creative strategies on the part of magazine distributors. Both newspapers and magazines include articles that fit in with the objectives of their advertisers. Some communities will not receive news coverage if they are considered to be outside a sought-after demographic or geographic range.[37] For a democracy that depends on knowledgeable voters, this is an unwelcome trend.

Joseph Turrow (1997) expresses concern about the media's power to shape our view of society and to describe the way things are in America. Advertisers, through their power over the media, have what Turrow describes as a monopoly on the description of America. Particularly disconcerting is that, in response to the dictates of advertising, the media are changing from a unifying social and cultural force to a divisive force intent on segmenting society.[38] If in the past the media promoted a sense of belonging to a national community, "society making," then in the past two decades, notes Turrow, a new trend has emerged that he calls "segment-making." The media seek to label and separate people in accordance with the needs of marketers to reach their target audience. Income, age, and lifestyles distinguish these nongeographic media communities, and television programs, newspapers, and magazines are created for them, thereby leading to sharper social divisions as people come to identify with their media communities and not their physical community.[39]

The U.S. media are characterized by the primacy of the freedom to profit. Unfortunately, this freedom at times clashes with the requirements of political freedom and competitive free markets. The success of large media firms is attributable in part to government policies, over which they have considerable influence, and not necessarily the invisible hand of the market. Yet government intervention to correct market failures or protect the public interest is on the decline, an unwelcome trend for both economic efficiency and democracy. Finally and hypothetically, if a complete media monopoly came about, some would accept this as the inevitable result of market forces that should not be tampered with, regardless of how the monopoly was attained. Others would see the danger to democracy and to competition in the marketplace of ideas, never mind the economic implications; yet their views would not prevail, especially if there were no media outlets willing to disseminate such views.

PART III

Markets

CHAPTER 10

Competition and Markets

In Adam Smith's view of the working of the invisible hand, competition plays a crucial role. Competition counters greed and by so doing ensures the provision of goods and services at relatively reasonable prices. More generally, there is a popular belief in competition as a dynamic process leading to greater efficiency and prosperity. It is regarded as a catalyst for new technologies and innovations while also weeding out the inefficient and antiquated. To economists and social Darwinists, competition and competitive markets have beneficial economic and social properties.

However, admiration for competition is far from universal. Competition has connotations with primordial struggles for survival and international conflicts over land and resources. It is seen as unavoidable, although not an uplifting or unifying aspect of civilization other than in the sports arena. Business competition also has its dark side involving at times fraud and deception.[1] Attitudes on competition reflect a contradiction, with admiration expressed for competitive markets, especially for the products and services people buy, but an abhorrence of competitive markets for the items they sell[2]—all should be subject to the discipline of markets except us and our endeavors. Not surprisingly many enterprises attempt to reduce or eliminate competition, whether they are professionals, retailers, or manufacturers.

In previous chapters, arguments were made on behalf of competitive free markets. In this chapter, actual markets are examined, and the question posed is whether they can be properly described as competitive free markets.

10.1 Competitive Markets

A perfectly competitive market structure is said to provide the best allocation of resources. Such markets have many producers and many consumers, none of whom can affect price by their own individual actions. Instead, prices are set through the impersonal interaction of numerous buyers and sellers. Existing firms cannot bar entry into the industry or exit from it, thereby ensuring mobility of resources. In addition, products are standardized (no brands based on real or perceived differences), and buyers and sellers are assumed to possess perfect information. Such markets are clearly more in the nature of an ideal or a theoretical construct than a realistic depiction of an economy. Yet the theoretical basis for the well-known assertion that market economies are superior to alternative systems is based on the model of perfect competition.

Critics complain that there is an excessive emphasis on price competition and the ensuing (static) allocative efficiency while the benefits of other forms of business competition are downplayed. An obsession with price competition is said to reflect a misunderstanding of the way business functions and competes for survival. A serious challenge to price competition and its allocative efficiency as an economic priority is the claim that it may result in fewer technological innovations and therefore require a sacrifice in the form of slower rates of economic growth. Economic studies suggest that technological progress is a primary contributor to long-term growth.[3] Schumpeter proposes that monopolies and oligopolies, as well as large firms, are more likely to engage in innovative activity leading to technological progress than firms in more competitive (price) markets. If true, then imperfect competition may result in higher rates of growth[4] and living standards that should more than compensate for the misallocation of resources arising from monopoly type pricing. However, support for the existence of a positive relationship between monopoly power and innovation as well as firm size and innovation, even on theoretical grounds, is not unanimous.[5]

The lure of monopoly profits leads firms to engage in R&D; but, according to Schumpeter, existing monopolists also will have greater incentive to undertake costly R&D projects[6] because they can appropriate the gains from innovation without fear of competitors imitating them and sharing in their rewards. However, without competitors, notes Scherer (1980), a monopolist may not have the incentive to carry out risky R&D, whereas firms in more competitive environs face greater pressures to engage in research. Although the monopolist may have the financial wherewithal and organizational ability to engage in risky inventions and innovations, as well as less fear of imitation, it does not necessarily have the pressure to do so.[7] At one extreme, too much competition and fear of imitation may result in relatively little R&D efforts despite a desire to gain a competitive advantage. At the other extreme, with too little competition, the pressure dissipates and with it the desire to innovate.

Statistical tests of the Schumpeterian hypothesis have, on the whole, been inconclusive, with some studies finding increases in R&D correlated with rising concentration (less competition) up to what might be described as moderate oligopoly levels.[8] Scherer and Ross (1990), however, note that once technological opportunities in different industries are accounted for, the positive correlation weakens. There are also documented cases of cartel-like arrangements and other noncompetitive agreements delaying or suppressing innovation.[9] On the whole, it would appear that there is little support for the technological supremacy of any one particular market structure. A qualification to the perceived advantages of technological competition is noted by Piore and Sabel (1984). They caution that the winning innovation is rarely the technologically superior model but more likely an outcome of circumstances and market power.

An additional argument that raises doubts about whether a more competitive economy necessarily improves allocative efficiency is the Theory of Second Best. The theory suggests that having more competition in some sectors of the economy may not always get the economy closer to the efficiency attained when all markets are perfectly competitive.[10] Nonetheless, economists tend to favor the application of the competitive pricing rule based on setting price equal to marginal cost. Another criticism is Galbraith's (1983) broader argument that competition does not resolve concerns about economic power in the U.S. economy. He dismisses suggestions that the market mechanism and competition steer power to socially desirable ends.

Despite the criticisms and exceptions, such as market failures, competitive economies, with an emphasis on price competition, are thought to experience a more efficient allocation of resources and display a greater awareness of consumer requirements than economies with less competitive markets.[11] Profit and price signals allow the economy to adjust automatically to changing conditions. Even if one were to decide that it is futile to promote more competition on efficiency grounds, there are additional arguments both economic and political that could be made on behalf of competition. In a competitive system, resource allocation and income distribution are determined through the impersonal workings of supply and demand, thereby restricting the influence of government and private parties over the livelihood of individuals. Competition tends to decentralize power—a highly regarded political principle in America. Another benefit of competition is freedom of opportunity resulting from not having barriers to entry or to resource mobility and people being able to choose their preferred occupation or business.

U.S. markets are not perfectly competitive. They possess neither the efficiency nor the fairness properties associated with such markets, at least not to the same extent. However, there is an argument that many industries, while not perfectly competitive, could be described as "workably competitive", meaning they are sufficiently competitive in the sense that public intervention would produce little in the way of social gains. Bruce Greenwald and Joseph Stiglitz (1986) suggest that market failures are more widespread than previously thought, especially, cases of imperfect information (and incomplete markets). Therefore, government intervention to correct different market failures, in addition to imperfect competition, may be justified in many more situations.

Despite, or perhaps because of, the difficulties surrounding definitions and tests, the notion that the United States has a workably competitive economy is common. The basis for this acceptance has been the belief that resources, generally, respond to price signals and end up where they are needed most, markets clear, and prices tend to reflect average, if not marginal costs. Notwithstanding the presence of many imperfectly competitive markets, the overall economy is said to display a satisfactory level of competition.[12] This interpretation of the state of competition has been influenced by the Chicago School of thought. In the second half of the twentieth century, it adopted a methodological approach that essentially rules out the existence of imperfect competition. It takes as given (tight prior) that actual markets are competitive (approximating long-run equilibrium in perfect competition) and the burden—and a heavy one at that—is placed on nonbelievers to prove otherwise.[13] Melvin Reder (1982) describes how the traditional method of determining the validity of a theory has been reversed. Instead of subjecting theory to empirical testing, the theory is used to reject the outcome of empirical tests.[14] Markets are predetermined as competitive. The inference is that, if the economy contains competitive markets, there is no need to worry about market power. Therefore, economic freedom (defined as no government intervention in the economy) is preserved. The forceful promotion of this viewpoint has affected scholarly inquiry on these issues.

Differences of opinion exist on what is a satisfactory level of competition, and there is an element of the glass being half-full or half-empty to this debate. Nevertheless, major U.S. industries are imperfectly competitive, more specifically, oligopolistic. There is evidence that oligopoly firms can enjoy consistently high profits over long periods.[15] New firms and smaller existing rivals are often an insufficient competitive force for reducing those profits to normal levels. If either a price close to marginal or average cost or just evidence of price competition is required for a finding of a competitive free market, then key industries would not fit the bill. Nonprice competition exists in the form of advertising, financial terms, terms of delivery, competition to obtain monopoly rents, and more. However, those forms of competition are not usually regarded as equally beneficial as price competition because the purpose of some of these types of competition is strictly redistributive.[16] It is also doubtful whether acceptance of a different definition of a free market, requiring only the lack of barriers to entry and exit, but without price competition, yields a more favorable diagnosis. Here too debates abound over what constitutes a barrier and whether the existence of only a small number of firms in an industry signifies their efficiency or their power to deter entry. In addition, bargaining power is frequently tilted in a contrived manner, sometimes even with government help, against buyers and smaller sellers. Not only is the economic freedom of many individuals and firms lessened as a result, but such markets are not in conformity with Adam Smith's original intent. One might add that, legal issues aside, fraud and deception and misleading advertising also violate some definitions of free markets. Finally, in evaluating whether an industry resembles a free market or not, the extent of government intervention is crucial. Regardless of the form of pricing, if an industry or some of its members receive subsidies and other forms of government help, (as discussed in Chapter 8), then this is inconsistent with the definition of a free market.[17] Government may not set the price, but its assistance affects it.

10.2 Competition in Manufacturing

Monopoly is relatively rare in U.S. manufacturing industries, but important industries are oligopolies. In analyzing the degree of competition, one measure used by economists is an industry's four firm concentration ratio (C4), which is the combined market share of the four largest firms. In 1992, less than 5 percent of industries had a C4 greater than or equal to 80 percent, while at the other extreme, less than 18 percent of industries had a C4 less than or equal to 20 percent.[18] Using a rough dividing line for oligopoly of C4 greater than or equal to 40 percent, then 176 out of 409 industries in 1992 could be described as oligopolies.[19] Keeping in mind that concentration ratios are only one of several possible structural indicators of competition (in addition to behavioral indicators such as price) and not necessarily the best, the numbers suggest that more than 40 percent of manufacturing industries are characterized by some market power.

Historically, the nation began with local markets in manufactured goods and probably without too much competition.[20] National markets were facilitated by the advent of the railroads as well as advances in communications, which brought about more competition.[21] The great merger wave of the late nineteenth and early twentieth centuries saw the creation of dominant firms in many industries through the acquisition of competitors. The opportunity for promotional profits was a key factor in those mergers.[22] Cartels were deemed unreliable for the purpose of maintaining stable prices.[23] In that period, as previously noted, 71 industries were turned into near monopolies through mergers. This was not accidental, because it resulted in a halt to the emerging price competition and hence reassured investors about the profit potential of the merged companies.[24] Those mergers and the resulting market dominance were to have a profound impact on American industry for most of the twentieth century.

According to Warren Nutter (1951), at the beginning of the twentieth century, U.S. manufacturing already experienced relatively high concentration; approximately a third of output came from industries with a C4 equal to or greater than 50 percent. Views differ on the trend of concentration for the next 50 years, whether it increased or remained unchanged. William Shepherd (1982) estimates (by taking into account factors other than concentration, such as behavioral factors relating to pricing) that, by 1980, 69 percent of manufacturing industries were effectively competitive compared with less than 56 percent in 1958. During that period, the degree of competition increased in every major sector—a trend attributed to imports and antitrust policy. However, according to Pryor (2001), from 1982 to 1992, the trend reversed and concentration in manufacturing rose.[25] The main reason for the increase was the merger waves of the 1980s and 1990s due in part to the easy availability of financing, lenient antitrust enforcement,[26] and, possibly, new standards for CEOs' compensation. From the perspective of competition, the merger waves had a disconcerting pattern: 75 percent of these mergers, economy wide, in terms of value consisted of firms producing in at least one identical four-digit standard industrial classification (SIC) industry.[27] Domestic mergers reduced competitiveness, as did mergers of domestic firms with foreign firms because those imports could now be controlled by domestic firms.

Pryor attempts to account for the impact of import competition on concentration ratios and starts out by assuming that all imports had a procompetitive influence. Even with this assumption, he finds that the trade-adjusted concentration ratios in manufacturing industries from 1982 to 1992 do not show a clear trend in either direction. Pryor notes that if adjustments could be made for the fact that a significant percentage of imports came from foreign subsidiaries of U.S. multinationals as well as from foreign multinationals to their U.S. subsidiaries, then the adjusted concentration ratios would have most likely increased. If Pryor is correct, then contrary to conventional wisdom, imports on average failed to inject a procompetitive stimulus strong enough to overcome the impact of mergers. Although the findings require additional corroboration, at the very least, they serve to caution against automatic acceptance of the commonly held belief that competition in U.S. manufacturing has been steadily increasing.

An examination of competition from a somewhat different perspective shows that dominant firms' market share in different industries has remained stable or else declined very slowly throughout most of the twentieth century. The percentage of the economy affected is small,[28] but such evidence does not seem to accord with Schumpeter's hypothesis of "gales of destruction." Analyzing leading firms' market share over time, Shepherd (1997) writes that a moderate decay process appears to exist, and a consensus estimate might be that high market shares decline at a rate of about 0.5 percentage points a year, ignoring antitrust action and keeping in mind some large individual variations. The decline may have been somewhat faster in recent decades as compared to midcentury rates in manufacturing and utilities. There have been exceptions to the decline, although toward the end of the twentieth century some firms that previously appeared impervious to market share erosion began to experience decline. Among the dominant firms to lose market share were Gillette in razor blades, Eastman Kodak in film, IBM in digital computers in the 1980s, Xerox in electrostatic copiers, and Boeing in large passenger airplanes.[29] However, the slow pace of decline and the realization that without international competition the decline might have been further delayed is noteworthy. Shepherd attributes the lack of decline (until 1980) to financial ties of these companies, as well as to public policies and defensive tactics employed by the firms. Examples of some leading firms with substantial market shares in 1996, some held for a long time and others less so, included IBM in main-frame computers with 70 percent, Du Pont in titanium dioxide with 65 percent, De Beers in diamonds with 75 percent, Campbell Soup in canned soup with 75 percent, Procter & Gamble in detergents with 48 percent, and Microsoft in software with 85 percent.[30]

For an economy to function efficiently, there has to be not only internal rivalry but also competition from new firms. The evidence for U.S. manufacturing industries points to considerable numbers of entry and exit. A study by Timothy Dunne, Mark Roberts and Larry Samuelson (1988) finds that over five-year time intervals, nearly 40 percent of firms were new. This would seem to suggest a robust competitive process with plenty of mobility. Yet such a conclusion would be misleading because most entrants, in comparison with existing firms, were much smaller in size and produced less output, and many did not survive beyond five years. So despite the large number of entrants, their relatively small size and quick exit, vigorous price competition did not take place. The exception of course was in new industries, especially high-tech industries. In fact, those industries became the hallmark of what was called in the 1990s the New Economy and involved industries such as telecommunications, computers, software, and biotechnology.

Economic theory suggests that above-normal profits serve as a signal for the entry of new firms. Yet there are industries where, despite persistently above-normal profits, little or no entry takes place, thus raising questions about obstacles to mobility of resources and the resulting inefficiencies. The industries in question are often concentrated oligopolies protected by barriers to entry or exit. Studies have shown, for example, that key U.S. manufacturing oligopolies in the 1950s and 1960s lacked meaningful domestic entry (government assistance aside) that could have led to price competition and challenged existing leaders.[31] In the 1970s and 1980s, there was the expectation that import entry would compensate for the lack of domestic competition from new and existing firms. Yet while imports had a strong procompetitive impact in some industries, as noted above, in other industries the anticipated price competition did not materialize.

The structure of American industry in the twentieth century was determined, to a large extent, by the great merger wave at the beginning of the century. Leading firms in some industries lost market share slowly if at all. Where significant change occurred, it was due more to changes in technology, international competition, and periodic antitrust intervention than to domestic rivalry. Economies of scale in production provide an incomplete explanation for leading firms' market shares. In addition, despite arguments on the importance of economies of scale in research and development, there is insufficient evidence of such economies to account for unchanging market shares. Access to investment capital may be a source of advantage for large corporations, as well as the ensuing financial ties. There may be economies in distribution, marketing, and promotion. Post–World War II concentration increased in consumer goods industries with highly differentiated products.[32] Product differentiation with its sunk cost characteristic can also act as a barrier to the entry of new firms.

What else may have protected those oligopolies? In a few cases, it may have been outstanding performance on the part of the firms involved. In other cases, it may have been luck. However, collusive agreements such as price fixing and other forms of competition suppression (legal and illegal) played some role, as known from cases prosecuted by the U.S. government (discussed in the next chapter). Obviously it is unknown what percentage of anticompetitive agreements the government prosecuted.

Oligopoly theory suggests that firms with market power can charge higher prices. Economists have attempted to test this relationship indirectly by examining profit data for manufacturing industries. The results, for the most part, point to a positive correlation between profits and concentration, especially in consumer goods industries, suggesting that large firms in concentrated industries protected by barriers to entry can raise prices above cost. A criticism of these results is that higher profits can be explained by lower costs rather than higher prices. However, later studies examining prices (instead of profits) and studying individual industries again find positive correlations with concentration[33] suggesting that firms with market power can raise prices above cost.

One additional source of advantage often taken for granted or else ignored is that industries and particularly powerful corporations seek and receive government help in a variety of forms as discussed above. Government can protect a firm's position and place smaller rivals, actual and potential, domestic and foreign, at a disadvantage. Large firms can obtain favorable laws, including laws that establish the rules of the game such as those relating to business behavior, corporate ownership, mergers, patents, bankruptcy, and limited liability.[34] Government at all levels—local, state, and federal—can provide subsidies, favorable tax policies, and their custom. In 2008, Americans became reacquainted with another powerful form of help—bailouts.

10.3 Competition in Services

The service sector includes medical, financial, educational, and legal industries. It also includes auto repair shops, hotels, restaurants, barbershops, dry cleaners, and many additional services. In several respects, service industries depart further from the perfectly competitive model than is commonly assumed. Scherer and Ross (1990) note that, despite the large numbers of sellers nationally, there is much more market power than would appear from a casual examination. They attribute this to strong product differentiation, tight restrictions on entry, and other noncompetitive practices that prevent price competition. A key problem here is the asymmetry in information between sellers and buyers. Buyers often are unsure whether they need the service and, on receiving it, may be unable to evaluate its quality. Given the hundreds if not thousands of professionals in specific fields in each metropolitan area, one would expect to observe strong price competition for customers. Yet that is not the case among lawyers, physicians, and dentists. In fact, there is relatively little in the way of discernible price competition among professionals in these fields, although some changes have taken place in the medical field. A 1975 antitrust case involving fixed fees for title searches among lawyers in Fairfax County, Virginia, provides some indication that the lack of competition is not always accidental.[35] In real estate, despite the large number of real estate agencies in large cities, the 6 percent fee paid by the seller of a house has remained fairly intact, with some exceptions, despite federal government inquiries. Retailing is seen as basically competitive,[36] ranging in large metropolitan areas from atomistic to moderately oligopolistic, although food retailing may be more oligopolistic.[37] In the 1980s and 1990s, there was some decline in the competitiveness of retailing due in part to mergers.[38]

Banking, nationally, is a loose oligopoly but less competitive in smaller local markets.[39] The trend toward national banking and Internet banking appears procompetitive, but the large number of mergers, as well as other factors discussed below, may counter that trend. Consumers have more choices in terms of services due to legal and technological changes such as Internet banking, yet banks have been able to charge higher fees for checks, wire transfers, ATMs, and returned checks. Credit card companies in the early 2000s charged higher interest despite a noninflationary environment. Financial institutions have been able to push more costs on to consumers, partly as a result of new laws. In 2008, major changes were occurring in investment banking where venerable institutions were failing or being forced to merge with large banks due to mortgage, derivative, and more generally leverage problems.

As discussed previously, the health-care industry is growing both in absolute terms and as a percentage of the GDP. In fact, in the not-too-distant future if current trends continue, expenditures on health care may exceed the total value of U.S. manufactured goods. Hospital bills have been increasing rapidly, and prices appear to bear little relation to marginal costs. The state of competition in the industry is worthy of a chapter by itself, and it is a complex industry combining private and public elements. A major change in recent decades has been the introduction of managed health care primarily by for-profit insurance companies where the physicians are often employees. HMOs provide health care for a fixed premium, and hence their incentive is to minimize costs.[40] An additional outcome of the new economic approach and heightened legal concerns has been the deterioration in the relationship between physicians and patients. HMOs, from an economic point of view, attempt to minimize moral hazard[41]—the problem being that customers want to maximize benefits and have little individual incentive to keep costs down. One way to reduce costs is to reduce the number of sick and elderly people insured, which leads to a conflict between profitability and society's responsibility.[42] Goddeeris (2001) writes that large employers with relatively younger or healthier workers are able to receive lower insurance rates, thereby exacerbating the plight of older and less healthy groups. In the 1980s, insurance companies moved from paying hospitals according to the cost of patient treatment to paying predetermined rates.[43] The outcome was that hospitals had an incentive to discharge their patients as quickly as possible. Whereas in 1980 the average stay in a hospital was 7.6 days, by 2003 it was 5.7 days.[44] HMOs' success in reducing costs is subject to debate. In addition, their impact on the quality of service remains unclear.[45] A 2005 law, which prohibited government agencies from bargaining with pharmaceutical companies over price when purchasing drugs, is indicative of another source of power in the health-care industry.

In the mid-twentieth century, as a result of the American Medical Association limiting the supply of medical schools combined with tight local control over physicians' access to hospitals, competition among physicians was effectively curtailed, resulting in high fees. Under managed care, physicians' incentives may have changed, and there may be more competition than before, although this rarely translates into direct price competition. One outcome is physicians forming group practices to have more bargaining power in dealing with insurance companies.[46] Hospitals, too, have been merging for cost-saving reasons, to gain market power in local markets, or else to improve their bargaining position with insurance companies. Overall, there is probably some competition for medical services in large cities but less so in rural areas,[47] and, as stated above, costs keeps rising faster than the overall rate of inflation.

10.4 Overall Competition

Competition levels in the U.S. economy—intra-industry and inter-industry along both price and technology dimensions—probably exceed that of many other nations. Intensified global competition over the past two decades as well as the advent of Internet commerce has improved matters in different markets. Yet the economy is not moving uniformly toward greater competition as was hoped 25 years ago. Competitive markets exist, especially where many small entrepreneurs operate. Nevertheless, oligopoly power prevails in key parts of manufacturing and services. Many cases of price coordination, both legal and illegal, have been reported during the past and present century, including pricing practices in autos, cigarettes, electric turbines, glass containers, steel, and vitamins. In those cases, it is not impersonal market forces that set prices, but rather tacit and explicit collusion.

Import competition has improved matters in some industries but has had little effect in others. Pryor (2001), surveying the different sectors of the economy from 1972 to 1992, does not discern a procompetitive trend. He notes that, once adjustments are made for structural changes in the economy such as the trend to services and away from manufacturing, overall market concentration increased. Contrary to the conventional view of deregulation as ushering in a new era of competition, Pryor claims that it may have led to increased concentration as a result of postderegulation mergers in industries such as railways, airlines, and telephone communications. Similarly, increased concentration through mergers has occurred in radio stations, media enterprises, and cable and Internet companies.

Pricing for the most part does not approximate the economic ideal of price equal to marginal cost.[48] The Adam Smith vision of an economy guided by an invisible hand appears unattainable, and there is no impetus for change. Quite the contrary, the emphasis has been on praising the current state of competition. Part of the problem, as argued earlier, is the recourse to political power to shield economic power. Although there are political institutions to protect competition, they have been either ineffective or insufficiently enforced to bring about a significant move toward a competitive free market economy.

A prevalent belief is that monopoly-type pricing does not cause much damage to the U.S. economy.[49] This view received support from Arnold Harberger's (1954) study, which calculated welfare losses (deadweight loss) due to monopoly pricing and found that, for 1924 to 1928, they amounted to only one-tenth of 1 percent of the gross national product (GNP). The tiny loss hardly justifies concern about market power. However, later studies find substantially higher welfare losses from imperfectly competitive pricing, suggesting that market power's impact on the economy is not inconsequential.[50] Among other types of inefficiencies resulting from market power are X-inefficiency[51] and competition for monopoly rents. X-inefficiency suggests that companies with market power may feel little pressure to minimize costs, and hence their costs are usually higher. There is some evidence from banks and utilities to support this phenomenon.[52] Companies competing for monopoly profits may devote resources to influencing politicians to obtain legal protection from competitors.[53] Tariff protection or the designation of a natural monopoly may be attained through campaign contributions, lobbying, bribes, legal tactics, and other expenditures.[54] Such spending, legal issues aside, is profitable to the company but of dubious value to society as a whole. If the amounts spent on these kinds of activities are added, the total welfare loss rises. There are arguments that exhortative advertising lacking informational content is wasteful, and such expenditures should also be counted as a welfare loss (although there is an opposing view that sees benefits in most types of advertising). A rather harmful effect arising from market power is the suppression of technology, and if this were measurable again, welfare loss would rise.

Finally, the findings from several key U.S. industries are unfavorable to a free market determination because of government intervention. Government involvement in the auto industry in the twentieth century was exceptionally strong. Taxpayers subsidized highway construction, which amounted to an indirect subsidy to automakers. Other examples of government involvement include limits on auto imports in the 1980s that, as noted above, raised the average price of an American car by $370 and Japanese cars by $900[55]; delays in requiring greater auto fuel economy, thereby incurring the social cost of greater oil consumption; limited funds for public transportation; and the acceptance of large social costs from pollution and highway deaths.[56] Those are only some of the more important examples of government help given to the auto industry. Eventually, imports injected more meaningful competition into the industry and weakened long-standing oligopolistic behavior, to the detriment of domestic firms and workers. Yet for most of the second half of the twentieth century, few industries received as much direct and indirect government support as the auto companies. It is difficult to claim that the industry met competitive free market standards.

Crucial government intervention took place in the steel industry through import protection in the late 1970s, 1980s, and 1990s. The oil industry experienced considerable government intervention, often with questionable economic objectives.[57] It was also subject to different rules than other industries in that it received immunity from antitrust laws for reasons of national security, and later on similar grounds, private antitrust lawsuits were dismissed.[58] The subsidies provided to ethanol producers offer another interesting case of government help. In the face of steeply rising energy costs, ethanol has been promoted as an alternative to petroleum-based gasoline. However, critics have questioned its cost effectiveness, particularly the fact that it requires large amounts of fossil fuel to produce.[59] Suggestions that the financial industry resembles a free market suffered a fatal blow in 2008. The use of a variety of government agencies to redistribute trillions of dollars to an assortment of investment banks, commercial banks, and insurance companies put to rest claims about the free market characteristics of the financial sector.

The above are just a few examples of government intervention, but they are consequential enough to void the free market appellation for the industries in question. Despite widespread use of price signals to direct resources, in major industries the guidance of the invisible hand is replaced with coordinated private economic power and public intervention. The conclusion, again, is that the freedom to profit of corporations takes precedence; in this case, it has priority over the freedom of markets.

CHAPTER 11

Competition Policy

11.1 Competition and Government

A long-held belief, going back to Thomas Jefferson, is that competition is necessary to prevent individuals or organizations from infringing on the economic liberties of others or undermining the freedom of the system.[1] A genuinely competitive free market economy has a built-in mechanism for preventing the rise of economic power through decentralized decision making of numerous economic units. Yet in the laissez faire environment of the past 30 years, competition and its protection have been relegated to a lesser role often in the name of economic efficiency. It would appear that when corporations' freedom to profit is paramount,[2] the importance of protecting competition becomes secondary, for all intents and purposes. Can competition survive in a completely laissez-faire environment? A competitive market's existence is not guaranteed and can be destroyed by its participants[3] so that laissez-faire does not ensure optimal economic performance.[4] Without competition, the public risks facing monopolies and cartels. Economic freedom without a modicum of public supervision may lessen market competition as well as other freedoms.[5] Specifically, in the context of the current framework, unrestricted freedom of corporations to profit by circumventing the market endangers both individual economic freedom and the freedom of markets.

Henry Simons, unlike many modern laissez-faire proponents, does not see a logical inconsistency in promoting market solutions while proposing government protection of competition.[6] He is aware that competitive markets can quite easily turn or be turned into monopolistic markets. Monopoly, he argues, must be fought against on both economic and political grounds. Private economic power, just like government, can engage in coercion, and a free market requires institutions to protect competition. Simons strongly opposes government intervention through price or quantity controls. Nonetheless, he approves of a government-backed framework to defend market competition , because in his opinion, it would reduce calls for direct government intervention in specific markets, especially on behalf of powerful groups.

From an economic perspective, government intervention in the economy is justified in cases of market failure , such as imperfect competition, where government can improve the allocation of resources. Government has several alternative policies at its disposal in protecting competition.[7] The options include imposing taxes on monopolists—price controls, public ownership, regulation of natural monopoly, consumer information programs, and antitrust laws discussed below.

11.2 Antitrust—Origins

The United States has rules of competition known as antitrust laws—a uniquely American invention. In the 1870s and 1880s, substantial private efforts were devoted to reducing or eliminating competition by establishing cartels, trusts, pools, and syndicates,[8] often nationwide. The numerous attempts to circumvent the market demonstrate that collusive practices were not the exception.[9] The courts, writes Roy (1997), came to the defense of markets and asserted that the state had an interest in their survival. Interestingly, many cases condemned as collusive were initiated by businesses that did not view such activities as illegal, suggesting again that they were fairly commonplace and raising doubts about how widespread was the idealized form of markets.[10]

There was support for pooling and cartels and sympathy for firms suffering from ruinous competition. John B. Clark defended pooling because he saw it as a natural defense against ruinous competition; and Attorney General Wickersham claimed that monopoly was preferable to a large group of weak firms.[11] The formation of trusts and the large merger wave of that era suggest that competitive markets may not survive without government support.[12]

The purpose of the antitrust laws is to provide rules of competition with a special focus on curtailing economic power and protecting competition. These laws served as a model for other nations. The most famous of the antitrust laws is the Sherman Act established in 1890. The act has two important sections. The first section outlaws competitors from fixing prices or otherwise colluding to reduce competition. The second section prohibits monopolization. Additional laws were later passed to strengthen antitrust and close loopholes by prohibiting certain types of behavior, such as price discrimination, exclusive dealing, and tying arrangements, if they reduce competition.

Explanations for the passage of the Sherman Act differ. Some contend that the law came about because of fears about the economic consequences of cartels, collusive agreements, and mergers that resulted in giant corporations in oil, meatpacking, whiskey, tobacco, gunpowder, and sugar. Farmers and small businessmen suffered from the trusts; they paid higher prices while receiving lower prices for their own products.[13] There were complaints about pricing designed to destroy competitors. To Roy (1997), antitrust laws, while dealing with some of the less-desirable consequences of giant firms, represented an idealistic effort to restore competition (perhaps to a state that never existed) while recognizing that the changes in industry structure were permanent and the corporations were here to stay. Chandler (1977) writes that antitrust legislation, while discouraging monopoly, encouraged oligopolies and the growth of giant firms.

While to some antitrust is an economic law focused on prices and output,[14] others see it as dealing primarily with issues of power, both economic and political. According to A.D. Neale (1970), the connection between economic concentration and political power was not lost on the legislators who passed the Sherman Act. Antitrust law is a manifestation of the American distrust of all sources of unchecked power. In this respect, it parallels the constitutional arrangements of political checks and balances and the separation of powers. It also represents another strongly held American belief, which is the preference for a government of laws and not of men.[15] Donald Dewey (1974) also sees the purpose of antitrust as more political than economic, based on curbing private economic power and not because of concern about economic efficiency. Its purpose is to hold down large concentrations of power as well as to prevent demands for greater government intervention in the economy. Dewey claims that the hostility to giant corporations and the support for antitrust is rooted in the belief that too much discretionary power is vested in the hands of giant corporations. People fear giant corporations because of their own unequal and inferior position in relation to these powerful organizations. Williamson (1975) and Brock (2001) also do not see concerns about economic efficiency or consumer welfare as the rationale for antitrust but rather a desire to disperse economic power.

Although the subtleties of maximizing either consumer or total welfare were perhaps unknown to the legislators, they understood the implications of concentrated economic power for individual freedom, both economic and political. The current judicial emphasis on economic efficiency suggests that the original purpose of the antitrust laws has been modified. Economists of the late nineteenth century were adherents of Darwinism, defended trusts, and most likely had little impact on public policy of that era.[16] Therefore, it is unlikely that allocative economic efficiency considerations were a concern of the legislators who passed the Sherman Act. According to Robert Lande (1982), production efficiency may have been a consideration but definitely secondary to the distributive goal of preventing "unfair" transfers of wealth from consumers to firms with market power.

11.3 Antitrust—Price Fixing

It was once argued that cartels are bound to fail because of cheating; however, recent theoretical work has shown that firms can prevent cheating and therefore collusive schemes may survive. Margaret Levenstein and Valerie Suslow (2006) find considerable variety in the type of products and industries where collusion appears and also suggest that there is no simple relationship between industry concentration and the likelihood of collusion. They find that trade associations play a large role in coordinating the activities of cartels in nonconcentrated industries and that the median duration of a cartel is about five to six years, although some last less than a year and others, decades. What causes the success or failure of a cartel and other forms of collusion? For cartels to succeed, it is important for them to invest in monitoring mechanisms, such as joint sales agencies or regular reporting to one another or third parties, because this helps minimize cheating. An additional requirement for success is the need to find ways to deal with changing economic conditions, such as cyclical fluctuations in demand that might also lead to a breakup.[17]

Section 1 of the Sherman Act prohibits pricefixing. This type of activity came to be considered by the courts as illegal per-se, meaning if defendants are found to have fixed prices, the courts do not look into the reason why this was done; mitigating circumstances are irrelevant. A couple of famous cases that fell under Section 1 are the electrical equipment conspiracy of 1961 and the vitamins case of 1999. The electrical equipment case drew nationwide attention and involved Senate hearings. It was found that 29 firms had engaged in price-fixing and bid rigging in about 20 different product lines including expensive turbine generators and power transformers.[18] A wide variety of collusive methods were used for the different products. This included meetings in remote Canadian motels, the use of code names, pay phone conversations, and bid rigging based on phases of the moon where it was decided in advance which company would win the bid.[19] The heaviest penalty came not from government fines but rather from private antitrust lawsuits initiated by customers.

The vitamin conspiracy was considered by the Justice Department as the most harmful criminal antitrust conspiracy ever uncovered.[20] The conspiracy involved European and Japanese companies selling vitamins in the United States. The companies limited competition by agreeing to share global markets. Each company was assigned a predetermined market share, thereby avoiding head on competition. They agreed to fix prices and price increases in the United States and also rigged bids. They held meetings in Switzerland and Germany and did their best to prevent cheating among themselves. What is remarkable about this case is the size of the fines negotiated with the Department of Justice, which amounted to almost one billion dollars. The companies also had to pay their customers large compensatory sums.

An Antitrust Division list of all Sherman Act violations resulting in a corporate fine of $10 million or more in recent years shows some substantial fines. The largest fine was $0.5 billion paid by Hoffman-La Roche in the vitamins case. Interestingly, of the 52 firms listed, a majority were foreign firms—some of which were fined more than once.

For most of the twentieth century, both enforcement agencies and the courts regarded price-fixing violations as a serious matter, and with one exception during the Great Depression, applied the aforementioned per-se rule. However, since 1979 (in the ASCAP/BMI case), the courts have become amenable to requests for exemption from the per-se approach based on mitigating circumstances, such as whether concerted action on price was perhaps indispensable to the sale of the product.[21]

11.4 Antitrust—Oligopoly

George Stigler (1950) cautions that acceptance of oligopoly as a reasonable economic structure is a weakness of antitrust law. He warns that, from the point of view of competition, an industry structure consisting of only a few firms cannot be ignored; therefore, mergers leading to oligopoly are socially undesirable. With only a few firms in an industry, the firms are bound to recognize their interdependence. Yet, antitrust, if it tackles oligopoly at all, usually applies behavioral remedies. In addition, since 1946, government has been unable to prosecute successfully cases involving tacit, rather than explicit, collusion[22] inferred from circumstantial evidence, for example, similar pricing. The explanation for this judicial outcome is that the courts do not want to risk outlawing what they consider might be normal business practices within an oligopoly.[23]

Those who see the problem in oligopoly as structural in nature regard the behavioral approach as useless because it requires behavior contrary to self-interest. They are of the opinion that some collusion is inevitable in highly concentrated oligopolies because it is inherent in the structure of the industry. They do not see the issue in terms of well-behaving versus badly behaving oligopolies. Consequently, there has been a long-standing concern that antitrust with its emphasis on a conduct approach cannot deal effectively with oligopoly. Those critics would prefer an economic law based on market share (structure) rather than the existing legal approach based on evidence of conspiracy (conduct). Simons (1947) and Carl Kaysen and Donald Turner (1959) propose, under certain conditions, restructuring oligopolies with market power to enhance competitiveness. Richard Posner (1975) disagrees with the structural approach, claiming that an oligopolistic market structure can help noncompetitive conduct, but this type of behavior is not inevitable. Oligopolists have to take specific actions, as in a regular cartel or any other conspiracy. Williamson (1975) also does not see collusive activities as unavoidable in an oligopoly. Tacit collusion, he argues, is not easy to accomplish and is probably less reliable than regular collusive agreements in both price and nonprice decisions. Presently, the courts, influenced possibly by numerous theoretical studies pointing to a myriad of possibilities in oligopoly,[24] have increasingly declared suspect behavior as innocuous and compatible with normal behavior rather than evidence of collusive oligopoly.

11.5 Antitrust—Monopolization

The Sherman Act Section 2 prohibits monopolization. It is not illegal to have a monopoly; however, it is illegal to attempt to acquire a monopoly, that is, to monopolize. The distinction is not always clear. Based on the Supreme Court's decision in the famous Standard Oil (1911) case, a finding of monopolization requires two things. First, a firm has to have a large or dominant market share; however, exactly how much is not specified. Second, there has to be evidence of anticompetitive practices, such as predatory pricing or other abusive and "unreasonable" business practices used to obtain the large market share. In a sense, two categories of monopolies—the "good" and the "bad" monopoly—were created, perhaps unintentionally (although the courts were not unanimous about this). The good monopoly attains its position by building or inventing a superior product or service and has many satisfied customers. The bad monopoly engages in abusive and anticompetitive practices to acquire or retain its position.

Unlike price-fixing cases, a rule of reason is applied in monopolization cases to determine whether there was intent to monopolize through anticompetitive practices. An inconsistency exists here in that a group of firms jointly setting a monopoly price is illegal, regardless of circumstances; yet a monopolist charging the same price could be considered legal. An argument in defense of this position is that a collusive oligopoly cannot claim economies of scale whereas the monopoly might be able to do so.[25]

In the Standard Oil case, the company was found guilty of violating both Sections 1 and 2 of the Sherman Act. The company had close to 90 percent of the market and had acquired its large share partly through mergers with 120 smaller companies. It was accused of a variety of anticompetitive practices, including predatory pricing and foreclosing competitors from crude oil supplies. The court ordered that Standard Oil be dissolved.

In 1945, ALCOA was accused of monopolizing virgin aluminum. In this case, Judge Learned Hand sorted out the economic issues involving the relevant market share, which was complicated by the availability of scrap metal. Judge Hand ruled that ALCOA, with its 90 percent market share, could be considered to possess a monopoly. As far as intent to monopolize, the judge made the following ruling: Despite the fact that ALCOA had not engaged in abusive practices, the company's construction of large amounts of manufacturing capacity, far in excess of its needs, and its accumulation of reserves of raw materials was a form of entry deterrence and could be construed as evidence of monopolization. The monopoly had not fallen into ALCOA's lap; they had actively pursued it. The remedy was that ALCOA had to sell two plants to new companies. The ruling left to future courts the task of deciding whether a firm's behavior constituted an acceptable business practice or an attempt to monopolize.[26]

In the past two decades, the most publicized monopolization case is that of Microsoft. Justice Thomas Jackson found the company guilty of monopolizing the PC operating system market for Intel-compatible personal computers. He found as follows: Microsoft had a dominant market share of 95 percent; it had barriers to entry to protect its position; it possessed the ability to raise price above marginal cost without attracting entry; it maintained its monopoly power by anticompetitive means; it attempted to monopolize the web browser market by unlawfully tying its web browser to its operating system (a finding overturned by the Appeals Court); it sought to prevent middleware from threatening Windows (Internet applications); it demanded that original equipment manufacturers not use Java and Navigator; and it prevented innovation. Judge Jackson ruled for a structural solution consisting of breaking up the company into two parts; however, he was overruled by the Appeals Court. According to some experts, there is little in the sentencing or final settlement to deter Microsoft, or for that matter future high-tech companies, from adopting anticompetitive practices. Microsoft acquired a monopoly position through a combination of first mover advantage, economies of scale, and network effects. The government did not claim that Microsoft had won its monopoly illegally but rather that it was protecting its position through the use of illegal tactics.[27] A monopoly position that has not been acquired or defended through illegal or anticompetitive practices appears to be beyond the reach of the law.[28] Williamson (1975) expresses concern about the advisability of allowing structural dominance positions based on past superiority to last indefinitely. He points out that persistent dominance can sometimes be construed as a market failure that might, under certain conditions, justify government intervention.[29]

11.6 Antitrust—Enforcement

The level of antitrust enforcement varied considerably over the twentieth century. An aggressive approach was applied before World War I and Standard Oil and American Tobacco, having been found guilty of violating both Sections 1 and 2 of the Sherman Act, were restructured. Competition was seen in a less favorable light during the Depression. The National Industry Recovery Act (NIRA) permitted cartel-like arrangements in the mistaken belief that such a policy would encourage industrial expansion and boost employment. Disenchantment with the NIRA and market power in the late 1930s prompted a rethinking about competition that led to renewed antitrust activity.[30] For a quarter of a century after World War II, the laws were strongly enforced. However, in the last two decades of the twentieth century and the first decade of the twenty-first century, enforcement has tended to be more lenient. Some point to the Microsoft case as an example of judicial zeal; to others, it represents an exception to generally lax enforcement, especially given the large number of uncontested mergers that have taken place.

The judiciary increasingly has accepted the Chicago School's efficiency explanations and has been willing to override laws protecting competition for alleged economic efficiencies.[31] Many judicial appointees during the Nixon Administration[32] and later Republican administrations[33] opposed a strong interventionist approach to antitrust matters. Adams and Brock (1986) note that antitrust agencies, rather than enforce the law, were acting more as consultants to facilitate mergers, regardless of their effect on competition. The trend was to gain strength. Department of Justice Merger Guidelines issued in 1982 and 1992 focus on economic efficiency; yet there is little evidence of efficiency in mergers, never mind that efficiency was not the intended purpose of antitrust laws. William Curran (2001) suggests that, notwithstanding claims of rationality and objectivity in support of efficiency and welfare maximization rules, dominant economic interests were promoting the new antitrust values.

When it comes to sentencing, antitrust is generally treated as a mild crime. Neither the individual sentences nor the fines imposed on companies in most cases are considered much of a deterrent. Given uncertainties about the economic viability of the newly formed companies (especially in high-tech industries[34]) and prospects for their shareholders, courts are reluctant to order structural remedies involving the breakup of a company. The courts do not relish the role of economic planner. However, the result all too often has been that remedies in monopolization cases seem an afterthought and address the symptoms and not the causes of monopoly.[35]

Increasingly, the objective of antitrust has become economic efficiency. As already noted, the original intent of antitrust laws was far broader than economic efficiency. The strictly economic argument started as a proposal by Robert Bork (1978) to maximize consumer welfare (surplus), although it has been pointed out that, in economic terms, his goal is more appropriately described as maximization of total welfare.[36] A review of the courts' decisions in antitrust matters over the past quarter century would suggest that, in practical terms, especially in the 2000s, the welfare criterion actually applied bears closer resemblance to producer welfare (surplus) maximization than either of the above two standards. From 1994 to 2007, every Supreme Court antitrust case was won by the defendant.[37] The Supreme Court's inclination for errors of omission over errors of commission conforms to the laissez-faire view that markets are fine the way they are.[38]

A sharp change in focus and a radical reinterpretation of congressional intent has taken place. Economic arguments bordering on the speculative are accepted regarding predatory actions and price fixing while allegations of anticompetitive practices, notwithstanding the evidence, are dismissed as impossible to determine.[39] The end result, invariably, is that the freedom of corporations to profit prevails over the freedom of markets and individuals.

11.7 Objections to Antitrust

Possibly coinciding with the economic prosperity and the stock market boom of the late 1980s and 1990s were calls for the elimination of the antitrust laws. Laissez-faire proponents see government interference, even on behalf of competition, as inconsistent with a free market. Private market power may have unattractive economic consequences, but on philosophical grounds, they still prefer private power to government intervention.[40] Modern laissez-faire supporters do not worry about corporations with dominant market power or about the power of large private organizations as long as they are subject to some market discipline. By and large, they see evidence of vigorous competition in many industries and in many forms, even if not of the perfectly competitive variety.[41] With regard to cartels and collusive arrangements, the argument is that they tend to collapse quickly because of cheating or buyer pressures.[42] In addition, they are not convinced that monopoly power is necessarily bad and may be justified on grounds of efficiency or innovation. They fear government, which they believe is easily corrupted. When government does act, it intervenes on behalf of powerful interest groups and therefore cannot serve to improve competition.[43] They claim that market power is usually the result of government intervention; therefore, minimizing government's role is preferable to an antitrust policy that may be used to protect and promote powerful interest groups.[44]

The above views are in contrast to conservative or free market advocates of the first half of the twentieth century who supported antitrust laws as well as regulation. The earlier conservatives were of the opinion that to ensure economic freedom and efficiency, strong government enforcement was necessary to deal with the intrusion of private economic power.[45] Modern laissez-faire arguments contain elements of status quo protection as well as a belief that history begins today. Private economic power is seen as legitimate, but government intervention to preserve competitive markets is rejected. This ignores the connection between private economic power and the attainment of political power. Vague references to interest groups and their influence over government tend to downplay the importance of the key interest group—large corporations and their overpowering effect on government. As previously noted large and powerful corporations emerged in the nineteenth century with considerable help from government and not necessarily as a free market response.

There are other objections to antitrust laws. Perhaps the severest criticism comes from Galbraith (1967b) who argues that these laws are essentially a charade because giant corporations with market power are shielded from antitrust. The law only applies to smaller firms aspiring, through mergers, for example, to the market power held by giants. Galbraith argues that antitrust laws do not preserve markets—only the illusion of markets; therefore, antitrust represents an exercise in futility in that the most serious violation of competition is exempted.

Arguments for abolishing antitrust laws are often rooted in economic Darwinism:—the superior firms will survive, and the inefficient firms will be weeded out by a natural market process. Therefore, intervention in the market is akin to interference with the natural order of the universe, and doing away with antitrust laws will improve the economy.[46] As argued in the previous chapter, equating superior efficiency or performance with surviving firms is troubling because the reason for their survival is unknown. It cannot be assumed automatically that survival was due to economic efficiency when, for example, it may have been because of political connections.[47] One could argue that, in a survival sense, they meet the test of efficiency. However, that is not what is meant by economic efficiency.

It is claimed that horizontal mergers enhance efficiency and may enhance society's welfare. The argument is that such mergers may result in cost savings that outweigh the damage from potential price hikes. Yet statistical studies on mergers in the second half of the twentieth century have, for the most part, been unable to find evidence of postmerger efficiencies. Instead, they find a relative loss of profitability and/or market share as more likely while shareholders of the acquiring firm mostly do not experience an increase in share value, and failure is not uncommon.[48] A study by *Business Week*[49] examined 302 large mergers from 1995 to 2001. The study finds that in 61 percent of those mergers, shareholders of the acquiring company lost as a result of the merger. One year after the merger, those companies' average return was substantially below their competitors. The gains of the companies profiting from mergers were not enough to offset the losses of the losers. Results did not improve much if a longer lag was used to determine profitability. Therefore, economic efficiency leading to higher profits does not appear to be the best explanation for recent corporate mergers.

Competition is an important element of free markets and it is doubtful whether competitive markets can survive without government protection such as antitrust laws. Aside from the inefficiencies resulting from a misallocation of resources, concentrations of economic power may use their economic and political clout to prevent new firms and new technologies from challenging them. Therefore, restrictions are necessary to prevent one generation's successful firms from placing obstacles in the path of the next generation of innovators and efficient firms.[50]

Jonathan Baker (2003) demonstrates that without antitrust laws, collusion takes place to the detriment of the public. Evidence from periods when the laws were not in effect includes the pre-antitrust era, which was fraught with collusive agreements and other forms of concerted action; the Codes of Fair Competition developed in the 1930s under the NIRA that led to collusion that persisted, at times, even after the statute was found to be unconstitutional; and the legalization of export cartels after 1918 that resulted in many cartels, some of which survived more than 15 years.

The events of 2008 suggest that greater corporate freedom to profit including the relaxation or non-enforcement of antitrust laws may have had severe consequences for the economy. More fundamentally, the noneconomic or nonefficiency goals of antitrust do not seem quite as naïve or misguided anymore, especially in light of "too big to fail" firms (some created through mergers) being rescued at tax payer expense.[51] Furthermore, inherent in the law's original goal may have been conditions for ensuring overall economic efficiency, far more than previously realized.

Antitrust appears to be an anomaly in comparison with other political-economic institutions, and perhaps that explains why it suffers from neglect. Firms should be rewarded for success; yet, the antitrust position, writes Marris (1970), is that while success is acceptable, successive success is illegal—a policy at odds with capitalism and the liberty of organizations. Antitrust laws were intended to protect both market freedom and individual economic rights from the profit-seeking activities of powerful organizations. However, the current justification for market power and anticompetitive practices, based on efficiencies that materialize all too infrequently, favors decidedly the economic freedom of large organizations over that of markets and individuals.

11.8 Protection from Imports

Autos and steel are oligopolistic industries that, for most of the twentieth century, were of unusual importance to the American economy. Accommodation among the major producers in each industry blunted meaningful competition and made them vulnerable to foreign competitors in the last third of the century.[52] With foreign competition threatening, both industries demanded and received protection. The steel industry received considerable import protection in the late 1970s, 1980s, and 1990s through the imposition of quotas on imports. This help came without any commensurate requirements to either modernize facilities or undertake other measures for the purpose of enhancing its global competitive position.[53] A similar story took place in the auto industry. As previously described, the 1980s saw the introduction of "voluntary" export quotas on Japanese auto manufacturers. The demand for protection continued in the 1990s with appeals to different government agencies including the U.S. International Trade Commission, which was asked to investigate whether Japanese minivans were causing injury to U.S. companies.

Cline (1986) finds that the granting of import protection is determined, among other factors, by the industry's political influence. Protection is usually regarded as a temporary measure to allow the industry time to adjust sufficiently to be able to compete. The type of adjustment envisioned is not clear, that is, whether it refers to an upward or downward adjustment, and Cline notes that, over a 20-year period, import protection for autos did not result in improved productivity.

Substantial costs are involved in import protection. Prices of the protected good rise as do prices of products using the protected item as an intermediate good. Protection results in income redistribution from consumers to protected domestic producers and their employees.[54] With the imposition of voluntary export quotas, income was transferred from U.S. consumers to foreign producers whose products became relatively scarce.[55] On a long-term basis, matters did not improve for the domestic industry. The Japanese auto manufacturers started importing larger and more expensive cars while meeting their allotted quotas. Even more ominous for U.S. manufacturers, foreign auto companies began to build production facilities in the United States. Whereas in the early 1990s, the import share of the market was less than 25 percent, by the end of the decade, the combined market share for imports and transplants rose to 43 percent.[56] In 2009, two of the big three, GM and Chrysler, were forced to declare bankruptcy. Notwithstanding the various types of protection, domestic automakers have not been able to compete effectively with foreign competitors.

11.9 Economic Regulation

Despite a preference for market solutions, when there is a strong enough demand for government intervention, whether from consumers, as in the case of rent controls in some cities, or more frequently from producers, the government steps in and replaces the market with regulation. To some extent, all businesses are subject to government regulation on matters such as worker safety, health, and protection of the environment. However, there is a sector of the economy known as the regulated sector where government, whether it is local, state, or federal, has a much greater say in how business is run than in the unregulated sector. Government involvement may include control over economic functions such as setting prices, profit rates, the type of services offered, and whether to allow the entry of new firms.

Many of the regulated industries are public utilities providing electricity, natural gas, and phone service, and as such, they are considered to be "affected with a public interest." For more than a century, it was argued that such businesses are vital to the public, so much so, that the public should have a say in how they are run. For decades, the Supreme Court debated what a state could or could not regulate and whether a particular industry was or was not affected with a public interest. In the Nebbia (1934) case, the Supreme Court decided that a state could regulate any business or economic activity, including prices charged.

One argument for economic regulation is that of natural monopoly. When a single firm can produce more cheaply than any other number of firms, it makes sense to allow a monopoly to produce. However, to avoid the inefficient allocation of resources and the possible unfairness of monopoly pricing while retaining production efficiency, a monopoly is permitted but its prices and profits are regulated. Each state has a regulatory commission from which public utilities are required to obtain permission to change rates and service. The regulatory system also has a federal counterpart where industries such as transportation, banking, and telecommunications have been subjected to varying degrees of regulatory supervision.

The regulatory system has been sharply criticized for being costly, inefficient, and ineffective. It is claimed that regulatory commissions fail to attain objectives such as setting prices equal to average costs[57] and providing incentives for efficient operation and innovation. It is also argued that regulation impedes the entry of new firms and hence stifles competition. Regulatory commissions all too often identify their mission with the welfare of the firms they regulate.[58] This has led them to set prices (rates) sufficiently high so as to ensure the survival of each and every firm under their supervision regardless of efficiency.

It was once thought that regulation was established primarily to protect the public; however, Stigler (1971) claims that industries themselves sought regulation. It may seem strange that firms would seek interference in their business. After all, there is the popular business refrain "let's get the government off our backs." The answer lies in the fact that government can provide considerable help. Regulatory commissions can bar new entrants from coming into the industry. That happened in industries such as the airlines and banking. In more than 30 years of regulation, there was little entry into the airline industry. Perhaps even more importantly, regulatory commissions have the power to set prices for the industry that nonregulated firms could not do jointly without violating the Sherman Act. So here is another way to avoid price competition—the government sets price.[59] If Stigler is correct, and there is evidence to support his theory, then an industry (and possibly other groups) under certain conditions may have an incentive to seek government protection from competition through regulation and thereby boost profits.

It is not only utilities that are regulated. Most professions and occupations, including physicians, lawyers, optometrists, and electricians, are also regulated by the states. When a professional or occupational group seeks government regulation, usually the justification is couched in terms of public interest. Yet the most likely reason for seeking regulation is to increase profits, whether by limiting entry or fixing prices.

Economists generally argue for less protective regulation with incentives for efficiency, innovation, good economic performance, and importantly, some pressure on regulated firms to approximate market competition.[60] Those opposed to regulation also argue that intermodal competition can compensate for lack of intra-industry competition and prevent excessive prices. If, for example, the airlines overcharge, then there will be a switch to trains; if electricity rates are excessive, there will be a greater use of natural gas and so on. Another argument is that potential competition can be as effective as actual competition in maintaining competitive prices.

In the past 30 years, there has been a move to deregulate, in part, because of the impact of the above criticisms and also because of economic and technological changes.[61] Deregulation is likely sought when some industry or its customers can gain from such a change. Regulated industries' share of the GNP in 1977 amounted to 17 percent, but by 1988, the share had declined to 6.6 percent.[62] Among the deregulated industries were the airlines and banks; also deregulated were the interest rates on deposits, interstate banking (partially), satellites, stock brokers' commissions, natural gas (partially), railroads, and trucking, and partial deregulation of the telecommunications industry, including cable television.[63]

Trucking was deregulated in 1980, and substantial entry took place followed by large decreases in prices.[64] Railroad deregulation improved the industry's precarious financial situation by enabling exits from unprofitable routes and more pricing flexibility.[65] Despite the praise for deregulation, the expected competitive outcomes have not quite materialized in some industries. In the airline industry, fares did come down, at least in large metropolitan areas. Initially, many new airlines entered the industry; however, some were unable to survive, especially when encountering, on occasion, anticompetitive practices.[66] Airline mergers resulted in increased concentration and concerns about the emergence of a tight oligopoly raising prices. California in 2001 experienced severe power shortages that led to blackouts and huge price increases following the deregulation of electricity. Suggestions have been made about possible collusion among out-of-state power suppliers.

Finding the right balance between regulation and deregulation to ensure a minimal level of competition has proven to be an elusive task. It was believed that antitrust laws would safeguard competition in the newly deregulated industries; yet it has not always worked out that way. Another approach undertaken by the government, with mixed success, has been the introduction of rules meant to encourage entry in some of the deregulated industries.[67]

The economic benefits from preventing greater concentrations of market power, cartels, and various anticompetitive practices appear to justify a framework for the protection of competition. Despite the ambivalence toward enforcement of antitrust laws over the past three decades, it is important to have safeguards against the more egregious forms of anticompetitive behavior, including price fixing and monopolizing. As noted before, the merits of competition policy go beyond economic concerns. There is the need to protect democracy—genuine democracy does not appear to be compatible with great concentrations of economic power. When massive amounts of resources are at the disposal of an organization, they can be used to manipulate the political process for gain and to turn government effectively into an agent of such an organization. A framework to defend competition is warranted to protect economic and political freedoms.

PART IV

Individuals

CHAPTER 12

Fortunes and Fairness

12.1 Opportunity and Change

For generations, America's image worldwide has been that of a land of opportunity. Americans enjoy a variety of freedoms ranging from religious to artistic freedom. Yet the most coveted of freedoms, to both residents and potential immigrants, is economic freedom. It includes the freedom to make a fortune, a livelihood, to apply one's skills, intelligence, and industry and be able to enjoy the fruits of one's work. The United States has far fewer legal or cultural obstacles standing in the way of those wishing to engage in business and pursue profits. People can elevate themselves beyond their ancestors' station in life. Parents' occupation does not restrict their children's choice of livelihood, and one's individual accomplishments matter more than one's background. There is a clear and widely accepted standard of success—financial success. Those who succeed are held in high regard; they certainly are not despised, thereby representing a turn from feudal and caste systems to a meritocracy. How success is attained is irrelevant; whether through hard work, cunning, sheer luck, or borderline legality, the outcome is admired and respected.

A more extreme vision of opportunities in America has captured people's imagination throughout the world and persists to this day. The idea is that, in the United States, any person can become fabulously rich. Fortunes can be made and hence the nicknames such as the golden mountain. There are numerous rags-to-riches stories, known in the United States as Horatio Alger stories. More so in the past, those stories dwelled on uneducated people who had a great idea, worked hard, or were just lucky and consequently became immensely wealthy. The belief in these possibilities of claiming the jackpot, winning the lottery's grand prize, or making a quick fortune in some business venture undoubtedly helps bolster the perception of America as a land of unlimited opportunities domestically and abroad. There is also a national dimension to this aspiration, what Slotnick (1992) calls the "bonanza" frontier or the "bonanza" economy with the prospect of huge and quick rewards for a relatively small investment. Examples range from the California gold rush of 1849 to the more recent "flipping" of houses.

Fortunes aside, the focus here is on whether economic freedom permits the attainment of a more modest version of the American dream: a comfortable middle-class existence. Contemporary America is a meritocracy, and education is the primary avenue to success. Although there are large differences in the availability of quality education at all levels, American children, until recently, have had more opportunities for higher education than elsewhere. There are second and third chances for those who do not perform well in high school. If they have the willingness and a small amount of financial resources, chances are that some institution of higher learning will find them worthy of admission. There is a tremendous amount of choice and flexibility; students can change their field of study as often as they want. The opportunities continue in adult life. Most colleges in urban areas have adult programs designed for people with day jobs, and America's system of higher education has served as a model to nations attempting to make higher education more widely available.

A high degree of job mobility characterizes the economy, and although contacts and networking help (especially for higher-level jobs[1]), as they do in all societies, people can find employment based on their own individual merit more so than in most other nations. There is a fluid and impersonal labor market for many jobs. There are part-time jobs, jobs for people wanting to work at home, and summer jobs for students. There are very fulfilling jobs that pay astronomical rewards and, of course, many more at the opposite extreme. Are the opportunities available to all? No, not to all. But they are available to a substantial number of Americans.

Immigrants have far more economic opportunities in the United States than in almost any other country, which helps explain in part why the U.S. image as a land of opportunity persists. This is particularly true for immigrants with entrepreneurial talents. It is easier to start a business and to obtain credit in the United States than elsewhere. Perhaps equally important is the issue of acceptance. Entrepreneurial success is not frowned upon, it is applauded. Similarly, business failure resulting in personal bankruptcy does not have the stigma it has in other nations. Then there is also the matter of broader acceptance. It was noted by an American president that an immigrant to the United States can become an American, whereas an immigrant to France or Germany will not become, or be accepted, as French or German. Opportunities on the entrepreneurial and production side are paralleled by possibilities on the consumption side where there is an astonishing variety of shopping venues, choices, and credit.

For generations, America stood out in terms of its rising affluence and opportunities for economic and social mobility; yet in the past 30 years, the quality of life, job opportunities, and the standard of living of many have been adversely affected. A growing sense of economic insecurity and anxiety has resulted in an un-American phenomenon:—diminished expectations. There are doubts over continuance of the famed mobility. Advancement without higher education has become difficult. Income and wealth inequality have risen sharply, and a "hereditary elite" with special access to top universities—a key to the good life—appears to be emerging. Many families require two income earners to maintain an adequate standard of living, and the prospects of a better life for the next generation are no longer taken for granted.

Several factors are responsible for the above changes. Technological innovations aside, the catalyst for change is not so much the invisible hand of the market as it is the deliberate hand of very large firms exercising to the fullest their freedom to profit. On the one hand, those firms insulate themselves from the discipline of markets and competition, often with government help; and on the other hand, they subject their employees, suppliers, and even customers to market forces and competitive pressures. Economic efficiency is said to be enhanced, but for many employees and their families, the outcome is a fall from the ranks of the middle class.

12.2 Work

The phenomenal rewards available to those at the top of their field or profession are well known, as are the rewards for entrepreneurial success.[2] Yet the vast majority of Americans are neither professionals nor entrepreneurs, but employees. Statistics point to the importance of education in determining income. In 2005, the median income of full-time U.S. workers with a high school degree was $31,209; for college graduates, $51,436; for holders of master degrees, $64,540; and for those with professional degrees, $100,000 plus.[3] The median wage in 2006 was $14.61 per hour; in real terms, it had not risen for many years, which helps explain the rising number of families with two income earners.

As noted previously, large oligopolistic corporations offer more stable jobs, while smaller firms in the more competitive sectors employ more part-time or seasonal workers.[4] Galbraith (1985) suggests that the latter workers pay the price for the stability and higher compensation given their counterparts in the oligopolistic sector with more frequent layoffs and inferior working conditions. Currently, benefits, pension plans, and job security are being reduced in both large and small businesses; but large firms still provide better jobs than small firms in most dimensions of employment. Small businesses, as noted in Chapter 5, pay less and are less likely to provide health insurance, retirement, training, and other benefits. They are often characterized by poorer working conditions.[5] However, workers in both sectors are more fortunate than another group for whom the inability to find employment results in poverty and social exclusion.[6]

A striking feature of work in the United States is the right to be terminated summarily or on short notice, regardless of sector. The phenomenon of mass layoffs in large firms began in the late 1970s.[7] This represented a fundamental change in the American workplace—the invalidation of the (unofficial) social contract that existed between corporations and their blue- and white-collar workers. With little protest, a century-old tradition of job security and loyalty disappeared. Many of the millions dismissed, have found new jobs that do not permit a middle-class existence.[8] A harsh new reality has emerged for employees. Globalization, foreign competition, deregulation, and technological change are blamed and, at times, justifiably so. However, there are additional factors. These include the greater attention paid to signals coming from financial markets, new incentives given CEOs, designed to maximize shareholder returns, and the social acceptance of unlimited compensation.

It is generally assumed that if an employee is laid off but finds a job elsewhere, then all is well and society is none the worse. Yet unemployment in and of itself causes damage beyond the monetary losses to the laid-off worker. Job losses affect self-esteem, endanger family life, and force an involuntary mobility. Another pernicious effect is that work used to be more than just a means to survival; it was also a means to worth and identity. But that is no longer the case.[9] Older laid-off workers and retirees are often forced to settle for much lower paying jobs in service industries, usually in the form of part-time work.[10] Harris Collingwood (2003) points to studies showing that 60 percent of people who change jobs end up with lower lifetime earnings than those who stay with the same employer; and this number may be biased downward because it includes people who move voluntarily.

The work environment in general, excluding the new high-tech industries and a few other innovative companies, represents a paradox. In a nation that holds strong egalitarian principles and takes prides in democracy, and where people of different backgrounds, education, and income feel reasonably comfortable with one another, an authoritarian philosophy and a lack of trust prevail in the workplace. The boss's power is well nigh absolute; this is true in factories and offices. The leader, upon his or her appointment, is seen as endowed immediately with remarkable gifts and powers. The source of these attributes lies in ownership and property rights, which, strictly speaking, is true for self-owned businesses more than for large corporations. It is further reinforced by Taylorist management principles and perhaps the weight of responsibility. Whatever the reason, the company leader is deemed worthy of the powers of an autocrat, including the right of mass layoffs. One wonders whether such power is crucial for enhancing profitability.

12.3 Mobility

Another aspect of opportunity is economic mobility throughout a person's life. Using the U.S. Census classification where the population is divided by income into five groups (quintiles), Isabel Sawhill (1999) finds evidence of income mobility. Every year about 25 to 30 percent of all adults move between income quintiles, and over a ten-year period, 60 percent move but not too far. In recent decades, income mobility may have slowed down.[11] Peter Gottschalk (1997), tracking a group of people over a 17-year period, finds evidence of some earnings mobility attributable to work experience. Yet over this long period, 42.1 percent of the people in the bottom quintile remained there, and those that did move usually moved only one quintile. The probability of staying in the top two quintiles was 79.3 percent.[12] The conclusion is that mobility is too low to undo the effects of yearly inequality. On a cross-country basis, several studies report a surprising result: U.S. mobility rates are probably not too different from those of major West European nations.[13]

Historic economic mobility, that is, increases in per capita income over time, has been responsible for America's reputation as the land of opportunity.[14] Yet as important as it was historically, economic mobility has been declining over the past few decades, in part, because the rate of economic growth has slowed. Adjusted for inflation, the median family income doubled between 1947 and 1973. However, from 1973 to 2003, it increased by only 23 percent, and most of the increase was due to wives either getting jobs or working longer hours.[15]

One of the stronger arguments for a meritocratic system is that children have an opportunity for a better life. Studies find that, in the United States, the relationship between family background and occupational success has declined over time.[16] Such evidence is consistent with rising intergenerational mobility and is attributed to education.[17] However, recent research suggests that the correlation between parents' and children's economic success may be stronger than was previously recognized.[18] The precise nature of the intergenerational transfer process is elusive, and a long list of recognized and unrecognized factors may be involved, including cultural factors that influence cognitive skills and traits valued in the labor market.[19]

While education is a key factor today in intergenerational mobility, family background still plays an important role in access to quality education. Some point to an education system increasingly divided by class, with children from low-income families attending schools with fewer resources and accountability.[20] Equally disconcerting is the fact that such differences do not disappear at the university level. Three-quarters of the students at the top 146 universities came from the 25 percent of the most well-to-do families, while only 3 percent of students came from families in the poorest 25 percent.[21] Such findings, combined with comparisons among other advanced industrial countries, cast doubts on the extent and uniqueness of America's intergenerational mobility.[22]

Nonetheless, the perception of intergenerational mobility is probably valid. However, American mobility is no longer exceptional, which by itself is not worrisome, except for indications that it may be on the decline. In fact, according to the *Economist* (2004), this is not accidental. American elites, in a manner reminiscent of earlier Britain, have learned how to preserve dynasties. If true, this does not bode well for meritocracy.

12.4 Equality

America is seen not only as a land of economic opportunity but also as a nation without classes and without an aristocracy, where one's origins, family social status, and accent are not barriers to success. Foreign observers like De Tocqueville marveled at America's egalitarianism,[23] and for nearly 200 years, it was regarded as one of the few nations where people (of European ancestry) were treated as equals. The rich person may have had more money but, more importantly, the penniless fellow could become rich.

Yet there is ambiguity about what is meant by equality. Egalitarian attitudes are very different from having equal incomes or equal access to top universities or hospitals. Three types of equality are commonly cited.[24] The first is equality of conditions. This refers primarily to civil and political liberties, such as equality before the law where equal treatment by a common standard is the principle. The second is equality of opportunity or means, which refers to equality of access to the means of attaining unequal outcomes such as equal access to education. According to Daniel Bell (1976), this has been the predominant definition of equality in the liberal societies of the West and, one might add, certainly in the United States. The third equality is that of outcomes, which Americans for the most part reject, because they believe that individuals are entitled to collect the rewards resulting from their efforts, whether they are financial rewards or otherwise.

A just meritocracy, according to Bell, is based on the idea that differences in outcomes are justified on the ground that they are freely gained and earned through effort. Consequently, attempts to make people equal in terms of outcome face strong opposition. John Locke's argument against income redistribution is based on liberty to one's property and freedom of contract.[25] The standard economic trade-off between efficiency and fairness bolsters this argument, suggesting that efforts to promote greater equality through income redistribution will distort work and investment incentives, thereby reducing economic growth and impoverishing the nation.[26] However, in recent years, doubts have arisen over the validity of this trade-off.

A related argument involves the trade-off between equality and liberty. If government takes away a person's money to create a more equal society, it diminishes their liberty. The classical liberal argument is that a distinction should be made between treating people equally and making them equal. Accomplishing the latter inevitably leads to a violation with respect to the former[27]—an idea with considerable appeal in the United States.

Arguments for fairness in distribution can be found in Jeremy Bentham and John Stuart Mill's utilitarian ideas that a dollar has more worth for a poor person than a rich person. There is John Rawls's well-known concept of social justice that society should maximize the well-being of its worst-off members.[28] On a more pragmatic level, there is the concern that excessive disparities in income and wealth may trigger social upheaval.

In the United States, the attainment of power is not necessarily connected with birthright, privilege, or class, although these factors do play a role. Money and, more recently, education give one a leg up; but the point is that upward mobility is seen as a distinct possibility—a source of great pride and hope. Money can change hands, but a class system is more difficult to uproot. Rightly or wrongly, there is a belief in a level playing field, that is, the competition is open to all and that anyone who is sufficiently motivated and willing to work hard can get to the top. Therefore, differences in outcome and inequalities are accepted. In other words, there is belief in a meritocracy and that the economic system is fair because most people have a chance to succeed. Consequently, there is less resentment of the power elite than in most nations.

According to a 1998 Gallup Poll,[29] the American perception was that the rich were getting richer, and the poor were getting poorer. Yet the public, although upset at the fate of the poor, was not bothered by the success of the rich. The plight of the poor was troubling to 43 percent of those questioned who had high incomes. Remarkably, even a majority of people in the lowest income group (52 percent) thought that the system was fair. A belief in the fairness of a meritocracy and the opportunities available leads to a rejection of a social welfare system. Americans accept large inequalities in income and wealth as necessary for the proper functioning of the system.[30] However, less benign explanations point to voter ignorance on economic policies and economic self-interest as the reason for not demanding more redistribution policies; and yet others blame media misinformation.[31] The media usually do not provide the necessary understanding of social and economic issues; the market system and large corporations are almost taboo subjects.[32]

12.5 Income and Wealth Inequality

Income inequality is a sensitive topic in the United States, which is surprising because inequality is part of the incentive and signaling mechanism of a market economy. Over the past 30 years, the distribution of income has worsened.[33] The widening gap between those at the top of the income and wealth pyramids and the rest has led to predictions about the demise of the American middle class[34] and a return to the type of society that existed in 1900.[35] Notwithstanding studies pointing to growing inequality, there is a well-financed effort to discredit such research.[36]

12.5.1 Evidence on Inequality

Thomas Piketty and Emmanuel Saez's (2003) findings also show a distinct rise in income inequality beginning in the 1970s. During the interwar period, the income share of the top 10 percent of earners was 40 to 45 percent; it fell during World War II and remained at 30 to 32 percent until the 1970s. This was the heyday of the American middle class. In the 1970s, income inequality began to increase, and by the mid-1990s, the income share of the top 10 percent surpassed 40 percent. Even more illuminating is what took place within the top quintile. The income share of the top 1 percent jumped from 8 percent of all income earned to 14.5 percent, while the shares of all others showed relatively little gain during the 1980s and 1990s.[37] The average income of families in the middle quintile, adjusted for federal taxes and inflation, actually declined by 1 percent between 1977 and 1994.[38] Such findings are not restricted to social scientists. Turrow (1997) reports that, by the 1980s, marketers became convinced that deeper divisions were forming in American society between those who could afford to live nicely and those who could not, and that the American middle class was fading.[39]

Because of the large gains in the U.S. stock markets in the 1980s and 1990s, there were widely publicized claims that the middle class had become bona fide investors and many Americans shared in the prosperity. Yet according to the *Wall Street Journal*, 42 percent of the stock market gains between 1989 and 1997 went to the top 1 percent of the population, while the top 10 percent received 86 percent of the gains.[40]

Perhaps there is some deterioration; but surely America still has greater economic equality than other nations. Unfortunately, income inequality appears to be greater in the United States than in Europe.[41] After-tax income inequality is much higher in the United States than in Europe due to less redistribution.[42] The percentage of the poor is also higher in the United States.[43] Once again, these comparative findings are not entirely unexpected because income differences are supposed to produce greater economic efficiency, although they do conflict with widely held ideas about the egalitarian nature of U.S. society. Yet it is difficult to accept that the middle-class society of midcentury may have been a transitory phenomenon and that currently other societies are overtaking the United States on this score.

12.5.2 Explanations for Income Inequality

Increases in top income shares since 1970 are a direct result of hikes in top wages.[44] For example, the wage income share of the top 0.1 percent went up from 1.06 percent in 1970 to 4.13 percent in 1998.[45] Inequality of wages increased, and wages grew more slowly than in the 1950s and 1960s.[46] Family income did not decline because of increased hours worked, especially by wives in families with two wage earners,[47] but family income inequality increased.[48] There are many explanations for the rise in income and wage inequality.

1. Advances in technology, particularly information technology, increased demand for highly skilled workers and led to rising wage differences between skilled and unskilled workers.[49] Empirical studies provide some support for this hypothesis in that education and experience appear to be strong determinants of increased inequality. Between 1973 and 1994, the difference between the earnings of college and high school graduates with some experience more than doubled.[50]
2. The globalization hypothesis links the rise in inequality to changes in world trade and the growth in imports of manufactured goods. The globalization factor can explain only part of the rise in inequality. However, given the prominent role of American corporations in

promoting globalization, it is hard to consider it as an entirely exogenous market factor.

3. Greater instability in employment is another explanation. Gottschalk (1997) finds that inequality increased *within* groups of workers with the same gender, race, education, and experience. He calculates that a third of the increase in within-group inequality reflects the rising instability of earnings because jobs were becoming less stable. Once again, market forces played a part, but the rise in part-time jobs without benefits as well as mass layoffs were not always a reflexive reaction to foreign or even domestic competition. As previously noted, heightened alertness to financial signals and newly created executive incentive plans helped bring about the changes.
4. The "winner takes all" or "superstar"[51] hypothesis is a technology-related explanation. Robert Frank and Phillip Cook (1996) suggest that technological changes afford considerably more leverage in terms of remuneration to those at the top of their field (for example, satellites allow millions around the world to watch a concert or sporting event), including everyday labor markets. Market forces are placing a higher value on the services of top performers and this, combined with much lower pay for lesser-ranked participants, accounts for the rise in inequality.[52]
5. Additional economic explanations include the decline in union membership, intensification of market processes, and economic deregulation. Corporations, again, play a key role in all these developments.
6. An alternative explanation involves changes in social norms,[53] particularly regarding what is an acceptable compensation package. In the past 15 years, the United States has witnessed unusually large pay raises in both absolute and relative terms for the upper echelon of income earners such as chief executives, investment bankers, and brokers. This reflects an unleashing of the profit motive through market and non-market means and disappearance of the obligation to set an example. The hefty bonuses of top executives at publicly traded companies have caught the attention of the public. The ratio of CEO pay to that of the hourly wages of production workers rose from 93 in 1988 to 419 in 1999.[54] The average real compensation of the top 100 CEOs rose from $1.3 million in the early 1970s to $37.5 million by 2004.[55] At times, such pay raises are linked to outstanding performance; but, more often than not, they simply reflect a general rise in stock market valuation rather than any brilliant decision-making. In more than a few instances, subpar performance has not been an obstacle to large pay raises. Given the latitude of many top executives

> to determine their own pay packages and because many corporate boards of directors merely rubber-stamp management decisions, there is some unease about the moral aspects of the situation, the fiduciary responsibility, or lack thereof, to stockholders as well as harmful economic effects.

Krugman (2002) notes that the prevalence of social norms regarding relative equality in pay at midcentury led to the broad-based middle-class society in which America took great pride and other nations were advised to emulate. Why did the change in norms take place? The large pay raises were not the work of Adam Smith's invisible hand (not market determined), but rather that of the "invisible handshake" in the boardroom. In the 1950s and 1960s, such compensation packages were unacceptable; today they are acceptable, and academicians played a role in bringing about, or at least sanctioning, this social change. The argument was that CEOs had to be provided with the proper incentives to maximize shareholders' interests. Others point to an uncritical corporate-owned media. Phillips (2002) blames the change in social norms on a change in the intellectual climate favorable to wealth, markets, and corporations brought about by conservative financial support for an ever-growing network of policy journals, university chairs, and think tanks. The intent was to counter the influence of the New Deal and a perceived liberal bias, and it was successful in terms of its impact on government policies and politics in general.

12.5.3 Government and Income Inequality

Despite government programs designed to reduce income inequality, the United States stands out among industrialized nations for an austere and relatively tight-fisted approach to society's needy. In addition, the redistribution programs created have rarely been immune from the profit motive of some firm or industry. The prevailing wisdom is that government should avoid redistributive activities from the rich to the poor. Redistributive flows to the rich and powerful, such as corporate welfare, rarely encounter the same fierce opposition. More than a few fortunes were amassed thanks to the visible hand of the U.S. government (a notion reinforced in 2008). Among the recent bailouts, the ones encountering vociferous opposition were those for auto companies and their workers, and help to home owners to pay the mortgage.

Alberto Alesina and George-Marios Angelotos (2002) compare U.S. and West European policies regarding redistribution programs and observe fundamental differences between Europeans and Americans in their attitudes and outlook on poverty and success. Americans, more so than Europeans, are willing to accept inequality because they attribute poverty to lack of effort and not to bad luck or social injustice. Similarly, wealth is attributed to hard work, talent, and entrepreneurship but not to family connections or luck. Consequently, Americans are less enthusiastic than Europeans about redistribution programs.[56] Europeans see poverty as due to bad luck, including being born to poor parents, and therefore unfair. Regardless of whether American perceptions are correct or the result of indoctrination, by the end of the twentieth century, redistribution to help the poor was perceived as economically and morally objectionable and as a violation of individual liberty.[57]

Large tax cuts were implemented in the 1980s and in 2001 and 2003. The arguments for the 1980s tax cuts, in particular, were based on boosting efficiency and spurring people to produce, invest, and work more. A faster-growing economy would allow all groups in society, including the poor, to enjoy more goods and services. Therefore, demands for any particular income ratio between rich and poor or between workers and CEOs are not only pointless but, in fact, are harmful to economic growth. Objections to the tax cuts in the name of income equality were dismissed as anti-free market and contrary to the American way. Similarly, a focus on income distribution among groups at a particular point in time has met with criticism.[58]

Recently, conventional wisdom that higher growth rates and higher employment come at the expense of fairness in the distribution of income has been challenged. Empirical studies have found that inequality might be detrimental to growth.[59] One argument is that when capital markets are imperfect, the trade-off may no longer exist; therefore, redistributive policies may have a positive impact on growth.[60]

12.5.4 Consequences of Income Inequality

Income inequality is blamed for the fact that the United States suffers from higher poverty rates than most advanced industrialized nations.[61] In 2005, the official poverty rate was 12.6 percent with 37 million people living below the poverty line. Krugman (2002) cautions that, despite America's comparatively higher per capita income, it would be misleading to infer that this also means a higher standard of living. The higher average is because rich Americans are much richer than the rest of the nation. However, if the rich get more, there is less for everyone else, and the share of the rich is no longer a small share of the total pie.

Suppose one accepts the notion that as a society Americans enjoy both unprecedented wealth and a large measure of egalitarianism. Questions posed by scholars from different disciplines include these: Can an egalitarian society last once great levels of wealth are attained? Could America remain a meritocracy without the support of a "middle-class-friendly" government? Most crucial, can democracy and great concentration of wealth coexist? Supreme Court Justice Louis Brandeis claimed that democracy was incompatible with great wealth in the hands of a few. Brandeis's view was rarely heard in the last quarter of the twentieth century, not until growing income inequality became evident, as did the role of money in influencing government to protect the wealthy.[62] Accompanying those two interacting trends was a substantial literature devoted to the cause of laissez-faire and against government economic intervention. Behind the ideological principles was a simple message: cut taxes on the rich and cut government programs for the needy.

12.5.5 Wealth

The total wealth owned by the richest 10 percent of American households around 1770 was 50 percent; it rose to 75 percent around 1870, and then declined to 50 percent in 1970.[63] Several developments in the first half of the twentieth century affected capital income adversely and wealth equality favorably. One factor was the progressive structure of taxes.[64] However, in the past few decades, the trend has reversed. The percentage of net worth owned by the richest 1 percent is rising while the net worth share of others in the top quintile and in the remaining quintiles is declining.[65]

In 1998, median household net worth was $61,000, and median financial net worth was only $18,000.[66] About 90 percent of the total value of stocks, bonds, trusts, and business equity was held by the top 10 percent of households, suggesting concentrated wealth. In fact, the United States had overtaken Europe in terms of wealth concentration. Concerns about rising wealth inequality mirror concerns about income inequality regarding the threat to the democratic process.

12.6 Uncertainty

In recent years, increased uncertainty and the anxiety it produces have intruded on Americans' lives. The economy has moved into an age where safety nets are disappearing. Due to corporate restructuring, large mergers, technological changes, and global competition, job security is vanishing, and this creates feelings of insecurity at all income levels.[67] Compounding the problem is the fact that companies are reluctant to hire people over 55 and sometimes even over 40.[68] There has been a trend away from hiring permanent employees with relative job security and benefits to hiring temporary employees with no benefits and quick termination. From 1992 to 1995, the number of workers in the employ of temporary help firms increased 50 percent whereas overall employment only rose by 8 percent.[69]

The increased frequency of job changes has adverse psychological and monetary effects. The new flexible firms that constantly restructure and reinvent themselves are no longer able to provide a "life narrative" to workers that would enable them to measure their career's progress. Frequent changes in management also mean that few managers are familiar with their workers' long-term performance, thereby aggravating feelings of anxiety and isolation.[70] Annual fluctuations in the incomes of families have increased, and a little bad fortune can easily cause a middle-class family to become poor.[71] The prevalence of job instability also softens wage demands.[72] Traditional pensions are disappearing, and people have to rely on their own financial acumen to invest for retirement; unfortunately, many do not have the education or training to do so. Then there are questions, much publicized in 2005, about the viability of social security. All this has led to increased anxiety and dissatisfaction.[73]

Businesses that are in a position to do so attempt to pass on the burden of risk or uncertainty to someone else.[74] Workers whose skills are least in demand and small businesses often end up carrying a disproportionate share of the risk. Insecurity has permeated the workplace, spreading from manufacturing workers to administrative workers. With increasing job insecurity, the health of those affected is also at risk because the human nervous system is not designed for lengthy bouts of uncertainty.[75] Many Americans today appear helpless in the face of significantly more uncertainty than they want.[76] Finally, there are also concerns about the economic prospects for the next generation in an increasingly global economy.

12.7 Quality of Life

America for decades has had one of the highest per capita GDPs in the world. Yet the typical American family does not necessarily enjoy a higher standard of living than citizens of other advanced industrial nations. A comparison based on *median* rather than mean incomes is perhaps more meaningful. Krugman (2002) notes that if Swedes choose to work fewer hours and take longer vacations, it does not mean that they have a lower standard of living. Typical families in both nations have roughly similar standards of living. However, people considered poor in Sweden have higher standards of living in comparison with poor Americans, especially if they have children. The same would also be true for comparisons with Holland, Norway,

Denmark, and Switzerland. Of course, taxes are higher in Sweden (as well as in most other West European nations), but in return, their citizens enjoy more public services and public health care as well as higher life expectancy rates, literacy rates, and lower infant mortality rates, as do citizens of several other nations. Even when adjusting for real income differences, the living standards of the poor in most rich OECD countries exceed those of the poor in the United States.[77]

The increased commercialization of life also boosts U.S. GDP per capita, thereby providing a somewhat misleading comparison of living standards. In nations where the extended family structure is intact, the elderly often live with their children, not in senior centers; hence, the cost of their care does not show up in GDP numbers.[78] The same applies when people eat out, have someone else clean their house, or care for the children. Robert Heilbroner (1986) suggests that much of what is considered "growth" in capitalist societies represents a commodification of life, rather than genuine increases in output.

If American workers once had a comparatively short workweek, labor figures suggest that by 1999, the typical American worked 350 hours per year more than the typical European, the equivalent of nine workweeks.[79] Notwithstanding embrace of the notion of bonanza economics, Americans are the hardest workers among Western democracies. Benefits, contrary to some reports, had not really improved. By 1998, only 27 percent of employers paid the full cost of health coverage as compared to 45 percent in 1983. In addition, health insurance for most people was contingent on employment, a rather unsatisfactory state of affairs. Many companies switched from conventional pensions to 401(k) plans, with employees bearing more risk regarding their retirement earnings. U.S. workers also had the least amount of vacation time and maternity leave and the shortest average notice of termination among Western industrial nations but the highest death rate from hypertension.[80]

One could argue that at least U.S. workers had jobs, meaning U.S. unemployment rates in the 1990s were much lower than those, for example, of West European nations; however, this might be partly due to differences in the definition of unemployment. Another change for the worse, noted above, was the increase in job instability. Workers, more so than in most other advanced industrialized nations, had to be ready to move, tear up roots, and relocate, sometimes without their families.

Since increases in the production of goods and services do not necessarily represent improved quality of life, let alone embody the sum total of human progress, alternatives to GDP per capita have been developed. One such index, the Index of Social Health, has generally shown declines in quality of U.S. life from the early 1970s up to the mid-1990s, with some increases in the late 1990s. Yet there is an almost unavoidable element of subjectivity in such indexes.

Janny Scott and David Leonhardt (2005) write that, even though America is increasingly a meritocracy, class is a powerful factor; furthermore, its importance over the past 30 years appears to be rising. Class influence is discernible in the correlations between class and educational success, class and health care, and class and longevity.[81] Higher levels of education and income are correlated with greater benefits from medical advances and thus lower incidences of death from heart disease, strokes, diabetes, and different types of cancer.[82]

The story about quality of life in America is not entirely gloomy, even for the past two decades. During this period, nutrition levels have improved, rates of mortality for birthrates have declined, education levels have increased, and more people are attending universities.[83] On a historical basis, due to advances in technology, as is true for many other nations, there have been numerous improvements in medicine, new consumer products, cheaper computers, and much cheaper long-distance phone calls.[84]

American standards of living improved throughout most of the twentieth century. However, it would seem that other industrialized nations have caught up with the United States, which by itself does not necessarily imply deterioration. America's standard of living may no longer be unique, but it is still high. Disconcerting is that standards of living for the middle class may have stopped advancing and poverty rates have not changed much over the past few decades. This is explained by stagnant growth in median wages and increasing inequality.[85] Timothy Smeeding (2006) notes that low-income families in the United States work far longer hours than similar families in other rich nations. However, a combination of low skill level and greater wage inequality condemns many low-income families in the United States, including their children, to a life of poverty.

12.8 Final Comments

America in many respects has been and still is a land of abundant opportunities. Business opportunities are plentiful, and business success is admired. There are open and impersonal job markets for many positions where hiring is based on merit. However, the nature of opportunity for many Americans has changed, and not for the better. Higher education has become increasingly the key to success as well-paying blue-collar jobs are disappearing. Greater economic freedom exercised by corporations means more limited economic opportunities for people, especially those without higher education and, consequently, rising income and wealth inequality. For millions, a stable middle-class existence has become a dream. Corporations' greater freedom to profit has been accompanied by the abandonment of paternalistic obligations toward employees and their families, notwithstanding the higher compensation provided. This discarding of responsibility, notes Richard Sennett (2006), is justified as enhancing individuals' freedom. Rising corporate political and legal power combined with changing values regarding executives' compensation have played a role in effecting those changes. Incentives based on short-term performance have added fuel to the fire and have resulted in corporations exposing their suppliers, customers, and employees to greater market pressures. This helps explain the increase in temporary workers, free agents, outsourcing, and downsizing.

The purported improvements in economic efficiency resulting from the above changes are narrowly defined. They do not account for the physical and psychological toll exacted on millions whose lives are uprooted and whose economic security is replaced with constant uncertainty, without, in most cases, the protective mechanisms available in other industrialized nations.[86] Of course, the counterfactual—that is, what would have happened if the efficiency-augmenting measures had not taken place—is unknown. However, a way of life agreeable to many Americans, as well as a source of pride, is disappearing with few complaints or debates. Market logic dictated—so goes the argument—and any intervention to reverse the trend would have been inefficient. The conclusion is that the economic freedom of large organizations is far better protected than individual economic opportunities and living standards.

PART V

Culture

CHAPTER 13

Culture and Values

The United States may be too large and too diverse to simply discuss and define as one culture. The social and cultural differences between the Atlantic and Pacific coasts and, for example, Texas, seem large enough to remind one that America consists of different regions with their distinct identities, values, and customs. Yet, agrarian values are often upheld as representing the "true" values and culture of America despite the shift away from agriculture throughout the twentieth century. An urban-rural division still separates America in important ways and is at the root of some of the more serious public policy conflicts, such as those over gun control, agricultural subsidies, and the disdain for welfare payments and their recipients.

Cultural differences came to the fore in the presidential elections of 2000 (and again in 2004) more strongly than they had in several decades, partly because the Republican Party perceived correctly that these issues could help galvanize voter support notwithstanding unprecedented economic prosperity. The issues were expressed as values, ethics, morality, and trust, and to some extent represented cultural differences between hinterland America and what has been described derisively as the coastal elites. After the 2004 election, the division became known as blue states (Democratic) versus red states (Republican).

A prevalent view is that in the past there was more of a shared and durable culture in the United States, less susceptible to the fleeting trends of recent decades. This was probably helped by the melting pot philosophy by which immigrants were expected to give up their native culture as opposed to contemporary approval of multiculturalism. Writers refer nostalgically to a distinct sense of community, which was more common. The role of the family was well defined as were the roles of individual family members. Men worked; women stayed at home and looked after the kids and the house. Families spent more time together. Organized religion was widely accepted, more so than today. The culture of the workplace was fairly uniform. The corporate mentality based on a hierarchical organization was considered efficient, and the boss's authority was unquestioned. Radio and movie houses provided entertainment to the general populace. Later, television provided acceptable, or at least inoffensive, family entertainment. Games and toys were uncomplicated, and books were more widely read. Baseball was the national pastime. Radio and newspapers were the main sources of information regarding national and international events.

The above is obviously a simplified description and reflects in part the more limited economic opportunities of that era that required greater closeness on the part of the extended family and more community support. The portrait of an idyllic life masks a lot of hardship, poverty, and fewer choices. Yet, on a comparative basis, American society and culture of 60 years ago seemed more uniform than they are today, despite the homogenizing influence of television. The changes that have taken place since are attributed in large part to economic factors. The profit motive was unleashed, and it permeated throughout all areas of life, overwhelming all other values. A society based on strong family and communal ties gave way to a money society founded on commercial transactions. Whether at the executive level, on the factory floor, in the lawyer's office or the physician's office, any appeals other than pecuniary have become a distant second to what, borrowing a financial term, has become the monetization or commercialization of life in America. Relationships are examined in light of or reduced to their monetary component. Professionalism, scholarship, craftsmanship, and workmanship, are regarded as of little value without a corresponding pecuniary component. Throughout the past century, the preeminence of commercial forces has changed American values. The transformation to a society based on commercial ties with materialism as its universal ethic is the focus of this chapter.

13.1 The Overseas Perspective

Despite regional cultural differences, there are enough common values and shared traits to establish a clear American identity. From a U.S. perspective, the nation prides itself on democracy, egalitarian attitudes, and faith in free markets. The approved American self-image includes individualism, love of freedom, pragmatism, the pursuit of happiness, and a belief that with sufficient effort all can be accomplished. In comparison with other nations, few would disagree that America has a unique identity.

Yet, if there is one characteristic that defines America to people around the world, it is not so much the egalitarian qualities contained in the stirring statement "We hold these truths to be self-evident, that all men are created equal," which Tocqueville (1900) saw as a fundamental feature of U.S. society. Neither is it the features revered by Americans, such as democracy, liberty, freedom of speech, religious tolerance, the separation of church and state, and a political system based on checks and balances. These qualities are regarded as an integral part of the U.S. mosaic, especially by educated people. The distinguishing feature of the United States to those outside America lies in two economic factors. The first is that America is a land of unlimited economic opportunities, or in its more mythical version, its streets are paved in gold. The second represents the other side of the coin; it is the price for the first factor. America is seen as a society based on the supremacy of the profit motive and moneymaking values. As such it has been considered for two centuries as a materialistic society by writers such as Charles Dickens and even the more approving Tocqueville, who writes that Americans "cling to this world's goods as if...certain never to die."[1] To keep matters in perspective, one should note that other nations are not immune from similar charges. For example, George Orwell describing the England of his childhood wrote, "The goodness of money was as unmistakable as the goodness of health and beauty, and a glittering car, a title or a horde of servants was mixed up in people's minds with the idea of actual moral virtue."[2]

The aspirations of American culture seem at times unimaginative and uninspiring to inhabitants of other nations. European intellectuals, dislike American consumerism, the shopping malls, and status purchases—the notion of keeping up with the Joneses, and spending one's leisure time at yard sales. They see a society of consumers brainwashed by incessant television commercials reveling in the pursuit of materialistic dreams financed with borrowed money. However, European societies and more traditional Asian nations have also adopted the culture of consumption, although the latter continue to maintain traditions, especially those relating to family ties.

A common criticism is that there is an excessive intrusion of business elements into all aspects of U.S. life; that the profit motive has been allowed to infiltrate areas outside its proper domain where financial considerations do not belong. This includes the presence of the profit motive in areas, such as, family relations, friendships, romance, movies, arts, and sports. Consequently, critics have gone so far as to infer that the United States is cultureless or a vacuous society, a nonsociety, because of its materialistic inclination. Yet a materialistic culture is nonetheless a culture, notwithstanding the preference to emphasize the spiritual and the artistic. To some extent, all cultures are either based on or have links with economic factors as well as factors relating to physical survival. It is often a question of the visibility or prominence of the economic link and just how direct it is. In the United States, no attempt is made to conceal the desire to succeed financially, no attempt is made to obscure or minimize the visibility of the economic drive. Vestiges of feudalism that are still present in parts of the world and whose values influence those cultures, do not exist in the United States. Americans are not ashamed to express their dreams of accumulating great wealth and see such expressions as healthy and honest. Wealth is strongly equated with success.

13.2 Changes in Values

Numerous Americans consider themselves religious and devout; and there is evidence to support their view.[3] If the statistics on religious and denominational affiliation are correct, then the majority of Americans still have ties with religion. Churches and places of worship seem to abound in most towns and cities, and in 1998 there were close to half a million clergy.[4] However, others argue that the numbers on church affiliation do not tell the whole story and that there has been a decline in the intensity of religious devotion. One manifestation of the decline is the discarding of religious rules that church worshippers feel are either antiquated or inconvenient.[5] Although there is an active marketplace for religious ideas with a large diversity of offerings, the role of religion in America in the past 40 years, especially in relation to the economic motive, has been on the decline.

More generally, a common contention is that in American society, the roles of factors such as history, tradition, patriotism, civic mindedness, voluntarism, and organized religion have declined in importance. The 1960s are often associated with the beginning of the slide, although it probably goes back further. Other nations have also been breaking away from centuries-old traditions, but the United States and its culture of materialism are often blamed. Despite the exhortations of civic and religious leaders, politicians, and academics, the trend continues unabated. Barring a severe and prolonged economic downturn or some other national calamity, the slide will continue argue social observers. To some, these social trends are not entirely discouraging in that it is a sign of economic prosperity when a society can afford to minimize the role of factors that strengthen the national identity. Yet this is of little comfort to Americans worried about an overly secular, materialistic society and to foreign observers who are anxious because they see this as a portent of things to come in their own nation. Cultures and societies are subject to change, but the pace of change appears quicker in the United States. Among the reasons given as to why Americans are more amenable to rapid change is a greater acceptance of what are regarded as market pressures. In addition, the United States is a nation of immigrants without strong common cultural roots who are less resistant to change. Immigrants presumably come in search of a different life and hence are willing to go against tradition.[6] Acceptance of change is considered a contributory factor to America's economic success. Bell (1976) argues that the phenomenon of cultural change itself has become an integral feature of U.S society; and Richard Brown (2005) proposes that contemporary socialization no longer involves training for traditional roles but preparation for never-ending change.

According to Max Weber, the Calvinistic—Puritan tradition characterized the United States in its formative years and gave the nation its work ethic, a desire to save, and, for individuals, the incentive and ambition to succeed in their endeavors.[7] Through the use of Calvinistic predestination, the traditional conflict between the secular and religious worlds was seemingly resolved. Yet there has always been a good deal of skepticism over the claim that there is no contradiction between the pursuit of profits and the worship of God and that God and Mammon can coexist. In the past few decades, America has turned more secular. A form of secular humanism appears to be replacing religion, primarily among the better-educated and wealthier segments of American society. Questions then arise as to the impact of secularization on the work ethic[8] and, more significantly, on capitalism itself because it is in the process of being separated from its moral-philosophical roots.[9]

The adoption of market logic with its corrosive cultural and social effects plays its part in the turn away from traditional values. According to Schumpeter (1962), the appearance of modern logic, rational attitudes, and behavior are due primarily to economic necessity and quantitative economic decisions associated with capitalism. With the adoption of an economic mentality came cost-profit calculations, which were bound to impart a logical, rationalist outlook to a person's view of the world. This frame of mind was applied to matters as diverse as medicine, beauty, justice, spiritual matters, and one's outlook on life. Schumpeter argues that the achievements of modern civilization, not the least of which are its cultural achievements, are a result of this type of scientific inquiry and therefore capitalism, directly or indirectly, deserves the credit. However, with the spread of the rational approach and the decline in sentimental attachments, individuals started to question and assess alternative options in their lives. A key option—parenthood—notes Schumpeter was affected by the realization of the economic sacrifices involved. Therefore, capitalism weakened an ancient institution and reduced the value of traditional family life. With increasing numbers of singles and childless couples, there was also less need for saving and capital accumulation. The trend had a worldwide impact but probably advanced more quickly in the United States than elsewhere.

Capitalism has also affected other aspects of culture and society. Mass consumption, facilitated by innovations in production and marketing, combined with what Bell (1976) regards as the most important social innovation of all—the spread of credit and installment buying—destroyed the religion-based disdain for debt. This was a major breach in the wall of values. An emphasis on consumption, a high standard of living, and ostentatious displays replaced moderation, saving, and frugality; all made possible by the introduction of credit, argues Bell. If in the past people were judged by the quality of their work, this now changed to one's spending and capacity for enjoyment which represents a departure from the Calvinist tradition and the Protestant ethic. In response to the needs of mass consumption, selling became a crucial activity in the new society.[10] A major transformation had taken place in the value system. The media played its part in promoting the new values and particularly the delights of consumerism. It provided a suitable inspirational framework for consumption by associating it with freedom and higher living standards.

Bell points to the contradiction between the serious Protestant ethic values retained on the production side and the new lighthearted, pleasure-seeking consumption values. An economic organization is run in accordance with principles of efficiency, rationality, and hierarchy whereas the consumption culture is antirational, appeals to the senses, and is based and judged on how pleasing it is to the individual. An individual is supposed to embrace two sets of conflicting values and keep them separate. One set is for work and the other is for consumption. Thurow (1999) points to a related inconsistency. Investments have to meet a profitability criterion but no such rule is applied or offered for individual consumption. Consumers are told to spend their money any way they like.

Yet there is no anomaly here because what these contradictory behaviors have in common is that they both tend to boost producers' profits. Therefore, there is little reason or incentive for change from the perspective of business. While enhancing profits all along the supply chain, ranging from production to retailing, the prescribed behavior could hardly be considered economically efficient. Nonetheless, strenuous efforts are made to defend existing consumption patterns on economic and ethical grounds.

A related economic issue is how much sovereignty consumers actually possess and whether consumerism reflects individual economic freedom or corporations' freedom to sell and persuade people to believe that that is what they want.[11] Given peer pressure to conform and indulge in the consumption race while simultaneously being bombarded with ads from all media sources and the advice of "experts" explaining the benefits of consumption, the extent of freedom of choice involved here is debatable. Economists have expressed reservations whether the promotion of spending over saving is in society's best interest. In addition, advertising, which has turned into a subculture of its own and is considered essential to the promotion of consumption, has several undesirable effects. Blumberg (1989) writes that advertising helps generate a culture of manipulation and deceit not only in the business world but also in society at large. An overarching question is whether the creation of culture should be left entirely to commercial forces.

Revolutions in transportation and communications—the spread of autos, radio, movies, and television—as well as the social innovations of advertising, planned obsolescence, and credit all shaped the new national culture and society. Equally significant, as noted above, cultural change has become a permanent feature of U.S. society. Initially, the changes were in consumption, fashion, and tastes; but gradually, they came to affect family roles and family structure, morals, and the criteria of success in society. The commonly accepted mobility of labor reflects forcefully adherence to the dictates of the profit criterion.

The change in values also affected corporate America. In the past two decades, as discussed before, an increasingly aggressive reward-seeking behavior and free-agency mentality have influenced corporations' top managers. Executives are rewarded with pay packages often unrelated to performance, outlandish bonuses, and golden handshakes. The ideas of responsibility to shareholders, loyalty to the company, and setting an example for workers and society as a whole seem to have almost disappeared. With downsizing, outsourcing, reduced benefits, an end to lifetime employment, age discrimination, the demise of the traditional pension, constant reorganizations, and redundancy of middle management, the loyalty and trust of employees, both blue and white collar, are also fading.

Not only are corporations affected by the change in values but they are also catalysts of these changes. Whyte (2002) blames corporations for the decline in traditional values, especially the Protestant ethic. Corporations (in the 1950s) claimed to stand for individualism while in reality they promoted a conformist culture involving the suppression of individuality. They created a bureaucratic collective society while constantly denying this. The methods of large economic organizations conflicted with the Protestant ethic. It was the latter that lost out, although this was not recognized or admitted until long after the fact, if at all. Contemporary corporations continue to hail individualism and freedom as primary American qualities.

America is undoubtedly an economic society. The interests of its citizens and their energies, efforts, and conversation, to a greater extent than in other democracies, are focused on commercial or financial activities; in short, on ways to make money. Despite the materialistic inclination its citizens are not necessarily greedy or greedier than those of other societies. Money does have a prominent place. It serves as the criterion of success and achievement. Although this may seem paradoxical, it is in line with America's egalitarianism, because here is a common denominator, a widely recognized and easily understood standard with which to measure success. It also has the modern American virtue of being open to all regardless of race, religion, or national origin.[12] Other types of achievement, professional and personal, are considered as secondary or ordinary in the pantheon of success. By and large, success is measured in terms of financial gain. The dollar is not only the coin of the realm, it is also the mark of success.

Not all social commentators view the change in values as resulting from corporate pressures, the market, technology, the sanctioning of greed, or laissez-faire ideology, at least not as the main contributory factor. Some suggest that it is a result of the loss of spiritual faith and morality.[13] Bork (1995) sees individualism and egalitarianism as leading to the present secularization as well as an unfriendly attitude toward religion coming from the courts, the media, and the intellectual elite. Others blame the decline in religion on churches and their leaders because of their rigid adherence to dogma, whereas others take the opposite position and blame the decline on the departure of churches from traditional teachings and attempts to compromise with or accommodate modern culture. Some have trouble reconciling science and rationality with myth and unquestioning faith. In an age where science is held in high esteem (not the least of which is that you can make money from it) and where many Western nations have experienced unprecedented prosperity, it becomes harder to promote religion.

However, blaming unfavorable social and cultural changes on liberalism, socialism, or intellectuals misses the point. The forces of change that have swept away all competing values, here and elsewhere, have clearly been economic forces guided by the profit motive. As the economic mode of thought enters more areas of life, change is bound to take place. Ties based on loyalty and commitments are replaced by commercial relationships.

Some writers rail against the breakdown in values, the narcissistic culture, and a lack of commitment to employers, family, and community, while at the same time advocating unfettered laissez-faire in the business arena where any and all behavior is acceptable. Yet there is an inconsistency about advocating tighter controls in the economic sphere but freedom from restraint in other areas of life. It is also doubtful whether one can separate one's economic persona from the values brought to bear in one's private life.

13.3 Consumption as Culture

One of the distinctive features of American life and culture, let alone the economy, is the importance of consumption. People work not necessarily to meet the basic needs of food, shelter, and children's education but to be able to afford to splurge, to indulge in the pleasure of impulse buying be it in the mall or on the Internet or at the car dealer's lot. Judging from the statistics on personal saving, one might assume, erroneously, that in the United States saving money is an illegal activity. If it is not illegal, then it is certainly frowned upon socially. There is a strong social and cultural impetus to shop, with warnings that the economy depends on it. Shopping for many is an important pastime. The love of shopping is certainly not restricted to Americans; millions around the world whose standard of living has risen have been doing their best to keep up with American shoppers. Consumerism is probably an outcome of an American form of capitalism based on mass production that, in turn, required mass consumption. In a relatively new nation, people were more amenable to mass-produced, instead of craftsman-produced, goods and, equally importantly, to the notion of consumer goods as status symbols. If one adds the twentieth century national predilection for economic growth and the modern preference for private over public spending, it becomes easier to understand the embrace of consumerism. Marketing efforts have been very successful in promoting and defending this behavior. Bagdikian (2000) points to the use of "sacred and semi-sacred symbols" to encourage the consumption craze as well as to advertising expenditures of $1,000 per household in order to break through the resistance of human senses, and sometimes of human intelligence.

The culture of consumption would not have been possible, at least not to the same extent, without the practice of buying on credit. Americans buy numerous goods and services with borrowed money. The goal is to maximize one's consumption potential by obtaining as much credit as possible. With the rise in home prices in the early twenty-first century, many borrowed money based on the rise in the value of their homes, often to boost their consumption. The connection between borrowing money for consumption purposes and eventually having to pay it back, often with a relatively high interest rate to boot, is sometimes lost. The possible loss of freedom through indebtedness, often for nonessentials, does not seem to bother many.[14] In their eyes and the eyes of their peers, they are judged not by the quality of their work, despite the significance attached to work, but by their purchases—the more expensive or the more luxurious, the better. The prevailing philosophy is that a lack of money (or liquidity) should not be an obstacle to spending. The levels of debt incurred and the financial risks taken are surprising especially in light of the fact that this is done mostly for the sake of maintaining a "satisfactory" consumption level, not for food and shelter.

The car became the most prominent symbol of mass consumption in the twentieth century.[15] Cars have played, and continue to play, an important role in American life, more so than in any other country. Stan Luger (1999) explains how billions of dollars were spent on advertising to establish, in the consumer's mind, an association between car ownership and freedom. Cars have become a distinctive feature of the American way of life. They have had an impact on social, cultural, and economic life; the development of cities; the easy mobility; the location of schools; teenage dating; the construction of the interstate highway system; the disdain for public transportation; the motel industry; restaurants; drive-in movies; and banks.

Whether it is the thrill of buying and possessing, the need for validation through conspicuous consumption, or a substitution for the fulfillment of more traditional joys such as those from family and friends, many throw caution to the wind and indulge in the consumption race wholeheartedly. Luttwak (1999) asks why there is not even the slightest moral outrage at the consumption craze, which he sees as violating the most important of Calvinist virtues. He suspects that traditional moralizers have either themselves succumbed to the delights of conspicuous consumption or else they believe that it is a just reward for virtue. Another possibility is the reluctance to antagonize powerful benefactors who in the overall scheme of things did favor religion when their ideological opponents did not. Consumerism does not appear to be restricted to one segment of society; both rich and poor partake. David Brook (2000) mocks the compromises of the affluent but socially conscious as they go about fulfilling their consumption objectives. They too are not immune from the obsession with consumption, although they do go to some lengths to disguise their materialistic tendencies.

Robert Frank (1999), as discussed previously, asserts that current consumption patterns are inefficient and unbalanced because they do not provide Americans with maximum satisfaction for their money. The problem is inadequate spending for inconspicuous goods, which include time spent with friends and family, leisure, clean air, clean water, uncongested traffic, urban parks, and public transportation. Frank suggests that a change in the direction of more inconspicuous consumption might yield lasting increases in satisfaction and represent a better use of society's resources. Unfortunately, U.S. society is moving in the opposite direction; people work longer hours, commute greater distances, and buy showy items such as larger homes without any resulting increases in happiness. Given a consumption race akin to an arms race, consumers do not want to unilaterally change their purchasing patterns.

13.4 Materialism as a Public Philosophy

Arthur Schlesinger (1988) asserts that modern democracies differ from the classical democracies in one key respect: the adoption of profit motive as the driving force. This has led to a major problem confronting modern nations: how to turn private interest into public virtue. Is it possible for a society or a nation to be totally dedicated to material well-being to the exclusion of all else? Is there no danger from the increasing intrusion of the profit motive into so many areas of life including politics, the justice system, and health care? Can a predominantly economic society survive?

A singular national focus on economic growth on the one hand and the individual goals of moneymaking and consumption on the other hand ensures the predominance of economic values. All other societal objectives, such as the public good, tradition, morality, and religion, are on the decline.[16] Legally and administratively nontraditional, rationalistic legal systems have been adopted to govern the nation, designed to promote efficiency rather than any ideology or morality.[17] The prevalence of economic values is a state of affairs conducive to corporate profitability and, therefore, these organizations ensure that the status quo is maintained.

In the twentieth century, affluence became the national objective. It was envisioned as an elixir for all that ailed America, social as well as economic, and appeared to be a rational and enlightened goal. However, argues Bell, with the increasing emphasis on affluence, materialistic hedonism replaced the Protestant ethic as the nation's social philosophy. Capitalism (and America) was being left without a transcendental ethic and without some ultimate meaning so essential to humans. After all, materialistic hedonism lacks a value system and could hardly represent the moral dimension of capitalism, notes Heilbroner (1986). Allan Bloom (1987) counters by suggesting that even if modern American society lacks the fanatical loyalty associated with a religious following, it does have a universal philosophy, of sorts, based on the rationality of its goals—the search for the good life. Although this is a reasonable defense of materialism, and possibly sufficient for a consensus on major aspects of the political-economic system, society probably needs a clear and accepted public philosophy that also contains civic duty and social responsibility.[18] Without such a transcendental ethic, notes Brown, freedom as the right to participate in civic life becomes the right to withdraw from civic life, thereby radically altering American values.

Materialism, argues Bell, has not provided the nation an ultimate meaning in its character, structure, work, and culture, and he sees this as a major weakness of American socioeconomic philosophy. Most activities are transacted through market exchange, and in addition, Americans place a high priority on cultural pluralism, individualism, and freedom. Yet these values do not lend themselves to acceptance of a universal transcendental ethic and social conformity.[19] One should add that a noneconomic universal ethic that conflicts with profit making would face strong opposition.

Attempts have been made to intensify religiosity, patriotism, and a focus on family, often oblivious to the fact that materialism is weakening them. The economic system and its underlying philosophy have been promoted, at times, not as a means to an end but as the ultimate goal itself, with only partial success. Heavy use is made of advertising, movies, television, and different media outlets to defend materialism and consumerism. The supremacy of jobs and economic considerations is stressed, such as the benefits of two-income families.

Given the presumed success and increasing global acceptance of American corporate capitalism, there does not appear to be any great sense of urgency in finding an acceptable public philosophy. Many around the world have been eager to adopt the U.S. formula, including nations that were formerly bastions of socialist ideology. In normal times, the problem is not acute, but in the face of a national crisis it becomes more of a concern. One might argue that a distinctly economic society is more flexible and adaptable (no transcendental ethic to discard), and it is conceivable that such a society could transform itself quickly to meet new challenges and threats. The nation-building, socially unifying factors that currently seem weak in the United States may be of less importance than in the past. With the possible exception of the Great Depression, few national crises in the twentieth century highlighted the lack of a public philosophy. It is also possible that, as long as a nation has sufficient military might (related to economic might), the arguments for domestic cohesion are less important, which perhaps also applies to the current trend toward global corporate capitalism.

America's economic opportunities and, even more so, its materialistic inclination are considered, especially overseas, as its distinguishing features. Family and communal ties gave way to a money society founded on commercial transactions. The profit motive seeped into nearly all areas of life and overwhelmed other values. An emphasis on consumption and ostentatious displays replaced more traditional and opposing values; materialistic hedonism became the new ethic. There is little impetus for change from big business, quite the contrary. Consumerism is promoted as representing economic freedom for individuals; yet Galbraith's argument that it is the seller's right to profit that is being protected appears more in line with both the profit motive and political reality.

CHAPTER 14

Final Thoughts

14.1 America's Economic Success

It is difficult not to be impressed by the economic achievements of the United States. Life expectancy and living standards have risen throughout most of the twentieth century. The specter of famine, which continues to haunt millions around the world, has sharply diminished in the United States. Most people are well housed and well clothed. A large variety of consumer products, high-tech devices, and numerous services are available. It is true that several industrialized nations have caught up with the United States in recent decades, and the standard of living of their poor has surpassed that of America's poor. Yet the United States has one of the highest per capita GDPs in the world, and even if median GDP per capita is more indicative of a typical person's economic welfare, the U.S. standard of living is still high. The educational and career opportunities for men and women serve as a model for other nations. By global standards, an unusually large percentage of U.S. high school graduates enroll in colleges and universities. Unemployment rates for several decades were lower than in most European nations.[1] The job market is probably more impersonal, open, and flexible than just about anywhere else. These accomplishments should not be taken for granted.

Improvements in living standards are associated with productivity, and for most of the twentieth century, the United States led the world in labor productivity.[2] After World War II, it led the world in total factor productivity as well.[3] The reasons for the productivity advantage are not entirely clear, but they may have included some combination of an abundance of natural resources enhanced by a great infrastructure, a large domestic market, increases in capital investment, technological advances, an emphasis on education, scientific research, and a switch away from a predominantly agricultural economy. Behind the direct factors were also cultural, financial, political, sociological, and institutional factors that provided the right environment for capital investments, technological discoveries, and their commercial applications. The contributions of three broad factors particularly relevant to the present theme are values, large corporations, and government.

14.1.1 Values

The Calvinistic-Puritan tradition is said to have been influential in early America and contributed to economic success by giving the nation its work ethic, a desire to save, and the incentive and ambition for people to succeed in their endeavors.[4] There is respect for business that was lacking in most of the world. An entrepreneurial ethos is said to play a part in business success by promoting alertness to business opportunities and encouraging new ventures. A devotion to economic matters is widespread and includes a willingness to make sacrifices such as uprooting one's family and having both spouses work. Disparities in income and wealth are accepted in the name of the common good—the overall efficiency of the economy. There is a belief in modernity, science, and the idea that scientific discoveries will benefit society. Social factors such as religious tolerance, cultural and social diversity, and a long-standing tradition of openness to immigration[5] are said to play a part in allowing America's diverse meritocracy.

An important value is the acceptance or tolerance of change, which is deemed crucial to a dynamic economy. Unlike tradition-bound Western European societies that blocked change and placed obstacles in the path of entrepreneurs, the American system permits greater flexibility in the use of resources.[6] Allowing resources to respond to price or profit signals is a key element of a free market. The ease of opening new businesses and the ease of closing down businesses, without the kind of political deliberations that took place in Europe, are considered essential to American economic success. The adoption of the above values led individuals to establish great enterprises and come up with revolutionary inventions

14.1.2 Large Corporations

Schumpeter (1962) and Chandler (1977) attribute America's economic success to capitalism and especially to large corporations. Schumpeter, reviewing the late nineteenth and early twentieth centuries, dismisses alternative explanations for economic success such as government intervention, gold, new land, population increases, and even technological progress. Instead, he argues that the reason for success lies in the businessman's pursuit of profits. The commercialization of new technologies was part of that process.

In the early part of the twentieth century, U.S. corporations led the world in mass production, which together with a productive agricultural sector resulted in higher standards of living and wages than elsewhere.[7] Mass consumption followed mass production, and American consumers enjoyed goods that in the past had been accessible to only a rich few—the striking example being ownership of automobiles.[8] Chandler points to cost-saving changes in management and organization and to mass production techniques adopted by large corporations as contributing to American economic success. Richard Nelson and Gavin Wright (1992) agree with Chandler but see a more important role for technology development. It has also been suggested that proficiency in mass production was critical to the war effort during World War II.

Mass production by large corporations probably played an important role in the economy and gave America a distinct industrial system. Yet the big increases in real GDP per capita occurred in the 1870s and 1880s, not in the three decades following the rise of large corporations. Piore and Sabel (1984) suggest that mass production success had more to do with the interplay of social and political forces rather than technical or efficiency considerations. Some even argue that America's "great takeoff" was before 1840 and therefore prior to the formation of corporations.[9]

14.1.3 Government

If corporations' contributions to the nation's economic success have been acknowledged, there is greater reluctance to accept the part played by government other than through the establishment and enforcement of property rights. However, the United States has had a history of stable government. Investors can be reasonably assured that their investments will be protected from revolutions, anarchy, and (compulsory) nationalization. The military power and global political power of the United States are seen at times as either a contributory factor or an outcome of the nation's economic success post–World War II. Another important development in the last half of the twentieth century has been the government taking responsibility for the nation's economy through the use of fiscal and monetary policies aimed at reducing unemployment and inflation. Despite complaints about a meddlesome government, the United States probably has a less stifling bureaucracy and less restrictive laws than most nations.

By providing funds for education and research and development, areas considered crucial for improved productivity, government has contributed to economic progress. Higher educational standards in the United States had a major impact on U.S. industrial productivity growth for the years from 1920 to 1960.[10] Throughout most of the twentieth century, in comparison with other industrialized nations, the United States had relatively higher enrollments in primary education and a higher percentage of young people enrolled in universities.[11] For many years, U.S. expenditures on R&D were much higher than those of its industrial rivals. Nelson and Wright see a link between the U.S. lead in high-technology industries, investments in R&D, and the training of scientists and engineers, areas in which government has been extensively involved. Thurow (1999) points to three decades of government funding for the development of the Internet, which gave American companies a lead in electronic commerce. If one accepts the hypothesis that technological advances were primarily responsible for U.S. productivity growth and that there is a link between technological innovations and R&D expenditures, then it is hard to dismiss the link between government funding and productivity growth. This, however, is not a popular argument because it is contrary to popular images of free markets, the importance of market incentives, and government inefficiency.

14.2 Relative Decline

In 1950, America's productivity leadership reached a peak, after which would start a long narrowing of the gap with industrial rivals. A common explanation for the relative decline is the transnational convergence hypothesis that, among other factors, is attributed to outdated management techniques and economic organization in the United States. Schumpeter himself began to have doubts whether large corporations were most conducive to bringing about innovations.[12] He worried over a bureaucratization of innovation and noted how the entrepreneur's role in innovation had been reduced.[13] There are claims that some early large corporations were more intent on controlling innovation and patent protection than developing new technologies.[14] Other researchers have pointed to inefficiencies in the corporate management monitoring process based primarily on takeover threats.[15] The scope for opportunistic behavior inside corporations may have widened. With managerial controlled corporations capturing a larger share of the economy throughout most of the twentieth century, the entrepreneurial spirit, involving initiative and risk taking, other than in new industries, could no longer be taken for granted. The possibility has been raised that the introduction of Taylorist style management in research labs had a negative effect on innovation in the 1960s and 1970s.[16] The imposition of barriers to competition and shades of European-type protection for institutions and organizations of the kind discussed by Olson (1982) became more discernible. Corporations' advantages may have become outweighed by disadvantages related to their market distorting influence over government and the political process.

14.3 Economic Freedom

Economic freedom defines America, yet, it is not distributed equally. The freedom afforded large corporations exceeds that of individuals and has precedence over the freedom of markets. In addition, the unrestricted economic freedom of corporations threatens individual economic freedom, free markets, and political freedom. An important aspect of unrestricted economic freedom is the liberty to influence the political system for gain. The rise of large corporations probably could not have occurred without substantial government assistance, and in the process, a class of privileged firms was created. Over the course of time, that help, mostly antithetical to a free market, would widen and deepen. Large corporations would come to dominate government and the political process at a prohibitive cost to democracy. This is not to suggest that large corporations are the only powerful interest group. There are also several professional organizations, among others, with considerable economic and political influence. Nonetheless their impact on the nation is secondary to that of large firms.

The clash between political and economic freedoms is evident in the media industry where corporations' freedom to profit triumphs over voters' informational needs. The success of large media firms is due, in no small part, to their influence over government. Yet government intervention to correct media market failures or to protect the public interest is on the decline, an outcome inimical to economic efficiency and democracy.

It is difficult to describe the economy as free market when it is dominated by giant firms. Those firms are often shielded from the discipline of the market and, in fact, their operations may well be detrimental to free markets and the rule of the invisible hand. Their power allows them to extract substantial government help in a variety of forms, including profits gained by preventing the correction of market failures. The recent bailouts are a prime example of unrestricted economic freedom resulting in unprecedented government help.

The success of the U.S. economy during the 1990s convinced many that the United States was on the right path because of its adherence to the discipline of the market. Suggestions that behind the free market façade was an economic system consisting of mini-planned corporate economies had been long dismissed. Yet despite widespread use of price signals, the guidance of the invisible hand is frequently replaced with private coordination and government intervention. Those alternative allocation mechanisms are prevalent enough to question the free market description. Notwithstanding pronouncements of abiding faith in free markets, it is the freedom of large corporations that is upheld, not the freedom of markets.

A similar conclusion is reached when one examines the enforcement of U.S. antitrust laws. The economic benefits from preventing greater concentrations of market power, cartels, and various anticompetitive practices justify a framework for the protection of competition. In addition, a policy to safeguard competition protects democracy. Great concentrations of economic power that can capture government are incompatible with democracy. Therefore, a framework to defend competition is warranted for the protection of both economic and political freedoms. However, in the past 30 years, antitrust laws have been only minimally enforced.

For the most part the economy does not correspond to a free market. Powerful groups can impose laws and rules that are far removed from free market principles or any other economic ideology other than a Darwinian style survival of the fittest, and not necessarily the economic fittest. Evidence of CEOs rewarding themselves handsomely, regardless of performance, and mergers beneficial only to management and investment banks support this line of reasoning. At some point the opportunities and choices for individuals and the power and freedom to profit of giant organizations were bound to clash and indeed, on several fronts, they already have, usually at a cost to individuals.

Individuals have freedom to profit by starting a business, and this has led to some spectacular successes, most recently in high-tech areas. However, since the 1990s, the greater economic freedom exercised by corporations in activities such as downsizing, merging, restructuring, outsourcing, and globalization have adversely affected many Americans, especially those without higher education. Many well-paying jobs and the accompanying benefits were lost, resulting in anxiety and uncertainty and loss of hope for realizing the American dream. Corporations' increased political and legal power combined with changing values regarding executives' compensation played a role in effecting the changes. The wrenching transformations are defended on efficiency grounds and the inescapability of market outcomes. Yet what can be ascertained with greater confidence is that the freedom to profit of large organizations is better protected than the economic opportunities and living standards of individuals.

Consumption possibilities abound but consumer spending often rests on a pyramid of debt. Economic freedom offers even consumers in the secondary economy options that might not have existed otherwise. Regrettably, this is done on onerous terms involving misinformation, deception, and sometimes exorbitant interest rates. Consumers in the secondary economy are vulnerable to commercial abuse, and when that happens because of either market power or lack of information, government intervention is justified on economic grounds. Yet political influence is used to minimize restrictions on business freedom to profit, including predatory practices. Nonintervention is justified as a free market solution.

More generally, the profit motive has overwhelmed all other values. Family and community ties have long given way to a society based on commercial transactions. An emphasis on consumption and ostentatious displays replaced contrary values, and materialistic hedonism became society's ethic. Consumerism, it is claimed, represents individual economic freedom; yet the evidence suggests that, as in other areas, protection of corporations' freedom to profit is a better explanation. It is not about choice but about profits.

The oft-repeated warnings about the dangers of big government seem off the mark in light of the influence exerted by large corporations over government. The complaints of laissez faire advocates are aimed at the servant but rarely the master. However, the economic and political power of large corporations are no less threatening or harmful than the powers held by big government. Lessening restrictions on big business can lead to an even greater imbalance in economic freedom between large organizations on one side and individuals and markets on the other. Notwithstanding these findings, large corporations are associated with the very ideals that, in practice, they have fought against, including free markets, individual economic freedom, and democracy.

14.4 Remedies

A thorough and comprehensive plan for enhancing economic freedom for individuals and markets is beyond the scope of the present book although in several areas, such as media and antitrust, a solution to the problem of declining economic freedom is implicit in the analysis provided. Here are outlined only a few suggestions. A competitive market system, as discussed before, has many economic, social, and political benefits. Such a system requires decentralized economic decision making; therefore, it is doubtful whether giant corporations, with political influence, market power and extensive leverage over suppliers and employees represent either a free market or efficiency. With this in mind, proposed here are limits on firm size; a more vigorous enforcement of competition laws; and reducing the links between economic organizations and government.

Economists study market power and the lack of competition but tend to avoid the issue of firm size. Restricting firms' size is seen as inefficient, antimarket, and even anti-American. A controversial aspect of limiting a firm's size is that such restrictions are seen as tantamount to placing limits on success[17] and are, therefore, in conflict with the American entrepreneurial ethos. Yet, the problem is not usually individual success but rather organizational success—a distinction blurred. Size restrictions would lessen firms' influence over politics and democracy and consequently over the economy. Such a policy, however, is bound to encounter strong opposition on grounds, partly correct, that efficiency requires the "market" to determine firm size and not the government. However, efficiencies for the economic system as a whole, resulting from greater decentralization and reduced attempts to have government distort the market mechanism, are not usually considered and neither are the cost of bailouts for "too big to fail" firms. In addition, as argued before, it is not always the invisible hand of the market that determines firm size.

Given the reluctance to tamper with what is perceived as market forces, it is unlikely that outright limits on firm size would be found acceptable. Therefore a milder alternative would be a prohibition on horizontal mergers,[18] other than for small firms. Firms should be allowed to expand through internal growth but not through mergers. Needless to say, this idea would not receive a warm reception on Wall Street.

A second area for improvement is competition. In the past 30 years, antitrust enforcement has been lax. Many megamergers that would not have been allowed in earlier years have been approved based on the argument that they may enhance efficiency. Occasionally, even collusive schemes and other anticompetitive practices have been left intact, again under a presumption of efficiencies. Existing antitrust laws need to be enforced more vigorously both by the antitrust agencies and by the judiciary. In recent years, the courts have given antitrust laws a narrow economic interpretation at odds with Congress's original intent. The Sherman Act calls for a competitive economy and seeks to limit concentrations of economic power.

Although the antitrust laws contain weaknesses, loopholes, and inconsistencies, they do provide some rules and standards with which to protect competition. It is conceivable, for example, that if large financial institutions had not been allowed to merge, then some of the giants recently bailed out might not have been considered "too big to fail" and hundreds of billions of dollars of taxpayer money would not have been risked. Paradoxically, to move closer to a free market requires more restrictions on corporations' freedom to profit.

The final suggestion is that limits be placed on firms' participation in the political process. To have genuine free markets, one has to protect not only the market from government intervention but also, as has been argued throughout the book, government from the intrusion of economic power and its rebounding impact on the economy. Even if government does not intervene directly in the economy, it can affect business through laws and policies on a multitude of issues such as how government money is spent; where roads, schools, and military installations are built; what products are prohibited; and how taxes are determined. In addition, access to political power is detrimental to democracy and has enabled economic organizations to shape too many aspects of the nation. Serious efforts should be made to minimize or eliminate lobbying and political donations as well as any other political activity for corporations. All business contacts with politicians and government agencies should be made through open communications and standard channels. Taxpayer-funded subsidies to businesses should be prohibited at both federal and state levels, including bailouts. More generally, there should be no laws, rules, or regulations designed for specific companies. The revolving door phenomenon also needs to be addressed more seriously. The above recommendations may improve chances for competitive free markets as well as for democracy.

Laissez-faire advocates focus on reducing government intervention in the economy. However, they are mostly oblivious to the problem of corporate control over government and intervention in the legislative process. Access to the corridors of political power needs equal vigilance. Both the supply and demand for political influence have to be addressed. "Everyone's dollar has equal say" is not consistent with democracy when organized groups are pitted against unorganized individuals in dealings with government. The danger, if it is not already too late, is the loss of democracy. Adherence to the principle of "might is right" is not synonymous with and should not be mistaken for economic freedom. Individuals are at a disadvantage when dealing with a large corporation. This is true of an individual's main asset—labor resources—and in the purchase of numerous products and services. Individuals, in their dealings with corporations, should have a greater balance of rights in both the law and the courts. Greater economic freedom for individuals requires contracts with full information for buyers, no small print and laws written in plain English, as should be all government rules and regulations. Truth in advertising should be enforced more seriously. People should not be dispossessed of property by government at the behest of a private corporation or any other business entity under the rules of eminent domain.

America's long-standing message to the world has been the idea that people could escape feudalism, theocracy and different forms of political and economic tyranny and be free to pursue their dreams and seek the good life. An important element of that pursuit involves the freedom to profit. However, a point emphasized here is, that economic freedom has to be restrained especially when it is skewed heavily in favor of one group in society. It cannot be allowed to undermine democracy, diminish the freedom of individuals and markets, shape society and determine singly the course of the nation. Presently, it is hard to envision a change in the system because the status quo is entrenched and government is beholden to large economic organizations. One obstacle to change is the lack of information about economic freedom and it has been the purpose of the book to address the issue.

Notes

1 Introduction

1. Scherer and Ross (1990).

2 We the People: Government and Politics

1. De Tocqueville (1945).
2. See McGuire and Ohsfeldt (1984, 1989) and McGuire (1988).
3. Beard (1986) cites the Massachusetts writer Cornelius: "I conceive a foundation is being laid for throwing the whole power of the federal government into the hands of those who are in the mercantile interest."
4. Creditors, public security holders, merchants, traders, and owners of Western lands favored a constitution with a stronger national government that would protect their interests, especially from the individual states. They became united by their common interest and were strongly represented at the Philadelphia Convention, partly because of their strong concerns and partly because of property qualifications for both voters and state legislators. The arguments contained in the Federalist, claims Beard, were designed to appeal to those groups. In addition, several delegates also expressed distinctly antidemocratic sentiments.
5. McDonald (1986).
6. McDonald (1986).
7. McDonald (1986).
8. Dahl (1977).
9. Dahl (1977).
10. Brown (2005).
11. Brown (2005).
12. See Schumpeter (1962).
13. One argument is that the system of primaries (first-pass through) makes matter worse as far as democracy is concerned. See Mueller (2003).
14. Mueller (2003).
15. See Mueller (2003) on the Condorcet and the utilitarian efficiency criteria.
16. Lijphart (1999).

17. Lijphart (1999); Mueller (2003) notes, however, that only two nations, Israel and the Netherlands, have a voting system where all voters, regardless of location, can select from a common list candidates and parties.
18. Mueller (2003).
19. Entman (1989).
20. See Downs (1957).
21. See Eisenstadt (1988).
22. Poole and Rosenthal (1997).
23. Mueller (2003); however, Phillips (2003) suggests that Republican presidents since the 1980s have used economic policies to reward corporate, wealthy, and big donor constituencies.
24. Olson (1982).
25. Prindle (2006).
26. See Lipset (2000).
27. See Prindle (2006) on Dahl's pluralism theory.
28. Although in 2008, there was an unusually high percentage of electoral participation.
29. Brown (2005).
30. Mueller (2003).
31. Mueller (2003).
32. As explained further on in the chapter, the health of the economy may be important for reelection.
33. Mueller (2003).
34. See Phillips (2002).
35. Nassmacher (2003).
36. Thoreau (2007) "On the Duty of Civil Disobedience."
37. See for example Brennan and Buchanan (1980). This is opposite to a view of government where officials and politicians are seen as working for the benefit of society and responding to the demands of citizens.
38. See Lindblom (1977).
39. See Heilbroner (1986).
40. See Prindle (2006).
41. See Bartels (1996) for a study on voters in U.S. presidential elections.
42. Bartels (2005) takes issue with Frank's hypothesis and suggests that cultural issues did not supersede economic issues for white working-class Americans.
43. Phillips (2002) writes that this approach had already been used successfully by Richard Nixon in 1968.
44. Thomas Frank (2005).
45. Thomas Frank (2005).

3 Ideology and Myths

1. These included Locke, Montesquieu, Burke, Bentham, and the Mills.
2. Lindblom (1977).

3. Dahl (1977).
4. Lindblom.
5. Prindle (2006).
6. Prindle (2006) also explains that Jefferson's views represent an American tradition that cherishes democracy but is wary of both capitalism and active government.
7. Prindle (2006).
8. Prindle (2006).
9. Dahl (1977).
10. Galbraith (1985).
11. Galbraith (1985).
12. See Rueschmeyer, Stephens, and Stephens (1992).
13. See Mueller (2003) and Acemoglou, Johnson, Robinson, and Yared (2005).
14. See M. Friedman (1962) and Heilbroner (1962).
15. Friedman (1962).
16. See Beard (1986) and Lindblom (1977).
17. Lindblom (1977).
18. Lindblom (1977).
19. See Greer (1993).
20. Other argument against government attempts to enhance competition include Joseph Schumpeter's well-known thesis on creative destruction and the primacy of innovation and economic growth over concerns about allocation efficiency and competition and Lipsey and Lancaster's (1956) Theory of the Second Best.
21. See for example Hayek (1994).
22. *Encyclopedia Britannica* (2001).
23. Prindle (2006).
24. Prindle (2006).
25. *Encyclopedia Britannica* (2001).
26. Samuelson and Nordhaus (1998).
27. Galbraith (1983).
28. See Heilbroner (1986).
29. Muller (2002).
30. Muller (2002).
31. See Adams and Brock (1986).
32. Schlesinger (1945) notes, for an earlier age, that business made use of laissez-faire terminology to defend monopolies.
33. Adams and Brock (1986).
34. See Potter (1954).
35. Bloom (1987).
36. Schumpeter (1962).
37. Perrow (2002).
38. Perrow (2002).
39. John (1997).

40. Brown (2005).
41. Luttwak (1999).
42. Luttwak (1999).
43. Luttwak (1999).
44. Prindle (2006).
45. Lindblom (1977).
46. Lindblom (1977).
47. See Bartels (1996).
48. Dahl (1977).
49. Galbraith (1985).
50. Slotkin (1992).
51. Slotkin (1992).
52. Slotkin (1992) suggests that Keynesian economics, by extending the economic frontier through fiscal policy, was also a bonanza of sorts.
53. Slotkin (1992).
54. Prindle (2006).
55. See Phillips (2002) and Krugman (2002).
56. Luttwak (1999) and Phillips (2002).
57. Thomas Frank (2000) and Phillips (2002).
58. Thomas Frank (2005).
59. Thomas Frank (2005).
60. Thomas Frank (2005).
61. See Luttwak (1999).
62. Yergin and Stanislaw (1998).
63. Prindle (2006).
64. Roy (1997).
65. See Friedman and Friedman (1980).

4 The Economy

1. One notable exception may be the housing market.
2. *CIA World Factbook* (2008), which is based on purchasing power parity
3. Baumol, Litan, and Schramm (2007).
4. 1999, *The New York Times Almanac.*
5. Walton and Rockoff (2005).
6. Bell (1976).
7. Galbraith (1985).
8. See Luttwak (1999).
9. Johnston (2003).
10. See Brown (2005).
11. Krugman (2003).
12. Phillips (2002).
13. Phillips (2002).
14. See Benabou (1996) and Forbes (2002).

15. See Aghion, Caroli, and Garcia-Penalosa (1999).
16. Krugman (2003).
17. Robert Frank (1999).
18. From Veblen (1997) to more recently Frank (1999) and Brooks (2000).
19. Robert Frank (1999).
20. *Statistical Abstract of the United States* (2004–2005).
21. Blumberg (1989).
22. Blumberg (1989).
23. These issues are discussed in greater detail in the following chapter.
24. Reinsdorf (2007).
25. Thurow (1999).
26. Thurow (1999).
27. Gross (2005).
28. Jorgenson, Ho, and Stiroh (2005).
29. See Polyani (2001).
30. Bell (1976).
31. *The New York Times Almanac 2006* (2005).
32. Fallows (1996) and Goddeeris (2001).
33. In 2008, several illustrious names such as GM appeared in danger.
34. Sennett (2006) notes that, despite the tremendous loss of jobs, steel production has actually increased.
35. Brown (2005).
36. Brown (2005).
37. Piore and Sabel (1984).
38. Piore and Sabel (1984).
39. Piore and Sabel (1984).
40. Brown (2005).
41. Acs and Gerlowski (1996).
42. Sennett (2006).
43. Brown (2005).
44. Frank and Cook (1995).
45. Anderson (1999) estimates the net annual burden of crime in the late 1990s was in excess of $1.0 trillion, while the aggregate burden of crime was $1.7 trillion.

5 The Secondary Economy

1. See Galbraith (1985) and Piore and Sabel (1984).
2. See Galbraith (1985) and Sennett (2006).
3. See SBA Office of Advocacy (2001), and Chichilinsky (2004).
4. Reynolds, Carter, Gartner, and Greene (2004) and Reynolds (2007).
5. See Brown, Hamilton, and Medoff (1990), Harrison (1994) and Pryor (2001).
6. Piore and Sabel (1984).
7. Piore and Sabel (1984).
8. Bowles and Edwards (1985).

9. Belman and Groshen (1998).
10. Prindle (2006).
11. Belman and Groshen (1998).
12. Brown (2005).
13. Pryor (2001).
14. U.S. Census Bureau (2006).
15. Reynolds (2007) and Shane (2008).
16. Shane (2008).
17. Reynolds (2007).
18. Although according to Reynolds (2007), the United States does lead advanced industrialized nations in the rate of entrepreneurship.
19. Shane (2008).
20. Shane (2008).
21. Shane (2008); Reynolds (2007) disputes this relationship.
22. Shane (2008).
23. Bregger (1996).
24. Shane (2008).
25. Moscowitz and Vissing-Jorgensen (2002).
26. Hamilton (2000).
27. Moscowitz and Jorgenen-Vissing (2002) point to more rewarding alternatives for high returns.
28. Shane (2008).
29. Kim, Aldrich, and Keister (2006).
30. Hurst and Luardi (2004).
31. See Parker and Belghitar (2006).
32. Reynolds (2007) discusses some of these factors.
33. See Karger (2005) and Rhine, Greene, and Tousaaint-Comeau (2006).
34. Rhine, Greene, and Toussaint-Comeau (2006).
35. Schultz and Francis (2008).
36. See Hudson (2003/2004); Karger (2005); Fernandez (2007); Farmer, Mussenden, and Gutierrez (2008).
37. Rhine, Greene, and Toussaint-Comeau (2006); Stegman (2007).
38. Hudson (2003/2004).
39. Stegman (2007).
40. See for example Brooks and Simon (2007).
41. Hudson (2003/2004).
42. Karger (2005).
43. Shipler (2004).
44. Karger (2005).
45. Stegman (2007).
46. Schultz and Francis (2008).
47. Karger (2005).
48. Stegman (2007).
49. Stegman (2007).

50. Stegman (2007).
51. Morgenson (2007a).
52. Karger (2005).
53. What economists call "the curse of debiasing."
54. See Gabaix and Laibson (2006).
55. Spitzer (2008).
56. See also Acohido and Swartz (2007) on how the Federal Trade Commission (FTC) allowed credit bureaus to keep selling listings with personal and financial data of prospective borrowers to lenders who then tried to sell them subprime mortgages.
57. Stegman (2007).
58. Karger (2005).
59. Cohen (2008).
60. Cohen (2008).

6 The Rise of Large Corporations

1. Adam and Brock (1986).
2. Chandler (1977).
3. Chandler (1977).
4. Piore and Sabel (1984).
5. Piore and Sabel (1984).
6. Piore and Sabel (1984).
7. Roy (1997).
8. Roy (1997).
9. Roy (1997) and Perrow (2002).
10. Later, according to Perrow, railroads requested government regulation to solidify and sanction their new status as well as protect their oligopolistic structure.
11. Perrow (2002).
12. Perrow (2002).
13. Perrow (2002).
14. Perrow (2002).
15. Roy (1997).
16. Roy (1997).
17. Roy (1997).
18. Roy (1997).
19. Perrow (2002).
20. Levenstein (1998).
21. See Shepherd (1967) for problems in the use of the survivor technique to determine the efficient plant size. Levenstein (1998) suggests that Chandler may have intended a broader efficiency criterion than one based solely on production efficiency.
22. Roy (1977) also makes this point.

23. Scherer and Ross (1990).
24. Greer (1993).
25. Markham (1955) saw its influence still intact 50 years later and arguably, its effects are still evident.
26. Scherer and Ross (1990).
27. Scherer and Ross (1990).

7 Large Corporations and Economic Power

1. Pryor (2002).
2. These numbers are based on *Fortune* 500 (2006). The employment numbers include both domestic and foreign employees.
3. The numbers are from *Fortune* 500 (2006).
4. Roy (1997).
5. See Servan Shreiber (1967).
6. See Adams and Brock (1986).
7. Chandler (1977).
8. De Long (1997).
9. See Adams and Brock (1986).
10. Galbraith (1985).
11. See Galbraith (1985).
12. Thomas Frank (2000) makes a similar observation.
13. Putterman, Roemer and Silvestre (1998).
14. See Marris and Mueller (1980).
15. Additional inefficiencies are noted by Monsen and Downs (1965), who suggest that information bias as well as risk aversion and expense preference could be prevalent in large corporations. It has also been proposed that diseconomies of large scale characterize the management of giant corporations with many layers of bureaucracy.
16. Milgrom and Roberts (1992).
17. Milgrom and Roberts (1992) explain that the objective of the transaction cost approach can be reconciled with value maximization by assuming that individual preferences are not subject to wealth effects.
18. Martin (1993).
19. See Morck, Wolfenson, and Yeung (2005).
20. Chandler (1977).
21. Adams and Brock (1986).
22. Nave (2003).
23. Thomas Frank (2000).
24. Perrow (2002).
25. Galbraith (1985).
26. Galbraith (1985).
27. Galbraith (1985) and Adams and Brock (1986).
28. Salamon and Siegfried (1977) and Baldani and Waldman (1990).

29. Other organizations, such as, professional associations, may also be able to take advantage of this freedom although, probably, not to the same extent.
30. Hartmann (2002).
31. See Hartmann (2002).
32. Galbraith claims that the imperative of technological advances also justifies large-sized firms.
33. Perrow (2002).
34. Scherer (1980).
35. Scherer (1980).
36. See Mansfield and Brandenburg (1966).
37. Scherer and Ross (1990).
38. Scherer and Ross (1990).
39. Waldman and Jensen (2001).
40. Acs and Audretsch (1990).
41. Acs and Gerlowski (1996).
42. Roy (1997).
43. For a discussion of this issue, see *Fortune*, June 21, 2001.
44. Geoffrey Colvin (2001), Carol J. Loomis (2001).
45. Mueller (2003).
46. Marris and Mueller (1980).
47. See Schumpeter (1962).
48. See Collins and Preston (1961) and Stonebraker (1979).
49. Waldman and Jensen (1998).
50. See Kaysen and Turner (1959) and Galbraith (1967b).
51. See Waldman and Jensen (2001).
52. Scherer and Ross (1990) find that aggregate concentration measured by assets increased from the mid-twentieth century until the mid-1980s. However, the authors note that when the asset measure is replaced with value-added data, the findings indicate no change from 1963 to the early 1980s. The difference in results is due to the inclusion of overseas subsidiaries and nonmanufacturing sectors in the asset data but not in the value-added data.
53. Perrow (2002).
54. Slotkin (1992).
55. See Slotkin (1992).
56. Acs and Gerlowski (1996).
57. See Hartmann (2002).
58. Acs and Gerlowski (1996).
59. These studies include both corporate and noncorporate workers.
60. Boisjoly, Duncan, and Smeeding (1998).
61. Neumark, Polsky, and Hansen (2001).
62. Neumark, Polsky, and Hansen (2001).
63. Farber (2005).
64. Whyte (2002).

8 Heads We Win, Tails You Lose: Large Corporations and Government

1. This is also noted by Adams and Brock (1986).
2. Heilbroner (1986).
3. See Lindblom (1977).
4. Adams and Brock (1986).
5. Lindblom (1977).
6. Morganthau (1960). The author also sees labor unions as capable of taking power from government.
7. Lindblom (1977).
8. Perrow (2002).
9. Perrow (2002).
10. See Ansolabehere, Figueiredo, and Snyder Jr. (2003) and Nelson (2002).
11. See Nelson (2002).
12. The Center for Responsive Politics. This figure, based on ten business sector groups, may be somewhat overstated because donations from individuals affiliated with corporations may have been given to either ideological groups or to labor unions.
13. According to the Center for Responsive Politics, unions by contrast only spent $90 million dollars, indicative perhaps of their decline in numbers and influence.
14. Mueller (2003).
15. Mueller (2003).
16. Ansolabehere, Figueiredo, and Snyder Jr. (2003).
17. See Wright (1990) and Ansolabehere, Figueiredo, and Snyder Jr. (2003).
18. The Center for Responsive Politics.
19. There is also an ideological dimension to this issue, such as the right to use one's money as one sees fit. However, in the case of corporations, the force of the argument is somewhat diluted because corporate managers are agents rather than principals.
20. Nassmacher (2003).
21. Attempts to change U.S. presidential elections from relying on private donations to receiving public funding have only been partially successful in that candidates have the option to refuse public money.
22. Klein (1999) suggests that a prohibition on paid political advertising in the broadcast media is the main reason for the relatively low cost of campaigns in Britain. However, arguments for limiting the influence of money by restricting political advertising are opposed by those contending that a complete ban on advertising might discourage or hinder the entry of new political parties.
23. Brown (2005).
24. Klein (1999).
25. Roy (1997).

26. Millon (2001).
27. Phillips (2002).
28. Perrow (2002).
29. Perrow (2002).
30. NSF (1996).
31. Krugman (2003).
32. Phillips (2002). Some of the money dispensed was obtained under false pretenses, and no railroad ever emerged.
33. Perrow (2002) and Phillips (2002).
34. See Adams and Brock (1986).
35. See Phillips (2002).
36. See Thomas Frank (2000).
37. Cohen (2008) and Spitzer (2008).
38. Cohen (2008).
39. Public Citizen (2001).
40. Stephen Moore (1999).
41. Laird and Reich (1998).
42. See Adams and Brock (1986).
43. See Sloan (1998); Siconolfi, Raghavan, and Pacelle (1998); Dowd (1999); and Edwards (1999).
44. Dowd (1999).
45. Dowd (1999).
46. See Edwards (1999).
47. Although it is also possible that a bailout was anticipated.
48. Macey (2008).
49. See Adams and Brock (1986).
50. Adams and Brock (1986).
51. Phillips (2002).
52. Perrow (2002).
53. Samuelson and Nordhaus (1998).
54. Perrow (2002). Although difficult to measure, there were, presumably, also positive externalities from the construction of railroads.
55. Fishlow (1965).
56. Goodrich (1970).
57. Perrow (2002).
58. See Perrow (2002) and Phillips (2002).
59. North (1965) goes further and expresses skepticism about whether economic development ever resulted from government investment in transportation.
60. Goodrich (1970) sees an impetus to growth arising from government's promotion of canals and railroads.
61. Luger (1999).
62. Although according to Chapman and Maynard (2008), the percentage of public schools funding student driver education has declined substantially since the 1980s.

63. Luger (1999).
64. Luger (1999).
65. Luger (1999).
66. Cline (1986).
67. Lindblom (1977).
68. Nace (2003).
69. Galbraith (1985) and Lindblom (1977).
70. Lindblom (1977).
71. Perrow (2002).
72. Lindblom (1977); Bagdikian (1983).
73. See for example Friedman (1962).
74. Adams and Brock (1986).
75. Hartmann (2004).

9 Media and Freedom to Profit

1. Owen argued in 1974 that media interests had been able to influence government policy to prevent competition in both newspaper and television industries.
2. McChesney (2008).
3. See Owen (1974) on the Newspaper Preservation Act of 1970; see also Liebling (1975) and Baker (2002).
4. See Entman (1989).
5. Bagdikian (2000) writes about the decision made by publishers Hearst and Luce to promote preacher Billy Graham.
6. See Bagdikian (2000).
7. See Bagdikian (2000).
8. See Bagdikian (2000).
9. See Bagdikian (2000).
10. See Fallows (1996).
11. Fallows (1996).
12. Fallows (1996).
13. Allen and Calderone (2009).
14. Fallows (1996).
15. See Entman (1989).
16. Owen (1974) writes that the very regulatory mechanism established to ensure, among other things, freedom of expression was used to try and suppress the *Washington Post* reports.
17. Thomas Frank (2000) points to newspaper publishers of the past who opposed Democratic presidential candidates Roosevelt and Truman by large margins. Auletta (1997) refers to the support given by the *New York Post* to Edward Koch in the New York City mayoral race in 1977, contrary to the wishes of many of the newspaper's own reporters.
18. Entman (1989).

19. See Bagdikian (2000).
20. Fallows (1996) also writes that journalists identify with the rich and middle class but not the poor.
21. See Owen (1974).
22. See Kurtz (2008).
23. See Folkenflik (2009).
24. Kurtz (2008).
25. McChesney (2008).
26. Corn-Revere and Carveth (2004).
27. McChesney 2008).
28. McChesney (2008).
29. Corn Revere and Carveth (2004).
30. McChesney (2008).
31. Kahn (1971).
32. Baker (2002).
33. Owen (1974).
34. *Consumer Reports* (2009).
35. Baker (2002) notes that a single newspaper may have advantages, such as being able to devote more resources to news because it does not have to share a fixed revenue base with competitors; alternatively, it may simply increase its profits.
36. However, government regulation has also been blamed for television's economic power.
37. See Bagdikian (2000).
38. Turrow (1997).
39. Turrow (1997).

10 Competition and Markets

1. See Blumberg (1989).
2. This is also noted by Friedman and Friedman (1980).
3. See Solow (1957) and Denison (1985).
4. See Schumpeter (1962).
5. In a theoretical study, Arrow (1962) demonstrates that competition could yield superior R&D effort.
6. See Scherer (1980).
7. Scherer (1980).
8. Scherer (1967) found this level to equal a four firm concentration ratio in the range of 50 percent to 55 percent; Levin, Cohen, and Mowery (1985) found it equal to 52 percent, and Scott (1984) found a somewhat higher level of 64 percent.
9. See Scherer (1980).
10. Lipsey and Lancaster (1956).
11. This paragraph draws on Scherer and Ross (1990).

12. The inconsistency has been noted by Galbraith (1983).
13. Reder (1982).
14. See also Martin (1993).
15. See, for example, Mueller (1986).
16. See Marris and Mueller (1980).
17. Subsidies meant to remedy a market failure may be an exception, although in most cases politics are the determining factor and not resource allocation.
18. Waldman and Jensen (2001).
19. Based on Waldman and Jensen (2001).
20. Scherer and Ross (1990).
21. See Chandler (1977).
22. See Stigler (1950).
23. See Chandler (1977).
24. Scherer and Ross (1990).
25. Pryor uses weighted concentration ratios.
26. Pryor (2001).
27. Pryor (2001).
28. Shepherd (1997).
29. Scherer and Ross (1990).
30. The numbers are taken from Shepherd (1997).
31. See, for example, Harris (1973) and Masson and Shaanan (1982).
32. Mueller and Rogers (1980).
33. See Waldman and Jensen (2006).
34. Some of these points are discussed in greater detail in chapter 8.
35. *Goldfarb et ux v. Virginia State Bar et al.*
36. Shepherd (1982).
37. Scherer and Ross (1990).
38. Pryor (2001).
39. Scherer and Ross (1990).
40. Goddeeris (2001).
41. Goddeeris (2001).
42. See Fallows (1996).
43. Goddeeris (2001).
44. *The New York Times Almanac 2006* (2005).
45. Goddeeris (2001).
46. Goddeeris (2001).
47. Goddeeris (2001).
48. See Hall (1988).
49. This is discussed by Marris and Mueller (1980) and Reder (1982).
50. See, for example, Cowling and Mueller (1978) and Masson and Shaanan (1984).
51. Harvey Leibenstein (1973).
52. See Edwards (1964) and Primeaux (1977).
53. See Posner (1975).

54. See Marris and Mueller (1980).
55. Cline (1986).
56. See Brock (2009).
57. Scherer (1996).
58. Martin (2009).
59. Krugman (2007).

11 Competition Policy

1. Adams and Brock (1986).
2. Marris (1970) suggests that, under capitalism, the liberty of the organization has top priority.
3. Simons (1947).
4. Adams and Brock (1986).
5. Simons (1947) and Adams and Brock (1986).
6. This discussion is based on De Long (1990).
7. This section is based on Scherer (1980).
8. Roy (1997).
9. Roy (1997).
10. DeLong (1990) and Roy (1997).
11. Roy (1997).
12. See Roy (1997) and Brock (2001).
13. Scherer (1980).
14. Bork (1966) and Posner (1975).
15. Neale (1970).
16. Scherer (1980).
17. Levenstein and Suslow (2006).
18. Greer (1993).
19. Greer (1993).
20. The section is based on Barboza (1999).
21. Kwoka and White (1999).
22. See, for example, Brock (2006) on the E. I. du Pont de Nemours & Co. v. Federal Trade Commission (1984).
23. Kwoka and White (1999).
24. Brock (2006).
25. Stigler (1982).
26. Greer (1993).
27. Pearlstein (2002).
28. See Oliver Williamson (1975) for an analysis.
29. Williamson (1975) also includes chance events in this category.
30. Adams and Brock (1986).
31. Kovacic and Shapiro (2000) and Baker (2003).
32. Kovacic and Shapiro (2000).
33. Scherer (2008).

34. Scherer (1980).
35. Adams and Brock (1986).
36. Shores (2001) and Carlton (2007).
37. Elhauge (2007).
38. Scherer (2008) describes this view as "everything that is, is good" and suggests that such views were held both by jurists and individuals who led the antitrust enforcement agencies under the Reagan and Bush II administrations.
39. Brock (2008).
40. Greer (1993).
41. Greer (1993).
42. See Baker (2003) for a critique of those views.
43. See De Long (1990).
44. Cabral (2000).
45. Greer (1993).
46. Bork (1978).
47. Shepherd (1967) and Brock (2001).
48. Mueller (1985), Scherer and Ross (1990) and Martin (1993).
49. Henry (2002).
50. This is also noted by Brock (2001).
51. McDonnell and Farber (2003) discuss, as part of a broader evaluation of the "rivalry" and "efficiency" approaches, the merits of antitrust based on wealth maximization and its social costs in the form of inefficient government policies.
52. Adam and Brock (1986).
53. Adam and Brock (1986).
54. Cline (1986).
55. Cline (1986).
56. Brock (2009).
57. This represents the lowest price feasible without bankrupting the regulated natural monopoly firm. The more desirable, socially, condition of price equal to marginal cost is usually not feasible in the context of natural monopoly unless special types of pricing are introduced, such as peak load pricing, a two-part tariff, or price discrimination.
58. Shepherd (1991).
59. Stigler also mentions direct subsidies for the industry and the power to influence substitute and complementary goods.
60. Scherer (1970).
61. Schiller (2000).
62. Winston (1993).
63. Carlton and Perloff (1999).
64. Greer (1993).
65. Greer (1993).
66. Greer (1993).
67. Pearlstein (2002).

12 Fortunes and Fairness

1. See Brown (2005).
2. Discussed in chapter 4.
3. U.S. Census Bureau (2006), Table 08.
4. Piore and Sabel (1984).
5. Popkin (2005).
6. Brown (2005).
7. Uchitelle (2006).
8. Uchitelle (2006).
9. Brown (2005) and Uchitelle (2006).
10. Thurow (1999).
11. Allen (1999), Sawhill (1999) and Ashenfelter and Rouse (2000).
12. Cox and Alm (1999), also using the Panel Study of Income Dynamics (PSID) for roughly the same period, arrive at a totally different conclusion regarding mobility. They suggest that low income is a transitory phenomenon and, as workers gain in experience and education, they mostly move up the income ladder so that upward mobility remains a distinct possibility.
13. See Gottschalk (1997).
14. Sawhill (1999).
15. Krugman (2005).
16. Sawhill (1999) and Hauser *et al.* (2000). Flynn's (2000) study offers a similar conclusion from a different perspective.
17. Sawhill (1999) and Ashenfelter and Rouse (2000), Brooks (2000), and Hauser *et al.* (2000).
18. Bowles and Gintis (2002). Solon (2002) reports on labor studies that have found the intergenerational elasticity between father and sons' earnings to be about 0.4.
19. Bowles and Gintis (2002) find that the genetic transmission of IQ is not an important factor. Sawhill (1999); and Bowles, Gintis, and Osborne (2001) suggest the importance of parenting skills and two-parent families.
20. *The Economist* (2004).
21. *The Economist* (2004). This is blamed, in part, on government assistance for higher education, which often benefits the well-to-do rather than the poor as well as "legacy preferences" at elite universities.
22. See Erikson and Goldthorpe (2002) and Solon (2002), who finds Canada, Sweden, and Finland to be more mobile than the United States.
23. There are arguments suggesting that De Tocqueville may have overstated his case. See Phillips (2002).
24. Bell (1976) and Friedman and Friedman (1980).
25. Lindblom (1977) and Case and Fair (2001).
26. Interestingly there have been arguments, both from those seeking tax decreases for the rich and from those seeking to raise taxes on the rich, that the trade-off does not necessarily hold.

27. Bell (1976).
28. Rawls (1972).
29. Jack Ludwig (1999).
30. Isabel Sawhill (1999).
31. Putterman, Roemer, and Silvestre (1998).
32. Bagdikian (2000).
33. For example, one widely used measure, the Gini coefficient, rose from 0.391 in 1969 to 0.457 in 1999. The trend is confirmed by other income inequality measures published by the U.S. Census Bureau.
34. Turrow (1997) and Phillips (2002).
35. Krugman (2002) and Phillips (2002).
36. Krugman (2006) warns that bringing up this issue exposes one to charges of class warfare.
37. Piketty and Saez also note that these groups' share showed much less fluctuation over the course of the twentieth century than the share of the top 1 percent.
38. Phillips (2002).
39. Turrow (1997) also refers to an article in *American Demographics* suggesting that middle-class income families fell from 62.4 percent in 1969 to 55.9 percent in 1983.
40. Cited in Phillips (2002).
41. See Atkinson (1995), Gottschalk (1997), and Solon (2002).
42. See Alesina and Angelotos (2002). The authors also report that the Gini coefficient for pretax income in the United States was 38.5 and 29 for Europe for the mid-1990s.
43. Alesina and Angelotos report that, in the United States, the percentage of the population with incomes less than half of the median income was three times as high as in Continental Europe.
44. Piketty and Saez (2003).
45. Gottschalk (1997).
46. Gottschalk (1997).
47. Thurow (1999).
48. There is an argument that if nonwage compensation, including health benefits and contributions to retirement, were included, real total compensation would have increased. Gottschalk (1997) dismisses this argument.
49. See Krugman (2002).
50. Gottschalk (1997).
51. See also Sherwin Rosen (1981).
52. Frank and Cook warn that if such market incentives attract too many people to certain occupations, possibly because people are unrealistic about the probability of success in "winner-takes-all" markets, society's total income may diminish. This would suggest nonoptimal career choices from both an individual and societal perspective. This finding leads Frank and Cook to question whether the conventional equity-efficiency trade-off holds. In

winner-takes-all markets, taxes on high earners may have a beneficial effect on efficiency.

53. See Piketty and Saez (2003).
54. Phillips (2002).
55. *Economist* (2004).
56. Alesina and Angelotos also believe that the choices made by Americans result in less economic distortions in equilibrium and hence a fairer distribution and less need for redistribution. Europeans' preference for redistribution programs, in equilibrium, results in economic distortions that in turn increase the role of luck and make outcomes unfair, thus justifying redistribution. Therefore, the authors see justification for both the American approach and the more extensive European redistribution policies.
57. Luttwak (1999).
58. See, for example, Cox and Alm (1999).
59. See Benabou (1996) and Forbes (2002).
60. See Aghion, Caroli, and Garcia-Penalosa (1999).
61. See Gotttschalk (1997) and Krugman (2002).

    Cox and Alm, (1999) based on Labor Department data, claim that when adjusting the poverty rate to include only those who have been there for two or more years, the rate falls to 4 percent, far below the official rate of 13.3 percent in 1997. Another argument presented by Cox and Alm and others is that the poverty rate does not account for other resources available to people in this income group, and they consume much more than their earnings.
62. See Phillips (2002).
63. Aghion, Caroli, and Garcia-Penalosa (1999).
64. See Piketty and Saez (2003).
65. Wolff (2000).
66. Wolff (2000). There has been some dispute about the evidence on changes in wealth. Some have pointed to increases in the average (mean) net worth. This of course does not imply that the median net worth rose. Cox and Alm (1999), however, claim that median net worth increased from 1970 to 1995.
67. Mandel (1996).
68. Thurow (1999).
69. Mandel (1996).
70. Sennett (2006).
71. Krugman (2005).
72. Mandel (1996).
73. Mandel (1996).
74. Mandel (1996).
75. Collingwood (2003).
76. Mandel (1996).
77. Gottschalk and Smeeding (1997).
78. Luttwak (1999).
79. See Phillips (2002).

80. Phillips (2002).
81. Janny Scott (2005).
82. Janny Scott (2005).
83. See Phillips (2002).
84. Cox and Alm propose examining consumption instead, in which case, they assert, the U.S. quality of life has improved considerably.
85. Hoynes, Page, and Stevens (2006).
86. For more details, see Luttwak (1999).

13 Culture and Values

1. Tocqueville (1945), p. 136.
2. George Orwell (1954).
3. Lipsett (1967) claims that the United States is the most religious among Christian nations.
4. *The New York Times Almanac 1999* (1999).
5. See Bork (1995).
6. See Brown (2005).
7. See Lipset (1967).
8. Fukuyama (1995) points to the decline in trust in American society as a consequence of the decline in associability that originally came about from America's Protestant sectarian heritage. Fukuyama sees potentially adverse consequences for economic development in general and industrial organization in particular as a result of the decline in trust levels.
9. See Bell (1976).
10. Bell (1976).
11. Galbraith (1984).
12. See Blumberg (1989).
13. See, for example, Bork (1995) and Brooks (2000).
14. Luttwak (1999).
15. Bell (1976).
16. Heilbroner (1986) makes a similar argument.
17. Brown (2005).
18. Bell (1976); the author sees the search for a public philosophy akin to the search for a sense of destiny noted by Thomas Jefferson in the formative years of the United States.
19. Brown (2005).

14 Final Thoughts

1. Some question these numbers because of differences in the measurement of unemployment between European nations and the United States.
2. Broadway and O'Mahony (2007) based on data from Angus Maddison.
3. Nelson and Wright (1992).

4. See Lipset (1967).
5. Landes (1999).
6. Thurow (1999).
7. See Nelson and Wright (1992).
8. Landes (1999).
9. See John (1997).
10. Nelson and Wright (1992).
11. Broadway and O'Mahony (2007).
12. Marris and Mueller (1980).
13. Marris and Mueller (1980).
14. Nelson and Wright (1992).
15. Putterman, Roemer, and Silvestre (1998).
16. See Acs and Gerlowski (1996).
17. Marris (1970).
18. Mueller (2008) has made similar recommendations.

Bibliography

Abramson, Jill (2001) "Gravy Trains: Soft Money Goes through the Roof," *New York Times*, July 8, p. 4.3.

Acemoglu, Daron, Simon Johnson, James A. Robinson and Pierre Yared (2005) "Income and Democracy," Working Paper, February.

Acohido, Byron and Jon Swartz (2007) "The FTC under Fire as Credit Bureaus Sell Consumers Data," *USA Today* (December 17), p. B3.

Acs, Zoltan and David B. Audretsch (1990) Innovation and Small Firms, Cambridge, MA: MIT Press.

Acs, Zoltan and Daniel A. Gerlowski (1996) Managerial Economics and Organization, Upper Saddle River, New Jersey: Prentice Hall.

Adair, Douglas (1957) "That Politics May be Reduced to a Science: David Hume, James Madison, and the Tenth federalist," *Huntington Library Quarterly*, Vol. 20, pp. 343–360.

Adams, Walter and James W. Brock (1986) *The Bigness Complex*, New York: Pantheon Books.

——— (1990) "Efficiency, Corporate Power and the Bigness Complex," *Journal of Economic Education* (Winter), pp. 30–50.

Aghion, Philippe, Eve Caroli, and Cecilia Garcia-Penalosa (1999) "Inequality and Economic Growth: The Perspective of the New Growth Theories," *Journal of Economic Literature*, Vol. 37 (December), pp. 1615–1660.

Allen Jodie T. (1999) "Yachts Still Float Higher than Dinghies," *U.S. New and World Report*, May 24.

Allen, Mike and Michael Calderone (2009) "WaPo Cancels Lobbyist Event," *Politico* (July 2). http://dyn.politico.com.

Alesina, Alberto and George-Marios Angelotos (2002) "Fairness and Redistribution: US Versus Europe," MIT Working Paper.

Anderson, David A. (1999) "The Aggregate Burden of Crime," *Journal of Law and Economics*, Vol. 42 (October), pp. 611–642.

Ansolabehere Stephen, John M. de Figueiredo, and James M. Snyder, Jr. (2003) "Why Is There So Little Money in U.S. Politics?" *Journal of Economic Perspectives*, Vol. 17, No. 1 (Winter), pp. 105–130.

Arrow, Kenneth J. (1962) Economic Welfare and the Allocation of Resources for Invention, in National Bureau of Economic Research conference volume, *The Rate and Direction of Inventive Activity*, Princeton: Princeton University Press.

Arrow, Kenneth, Samuel Bowles, and Steven Durlauf (editors) (2000) *Meritocracy and Income Inequality*, Princeton: Princeton University Press.

Ashenfelter, Orley and Cecelia Rouse (2000) Schooling, Intelligence and Income in America, in *Meritocracy and Income Inequality*, edited by Kenneth Arrow, Samuel Bowles and Steven Durlauf, Princeton: Princeton University Press.

Atack, Jeremy (1986) "Firm Size and Industrial Structure in the United States during the Nineteenth Century," *Journal of Economic History*, Vol. 46 (June), pp. 463–475.

Atkinson, A. B. (October 1995) "Income Distribution in Europe and the United States," Working Paper 133, Luxembourg Institute Studies.

Auletta, Ken (1997) *The Highwaymen*, New York: Random House.

Bagdikian, Ben H. (1983, 2000) *Media Monopoly*, Boston: Beacon Press (first and sixth editions).

Bain, Joe (1956) *Barriers to New Competition*, Cambridge, MA: Harvard University Press.

Baker, C. Edwin (2002) *Media Markets and Democracy*, Cambridge: Cambridge University Press.

Baker, Jonathan B. (2003) "The Case for Antitrust Enforcement," *Journal of Economic Perspectives*, Vol. 17, No. 4 (Fall), pp. 27–50.

Baldani, Jeffrey and Don E. Waldman (1990) "Market Structure, Opportunity Costs and Tax Avoidance," *Review of Industrial Organization*, Vol. 5 (Spring), pp. 1–29.

Barboza (1999) "$1.1 Billion to Settle Suit on Vitamins," *New York Times* (November 4), p. C1.

Bartels, Larry M. (1996) "Uninformed Votes: Information Effects in Presidential Elections," *American Journal of Political Science*, Vol. 40, No. 1 (February), pp. 194–230.

——— (2005) "What's the matter with What's the Matter with Kansas? Paper presented at the American Political Science Association, Washington, DC (September 1–4).

Baumol, William J., Robert E. Litan, and Carl J. Scramm (2007) "Sustaining Entrepreneurial Capitalism," *Capitalism and Society*, Vol. 2, No. 2, pp. 1–36. http://www.bepress.com/ cas/vol2/iss2art1/.

Beard, Charles A. (1986) *An Economic Interpretation of the Constitution of the United States*, New York: Free Press.

Bell, Daniel (1976) *The Cultural Contradictions of Capitalism*, New York: Basic Books.

Belman, Dale and Erica L. Groshen (1998) Is Small beautiful for Workers? in *Small Consolation, the Dubious Benefits of Small Business for Job Growth and Wages*, Washington, DC: Economic Policy Institute (http://epinet.org).

Benabou, Roland (2000) "Unequal Societies: Income Distribution and the Social Contract," *American Economic Review*, Vol. 90 (March), pp. 96–129.

Berger, Mark C., Dan A. Black, Frank A. Scott, and Steven N. Allen (2000) "Distribution of Low Wage Workers by Firm Size in the United States," *Small Business Research Summary*, Office of Advocacy, United States Small Business Administration (March).

Berle, Adolf A. and Gardiner Means (1932) *The Modern Corporation and Private Property*, New York: MacMillan.

Bernasek, Anna (2005) "Do Taxes Thwart Growth? Prove It," *New York Times* (April 3), p. 3.6. www.nytimes.com/2005/04/03business/yourmoney/03view.html?/.

Block, Fred and Margaret R. Somers (1984) Beyond the Economistic Fallacy: The Holistic Social Science of Karl Polanyi, in *Vision and Method in Historical Sociology*, eds. Theda Skocpol, New York: Cambridge University Press

Bloom, Allan (1987) *The Closing of the American Mind*, New York: Simon & Schuster

Blumberg, Paul (1989) *The Predatory Society*, New York: Oxford University Press

Boisjoly, Johane, Greg J. Duncan, and Timothy Smeeding (1998) "The Shifting Incidence of Involuntary Job Loss from 1968 to 1992," *Industrial Relations*, Vol. 37 (April), pp. 207–231.

Bork, Robert H. (1966) "Legislative Intent and the Policy of the Sherman Act," *Journal of Law and Economics*, Vol. 6, pp. 7–48.

——— (1978) *The Antitrust Paradox*, New York: Basic Books.

——— (1996) *Slouching towards Gomorrah*, New York: Regan Books.

Bovard, James (1995) "Archer Daniels Midland: A Case Study in Corporate Welfare," Cato Policy Analysis No. 241 (September 26). http://www.cato.org/pubs/pa-241.html.

Bowles, Samuel and Richard Edwards (1985) *Understanding Capitalism*, New York: Harper and Row.

Bowles, Samuel and Herbert Gintis (2002) "The Inheritance of Inequality," *Journal of Economic Perspectives*, Vol. 16 (Summer), pp. 3–30.

Bowles, Samuel, Herbert Gintis, and Melissa Osborne (2001) "The Determinants of Earnings: A Behavioral Approach," *Journal of Economic Literature*, Vol. 39 (December), pp. 1137–1176.

Bregger, John E. (1996) "Measuring Self-Employment in the United States," *Monthly Labor Review* (January/February), pp. 3–9.

Brennan, Geoffrey and James M. Buchanan (1980) *The Power to Tax: Analytical Foundations of a Fiscal Constitution*, Cambridge: Cambridge University Press.

Broadway, Stephen and Mary O'Mahony (2007) Britain's Twentieth Century Productivity Performance in International Perspective, in *Work and Pay in 20th Century Britain*, eds. N. F. R. Crafts, Ian Gazeley, and Andrew Newell, Oxford: Oxford University Press.

Brock, James W. (2001) "Public Policy in a Free Enterprise Economy" Ch. 13 in the Structure of American Industry (tenth edition), eds. Walter Adams and James W. Brock, Upper Saddle River, NJ: Prentice Hall.

——— (2006) "Antitrust Policy and the Oligopoly Problem," *The Antitrust Bulletin*, Vol. 51, No. 2 (Summer), pp. 227–280.

Brock, James W. (2008) "Market Power, Antitrust Policy, and the Roberts Court," *The Antitrust Bulletin*, Vol. 53, No. 1 (Spring), pp. 179–202.

——— (2009) "Automobiles" Ch. 6, in *The Structure of American Industry* (twelfth edition), ed. James W. Brock, Upper Saddle River, NJ: Pearson Prentice Hall.

Brooks, David (2000) *Bobos in Paradise*, New York: Simon & Schuster.

Brooks, Rich and Ruth Simon (2007) "Subprime Debacle Traps even very Creditworthy," *Wall Street Journal* (December 3), p. A1.

Brown, Charles (2001) "Review of Meritocracy and Economic Inequality," *Journal of Economic Literature*, Vol. 39, March, pp. 93–104.

Brown, Richard Harvey (2005) *Culture, Capitalism and Democracy in the New America*, New Haven, CT: Yale University Press.

Burns, Malcolm R. (1986) "Predatory Pricing and the Acquisition Cost of Competitors," *Journal of Political Economy*, Vol. 94 (April), pp. 266–296.

Cabral, Luis M. B. (2000) *Introduction to Industrial Organization*, Cambridge, MA: MIT Press.

Canterbery, E. Ray (1980) *The Making of Economics*, Belmont, CA: Wadsworth.

Carlton, Dennis W. (2007) "Does Antitrust Need to be Modernized?" *Journal of Economic Perspectives*, Vol. 21, No. 3 (Summer), pp. 155–176.

Carlton, Dennis W. and Jeffrey M. Perloff (2000) *Modern Industrial Organization*, Reading, MA: Addison Wesley Longman.

Case, Karl E. and Ray C. Fair (2001) *Principles of Microeconomics* (sixth edition), Upper Saddle River, NJ: Prentice Hall.

Center for Responsive Politics (2005a), "The Big Picture, 2000 Cycle" www.opensecrets.org/bigpicture/sectors.asp?cycle=2000.

——— (2005b), "Lobbying Database" www.opensecrets.org/lobbyists/index.asp?year=2000.

——— (2009) "2008 Overview: Stats at a Glance' " www.opensecrets.org/overview/index.php.

Chandler, Alfred D. (1977) *The Visible Hand*, Cambridge, MA: Belknap Press of Harvard University Press.

Chapman, Mary M. and Micheline Maynard (2008) "Fewer Youths Jump Behind the Wheel at 16" *New York Times*, February 25, p. A1.

Cline, William R. (1986) U.S. Trade and industrial Policy: The Experience of Textiles, Steel and Automobiles in *Strategic Trade Policy and the New International Economics*, ed. Paul R. Krugman, Cambridge, MA: MIT Press.

Citizens for Tax Justice (2005) "International Tax Comparisons, 1965–2003," April 21, www.ctj.org/html/oecd05.htm.

Coase, Ronald (1937) "The Nature of the Firm," *Economica*, Vol. 4 (November), pp. 386–405.

——— (1960) "The Problem of Social Cost," *Journal of Law and Economics* Vol. 3 (October), pp. 1–44.

Cohen, Adam (2008) "Whatever Happened to (the Good Kind of) States' Rights? *New York Times* (May 23), p. A24.

Collingwood, Harris (2003) "The Sink-or-Swim Economy," *New York Times*, June 8, Magazine section 6, p. 42.

Collins, Norman R. and Lee E. Preston (1961) "The Size Structure of the Largest Industrial firms, 1908–1958," *American Economic Review*, Vol. 51 (December), pp. 986–1011.

Colvin, Geoffrey (2001) "The Great CEO Pay Heist," *Fortune*, June 25, pp. 64–70.

Congress Watch (2001) Corporate Welfare, *Public Citizen*, June 21, www.citizen.org/congress/welfare/index.cfm.

Corn-Revere, Robert and Rod Carveth (2004) Economics and Media Regulation, in *Media Economics* (third edition), eds. Alison Alexander, James Owers, Rod Carveth, C. Ann Hollifield, and Alberto N. Greco, Mahwah, NJ: Lawrence Erlbaum Associates.

Consumer Reports (May 2009) "Cable Rates Endless Rise."

Cowling, Keith and Dennis C. Mueller (1978) "The Social Costs of Monopoly," *Economic Journal*, Vol. 88 (December), pp. 727–748.

Cox, Michael W. and Richard Alm (1999) *Myths of Rich and Poor*, New York: Basic Books.

Curran III, William J. (2001) "Markets, Morals or Wealth? Delusions of a Standardized Antitrust Value?" *Review of Industrial Organization*, Vol. 19, pp. 3–18.

Dahl, Robert (1977) "On Removing Certain Impediments of Democracy in the United States," *Political Science Quarterly*, Vol. 92, No. 1 (Spring), pp. 1–20.

David, Paul A. (1990) "The Dynamo and the Computer: An Historical Perspective on the Modern Productivity Paradox," *American Economic Review*, Vol. 80 (May), pp. 355–360.

Davis, Lance E., and Douglass C. North (1971) *Institutional Changes and American Economic Growth*, London: Cambridge University Press.

De Long, J. Bradford (1990) "In Defense of Henry Simon's Standing as a Classical Liberal," *Cato Journal*, Vol. 9, No. 3 (Winter), pp. 601–618.

——— (1997) "The Corporation as a Command Economy," working paper, University of California Berkeley.

——— (1998) "Robber Barons," working paper, University of California Berkeley.

Denison, Edward F. (1985) *Trends in American Economic Growth 1929–1982*, Washington, DC: Brookings.

Dewey, Donald J. (1974) The New Learning: One Man's View, in *Industrial Concentration: The New Learning*, eds. Harvey J. Goldschmid, H. Michael Mann, and J. Fred Weston, Boston: Little Brown.

Dowd, Kevin (1999) "Too Big to Fail? Long Term Capital Management and the Federal Reserve," Cato Institute Briefing Papers, No. 52 (September 23), pp. 1–12.

Downs, Anthony (1957) *An Economic Theory of Democracy*, New York: Harper and Row.

Duhigg, Charles (2007) "Data on the Elderly, Marketed to Thieves," *New York Times* (May, 20), p. 1.1. www.nytimes.com/2007/05/20business/20tele.html?.

Dunn, Stephen P. and Steven Pressman (2005) "The Economic Contribution of John Kenneth Galbraith," *Review of Political Economy*, Vol. 17, No. 2 (April), pp. 161–209.

Dunne, Timothy, Mark J. Roberts, and Larry Samuelson (1988) "Patterns of Firm Entry and Exit in US Manufacturing Industries," *Rand Journal of Economics*, Vol. 19 (Winter), pp. 495–515.

The Economist (2004) "Ever Higher Society, Ever Harder to Ascend," December 29.

Edwards, Franklin R. (1999) "Hedge Funds and the Collapse of Long Term Capital Management," *Journal of Economic Perspectives*, Vol. 13, No. 2 (Spring), pp. 189–210.

Edwards, Richard, C. (1975) "Stages in Corporate Stability and the risks of Corporate Failure," *Journal of Economic History* (June), pp. 428–457.

Eisenstadt, Abraham S. (1988) Bryce's America and Tocqueville's, in *Reconsidering Tocqueville's Democracy in America*, ed. Abraham S. Eisenstadt, New Brunswick, NJ: Rutgers University Press.

Elhauge, Einar (2007) "Harvard, Not Chicago: Which Antitrust School Drives Recent U.S. Supreme Court Decisions?" *Competition Policy International*, Vol. 3, No. 2 (Autumn), pp. 59–77.

Encyclopedia Britannica (2001) "Capitalism," CD.

Entman, Robert M. (1989) *Democracy without Citizens*, New York: Oxford University Press.

Fallows, James (1996) *Breaking the News*, New York: Pantheon.

Farber, Henry S. (2005) "What Do We Know about Job Loss in the United States? Evidence from the Displaced Workers Survey, 1984–2004," *Economic Perspectives*, Q II, pp. 13–28.

Farmer, Robin, Sean Mussenden, and Bertrand M. Gutierrez (2008) "A Racial Bias in Subprime Loans?" *Richmond Times-Dispatch* (March 9), p. A1.

Ferguson, Roger W., Jr. and William L. Wascher (2004) "Distinguished Lectures on Economics in government: Lessons from Past Productivity Booms," *Journal of Economic Perspectives*, Vol. 18 (Spring), pp. 3–28.

Fernandez, Manny (2007) "Racial Disparity Found among New Yorkers with Higher Rate Mortgages," *New York Times* (October 15), p. B1.

Ferrie, Joseph P. (2005) "History Lessons: The End of American Exceptionalism? Mobility in the United States since 1850," *Journal of Economic Perspectives*, Vol. 19, No. 3 (Summer), pp. 199–215.

Fishlow, Albert (1965) *American Railroads and the Transformation of the Antebellum Economy*, Cambridge, MA: Harvard University Press.

Flynn, James (2000) IQ Trends Over: Intelligence, Race and Meritocracy, in *Meritocracy and Economic Inequality*, eds. Kenneth Arrow, Samuel Bowles, and Steven Durlauf, Princeton: Princeton University Press.

Fogel, Robert W. (1964) *Railroads and American Economic Growth: Essays in Economic History*. Baltimore: Johns Hopkins University Press.

Folkenflik, David (2009) "Where Were the Media as Wall Street Imploded?" *NPR* (March 10) (npr.org)

Fortune 500, A Database of Every Year of Fortune's List of America's Largest Corporations (money.cnn.com.magazines/fortune/fortune500_archive/full/2002/).

Frank, Robert (1994) *Microeconomics and Behavior*, New York: McGraw-Hill.

——— (1999) *Luxury Fever*, New York: Free Press.

Frank, Robert H. and Philip J. Cook (1995) *The Winner-Take-All Society*, New York: Free Press.

Frank, Thomas (2000) *One Market under God*, New York: Doubleday.

——— (2005) *What's the Matter with Kansas?* New York: Metropolitan Books.

Frey, Bruno S. and Alois Stutzer (2002) "What Can Economists Learn from Happiness Research?" *Journal of Economic Literature*, Vol. 40 (June), pp. 402–435.

Friedman, Milton (1962) *Capitalism and Freedom*, Chicago: University of Chicago Press.

——— (1970) "The Social Responsibility of Business Is to Increase its Profits," *The New York Times Magazine*, September 13, pp. 122–126.

Friedman, Milton and Rose D. Friedman (1980) *Free to Choose*, San Diego: Harvest Book, Harcourt Brace.

Fukuyama, Francis (1995) *Trust*, New York: Free Press.

Gabaix, Xavier and David Laibson (2006) "Shrouded Attributes, Consumer Myopia, and Information Suppression in Competitive Markets," *Quarterly Journal of Economics* (May), pp. 505–540.

Galbraith, John Kenneth (1967) "The New Industrial State and Comments on Galbraith's New Industrial State," *Antitrust Law and Economics Review*, Vol. 1, No. 2, pp. 11–20.

——— (1983) *The Anatomy of Power*, Boston: Houghton Mifflin.

——— (1985) *The New Industrial State* (fourth edition), Boston: Houghton Mifflin.

——— (1988) "The New Industrial State" after Twenty Years, *American Economic Review*, Vol. 78, No. 3 (May), pp. 373–382.

Goddeeris, John (2001) Health Care in *the Structure of American Industry* (tenth edition), eds. Walter Adams and James W. Brock, Upper Saddle River, NJ: Prentice Hall.

Goodman, Peter S. (2008) "Taking Hard New Look at a Greenspan Legacy," *New York Times* (October 9), p. A. 1.

Goodrich, Carter (1970) "Internal Improvements Reconsidered," *Journal of Economic History*, Vol. 30, No. 2 (June), pp. 289–311.

Gottschalk, Peter (1997) "Inequality, Income Growth, and Mobility: The Basic Facts," *Journal of Economic Perspectives*, Vol. 11 (Spring), pp. 21–40.

Gottschalk, Peter and Timothy M. Smeeding (1997) "Cross-National Comparisons of Earnings and Income Inequality," *Journal of Economic Literature*, Vol. 35, pp. 633–687.

Grant II, Don Sherman (1996) "The Political Economy of New Business Formation across the American States, 1970–1985," *Social Science Quarterly*, Vol. 77, No. 1 (March), pp. 28–42.

Greer, Douglas F. (1993) *Government, Business and Society* (third edition), New York: Macmillan.

Greenspan, Alan (1998) Antitrust, in *Capitalism: The Unknown Ideal*, by Ayn Rand http://www.polyconomics.com/searchbase.

Greenwald, Bruce C. and Joseph E. Stiglitz (1986) "Externalities in Economies with Imperfect Information and Incomplete Markets," *Quarterly Journal of Economics*, Vol. 101 (May), pp. 229–264.

Gross, Daniel (2005) "What Makes a Nation More Productive?" *New York Times* (December 25), p. 3.3.

Groves, Martha (1997) "Push Grows for Law on 'Veggie Libel,'" *Los Angeles Times*, August 20, p. A1.

Hall, Robert E. (1988) "The Relation between Price and Marginal Cost in U.S. Industry," *Journal of Political Economy*, Vol. 96 (October), pp. 921–947.

Hamilton, Barton H. (2000) "Does Entrepreneurship Pay? An Empirical Analysis of the Returns to Self Employment," *Journal of Political Economy*, Vol. 108, No. 3, pp. 604–631.

Handfield, Robert B. and Mark D. Pagell (1995) "An Analysis of the Diffusion of Flexible Manufacturing," *International Journal of Production Economics*, Vol. 39, pp. 243–253.

Harberger, Arnold (1954) "Monopoly and Resource Allocation," *American Economic Review*, Vol. 44 (May), pp. 73–87.

Harris, Maury N. (1973) Entry, Barriers to Entry, and Limit Pricing, Unpublished Ph.D. Thesis, Columbia University.

Hartmann, Thom (2002) *Unequal Protection*, Emmaus PA: Rodale Books.

Hauser, Robert, John Robert Warren, Min-Hsiung Huang, and Wendy Carter (2000) Occupational Status, Education and Social Mobility in the Meritocracy, in *Meritocracy and Economic Inequality*, eds. Kenneth Arrow, Samuel Bowles, and Steven Durlauf, Princeton: Princeton University Press.

Hausman, Daniel M. (1989) "Economic Methodology in a Nutshell," *Journal of Economic Perspectives*, Vol. 3, No. 2 (Spring), pp. 115–127.

Hawley, Ellis W. (1995) The New Deal and the Problem of Monopoly, New York: Fordham University Press.

Hay, George A. and Daniel Kelley (1974) "An Empirical Survey of Price-Fixing Conspiracies," *Journal of Law and Economics*, Vol. 17 (April), pp. 13–38.

Hayek Friedrich (1994) *The Road to Serfdom*, Chicago: University of Chicago Press.

Heilbroner, Robert L. (1968) *The Making of an Economic Society*, Englewood Cliffs, NJ: Prentice-Hall .

Heilbroner, Robert L. (1986) *The Nature and Logic of Capitalism*, New York: W.W. Norton.

Henry, David (2002) "Mergers: Why Most Big Deals Don't Pay Off," *Business Week* (October 14), pp. 60–65.

Herrnstein, Richard J. and Charles Murray (1994) *The Bell Curve*, New York: Free Press.

Hibbs, Douglas A., Jr. (1982a) "The Dynamics of Political Support for American Presidents among Occupational and Partisan Groups," *American Journal of Political Science*, 26 (May), pp. 312–332.

——— (1982b) "Economic Outcomes and Political Support for British Government among Occupational Classes: A Dynamic Analysis," *American Political Science Review*, No. 76 (June), pp. 259–279.

Hipple, Steven (2004) "Self-Employment in the United States: An Update," *Monthly Labor Review* (July), pp. 13–23.

Hochman, Harold M. (2002) Is Democracy an Antidote to Extremism? in *Political Extremism and Rationality*, eds. Albert Breton, Gianluigi Galeotti, Pierre Salmon, and Ronald Wintrobe, Cambridge: Cambridge University Press.

Von Hoffman, Nicholas (1992) *Capitalist Fools*, New York: Doubleday.

Hout, Michael (1993) Social Mobility, in *The Oxford Companion to Politics of the World*, ed. Joel Krieger, New York: Oxford University Press.

Hoynes, Hilary W., Marianne E. Page, and Ann Huff Stevens (2006) "Poverty in America: Trends and Explanations," *Journal of Economic Perspectives*, Vol. 20 (Winter), pp. 47–68.

Hudson, Michael (2003/2004) "Driven to Misery," *Southern Exposure*, Vol. 31, No. 3 and 4 (Winter), pp. 1–11.

Hurst, Erik and Annamaria Lusardi (2004) "Liquidity Constraints, Household Wealth, and Entrepreneurship," *Journal of Political Economy*, Vol. 112, No. 2, pp. 319–347.

Jewkes, David, David Sawers, and Richard Stillerman (1958) *The Sources of Invention*, New York: St Martin's Press.

John, Richard R. (1997) "Elaborations, Revisions, Dissents: Alfred D. Chandler, Jr.'s The Visible Hand after Twenty Years," *Business History Review*, Vol. 71 (Summer), pp. 151–200. www.thebhc.org/publicationsrjbhr.html.

Johnston, David Cay (2003) "Very Richest's Share of Income Grew Even Bigger, Data Show," *New York Times*, June 26, p. A1. www.nytimes.com/2003/06/26/business/26/business/26TAX.html.

Jorgenson, Dale W., Mun S. Ho, and Kevin J. Stiroh (2005) Growth of US Industries and Investments in Information Technology and Higher Education, in *Measuring Capital in the New Economy*, eds. C. Corrado, J. Haltiwanger, and D. Sichel, Chicago: University of Chicago Press.

Joseph, Antoine L. (2005) *The Dynamics of Racial Progress*, Armonk, NY: M. E. Sharpe.

Judis, John B. (2002) "Decline and Fall," *New York Times* Book Review, May 12, p. 12.

Kahn, Alfred E. (1971) *The Economics of Regulation*, Vol. 2, New York: John Wiley and Sons.

Karger, Howard (2005) *Shortchanged*, San Francisco: Berrett-Koehler.

Kaysen, Carl and Donald F. Turner (1959) *Antitrust Policy*, Cambridge, MA: Harvard University Press.

Klein, Lisa E. (1999) "Political Party Funding in Britain," *Case Western Reserve Journal of International Law*, Vol. 31, No. 1, pp. 1–46.

Kim, H. Phillip, Howard E. Aldrich, and Lisa A. Keister (2006) "Access (Not) Denied: The Impact of Financial, Human and Cultural Capital on Entrepreneurial Entry in the United States," *Small Business Economics*, Vol. 27, pp. 5–22.

Kovacic, William E. and Carl Shapiro (2000) "Antitrust Policy: A Century of Economic and Legal Thinking," *Journal of Economic Perspectives*, Vol. 14, No. 1 (Winter), pp. 43–60.

Krugman, Paul (1996) *Pop Internationalism*, Cambridge, MA: MIT Press

——— (2002a), "Greed is Bad" *New York Times*, June 4, p. A. 19.

——— (2002b), "For Richer," *New York Times*, October 20, p. 62. www.nytimes.com/2002/10/20magazine/20INEQUALITY.html?

——— (2003) "The Tax Cut Con," *New York Times*, September 14, p. 57. www.nytimes.com/2003/09/14magazine/14TAXES.html?/.

——— (2005) "Losing Our Country," *New York Times*, June 10, p. A21.

——— (2007) "The Sum of All Ears," *New York Times*, January 29, p. A19.

Kurtz, Howard (2008) "Press May Own a Share in Financial Mess," *The Washington Post*, October 6, p. C1.

Kwoka, John E. and Lawrence J. White (editors) (1999) *The Antitrust Revolution*, New York: Oxford University Press.

Laird, Frank N. and Robert Reich (1998) "The Rhetoric of Corporate Welfare," *The American Prospect*, September/October, pp. 74–77.

Lamoreaux, Naomi R. (1992) "Martin Sklar's The Corporate Reconstruction of American Capitalism: An Economic Historian's Perspective." *Business and Economic History*, Second Series, 21, pp. 36–39.

Lande, Robert H. (1982) "Wealth Transfers as the Original and Primary Concern of Antitrust: The Efficiency Interpretation Challenged," Hastings Law Journal, Vol. 34 (September), L.J. 65.

Landefeld, Steven J. and Barbara M. Fraumeni (2001) "Measuring the New Economy," *Survey of Current Business*, 81 (March), pp. 23–40.

Landes, David S. (1999) *The Wealth and Poverty of Nations,* New York: Norton.

Leibenstein, Harvey (1966) "Allocative Efficiency versus X-Efficiency," *American Economic Review*, Vol. 56 (June), pp. 392–415.

Leonhardt, David (2005) "The College Dropout Boom," *New York Times*, May 24, p. A1.

Levenstein, Margaret (1998) "Review of William G. Roy Socializing Capital: The Rise of the Large Industrial Corporation in America," Economic History Services, *H-Business, H-Net Reviews*, August 12. http://www.eh.net/bookreviews/library/0114.shtml.

Levenstein, Margaret C. and Valerie Y. Suslow (2006) "What Determines Cartel Success?" *Journal of Economic Literature*, Vol. 44 (March), pp. 43–95.

Levin, Richard C., Wesley M. Cohen, and David C. Mowery (1985) "R&D Appropriability, Opportunity and Market Structure: New Evidence on Some Schumpeterian Hypotheses," *American Economic Review*, Vol. 75 (May), pp. 20–24.

Lichtblau, Eric (2008) "In Justice Shift, Corporate Deals Replace Trials," *New York Times* (April 9) p. A1.

Liebling, A. J. (1975) *The Press*, New York: Ballantine Books.
Lijphart Arend (1999) *Patterns of Democracy*, New Haven: Yale University Press.
Lindblom, Charles E. (1977) *Politics and Markets*, New York: Basic Books.
Lipset, Seymour Martin (1967) *The First New Nation*, New York: Doubleday Anchor Book.
——— (2000) "Still the Exceptional Nation," *Hoover Digest*, No. 2. www.hooverdigest.org/002/lipset.html.
Lipsey, R.G. and Kelvin Lancaster (1956) "The Theory of Second Best," *Review of Economic Studies*, Vol. 24, pp. 11–32.
Loomis, Carol J. (2001) "This Stuff Is Wrong" *Fortune*, June 25, pp. 72–84.
Ludwig, Jack (1999) "Economic Status: Americans Assess Opportunity, Fairness and Responsibility," The Roper Center for Public Opinion Research, April. www.globalpolicy.org/socecon/inequal/poll-usa.html.
Luger, Stan (1999) *Corporate Power, American Democracy and the Automobile Industry*, Cambridge: Cambridge University Press.
Luttwak, Edward (1999) *Turbo Capitalism: Winners and Losers in the Global Economy*, New York: Harper Collins.
Macey, Jonathan (2008) "Brave New Fed," *Wall Street Journal* (March 31), p. A19.
Madrick, Jeff (2002) "Economic Scene: If Taxes Were Lower, the Economy Would Grow Faster, Right? Economists Say Not Necessarily," *New York Times* (October 31), p. C2.
Major, Russell J. (1966) *Civilization in the Western World*, Philadelphia: J.B. Lippincott.
Mandel, Michael (1996) *The High Risk Society*, New York: Times Books.
Mansfield Edwin (1993) "The Diffusion of Flexible Manufacturing Systems in Japan, Europe and the United States," *Management Science*, Vol. 39, (February), pp. 149–159.
Mansfield E. and R. Brandenburg (1966) "Allocation, Characteristics and Outcome of Firms' Research and Development Portfolio—Case Study," *Journal of Business*, Vol. 39, No. 4, pp. 447–464.
Marris, Robin (1970) "Is the Corporate Economy a Corporate State?" *American Economic Review*, Vol. 40 (May), pp. 103–115.
Marris, Robin and Dennis C. Mueller (1980) "The Corporation, Competition and the Invisible Hand," *Journal of Economic Literature*, Vol. 18 (March), pp. 32–63.
Martin, Stephen (1993) *Advanced Industrial Economics*, Cambridge, MA: Blackwell.
——— (2009) "The Petroleum Industry," Ch. 2, in the *Structure of American Industry* (twelfth edition), ed. James W. Brock, Upper Saddle River, NJ: Pearson Prentice Hall.
Masson Robert and Joseph Shaanan (1982) "Dynamic-Stochastic Limit Pricing: An Empirical Test," *Review of Economics and Statistics*, Vol. 64, No. 3 (August), pp. 413–423.
——— (1984) "Social Costs of Oligopoly and the Value of Competition: An Empirical Analysis," *Economic Journal*, Vol. 94, No. 375 (September), pp. 520–535.

McChesney, Robert W. (1999) *Rich Media Poor Democracy*, Urbana: University of Illinois Press.
——— (1999) *The New Global Media*, The Nation. (November 29). http://past.thenation.com/issue/991129mcchesney.shtml.
——— (2008) *The Political Economy of the Media*, New York: Monthly Review Press.
McDonald, Forrest (1986) A New Introduction, in *An Economic Interpretation of the Constitution of the United States*, by Charles A. Beard, New York: Free Press.
McDonnell, Brett H. and Daniel A. Farber (2003) Are Efficient Antitrust Rules Always Optimal?" *The Antitrust Bulletin* (Fall), pp. 807–835.
McFadden, Daniel (2006) "Free Markets and Fettered Consumers," *American Economic Review* (March), pp. 5–29.
McGuire, Robert A. (1988) "Constitution Making: A Rational Choice Model of the Federal Convention of 1787," *American Journal of Political Science*, Vol. 32 (May), pp. 483–522.
McGuire, Robert A. and Robert L. Ohsfeldt (1984) "Economic Interests and the American Constitution: A Quantitative Rehabilitation of Charles A. Beard," *Journal of Economic History*, Vol. 44, No. 2 (June), pp. 509–519.
——— (1989) "Self Interest, Agency Theory, and Political Voting Behavior; the Ratification of the United States Constitution," *American Economic Review*, Vol. 79 (March), pp. 219–234.
Milgrom, Paul and John Roberts (1992) Economics, Organization and Management, Englewood Cliffs, NJ: Prentice Hall.
Millon, David (2001) "The Ambiguous Significance of Corporate Personhood," *Stanford Agora*, Vol. 1, No. 2. http://agora.stanford.edu/agora/cgi-bin/article2_corp.cgi?library=millon.
Monsen, R. Joseph Jr., and Anthony Downs (1965) "A Theory of Large Managerial firms," *Journal of Political Economy*, Vol. 73, No. 3 (June), pp. 221–236.
Moore, Stephen (1999) Welfare for the Well-Off: How Business Subsidies Fleece Taxpayers, in *Essays in Public Policy*, Hoover institution. www-hhover.stanford.edu/publications/epp/88/88b.html.
Morck, Randall, Andrei Shleifer and Robert W. Vishny (1988) Characteristics of Targets of Hostile and Friendly Takeovers, in Alan Auerbach, ed., *Corporate Takeovers: Causes and Consequences*, Chicago: University of Chicago Press.
Morck, Randall, Daniel Wolfenzon, and Bernard Yeung (2005) "Corporate Governance, Economic Entrenchment, and Growth," *Journal of Economic Literature*, Vol. 43 (September), pp. 655–720.
Morgenson, Gretchen (2007a) "Crisis Looms in Mortgages," *New York Times* (March 11), p. 1.1.
——— (2007b), "Home Loans: Nightmare Grows Darker," *New York Times* (April 8), p. 3.1.
Morgenthau, Hans Joachim (1960) *The Purpose of American Politics*, New York: Alfred A. Knopf.

Moscowitz, Tobias J. and Annette Vissing-Jorgensen (2002) "The Returns to Entrepreneurial Investment: A Private Equity Premium Puzzle?" *American Economic Review*, Vol. 92, No. 4 (September), pp. 745–778.

Mueller, Dennis C. (1985) "Mergers and Market Share," *Review of Economics and Statistics*, Vol. 67 (May), pp. 259–267.

——— (1986) *Profits in the Long Run*, New York: Cambridge University Press.

——— (2001) "Delusions Regarding the Proper Role of Markets and Antitrust Policy," *Review of Industrial Organization*, Vol. 19, pp. 27–36.

——— (2003) *Public Choice III*, Cambridge: Cambridge University Press.

Mueller W. F. and R. T. Rogers (1984) "Changes in Market Concentration in manufacturing Industries, 1947–1977," *Review of Industrial Organization*, Vol. 1 (Spring), pp. 1–14.

Muller, Jerry Z. (2002) *The Mind and the Market*, New York: Alfred A. Knopf.

National Science Foundation (1976) *Research and Development in Industry 1974*. Washington, DC: U.S. Government Printing Office.

Nace, Ted (2003) *The Gangs of America*, San Francisco: Berrett-Koehler.

Nassmacher, Karl-Heinz (2003) Party Funding in Continental Western Europe, in Ch. 7, *Funding of Parties and Election Campaigns*, eds. Reginald Austin and Maja Tjernstrom, Stockholm: IDEA. www.idea.int/publications/funding-parties/index.cfm.

Neale, A. D. (1970) *The Antitrust Laws of the United States of America* (second edition), London: Cambridge University Press.

Nelson, Candice J. (2002) Spending in the 2000 Election in *Financing the 2000 Election*, ed. David B. Magleby, Washington, DC: Brookings Institute Press. www. Brookings.edu/gs/cf/Financing2000/ch02.

Nelson, Richard R. and Gavin Wright (1992) "The Rise and Fall of American Technological Leadership: The Postwar Era in Historical Perspective," *Journal of Economic Literature*, Vol. 30 (December), pp. 1931–1964.

Neumark, David, Daniel Polsky, and Daniel Hansen (1999) "Has Job Stability Declined Yet? New Evidence for the 1990s," *Journal of Labor Economics*, Vol. 17, No. 4, Pt. 2, pp. S29–64.

North Douglass C. (1965) "The State of Economic History," *American Economic Review*, Vol. 55, No. 80, pp. 86–91.

Nutter, Warren G. (1951) *The Extent of Enterprise Monopoly in the United States: 1899–1939*, Chicago: University of Chicago Press.

Olson, Mancur (1965) *The Logic of Collective Action*, Cambridge, MA: Harvard University Press.

——— (1982) *The Rise and Decline of Nations*, New Haven: Yale University Press.

Owen, Bruce M. (1975) *Economic of Freedom of Expression*, Cambridge, MA: Ballinger.

Parker, Simon C. and Yacine Belghitar (2006) "What Happens to Nascent Entrepreneurs? An Econometric Analysis of the PSED," *Small Business Economics*, Vol. 27, pp. 81–101.

Pascoe, George and Leonard W. Weiss (1983) "The Extent and Permanence of Market dominance," Federal Trade Commission, Washington, DC: working paper.

Pearlstein, Steven (2002) "Regulation Vs Competition: No Winner Yet," *Washington Post* (November 2), p. A14.

Perrow, Charles (2002) *Organizing America*, Princeton: Princeton University Press.

Phillips, Kevin (2002) *Wealth and Democracy*, New York: Broadway Books.

Piketty, Thomas and Emmanuel Saez (2003) "Income Inequality in the United States, 1913–1998," *Quarterly Journal of Economics*, Vol. 117 (February), pp. 1–39.

Piore, Michael J. and Charles F. Sabel (1984) *The Second Industrial Divide*, New York: Basic Books.

Polyani, Karl (2001) *The Great Transformation*, Boston: Beacon Press.

Poole, Keith T. and Thomas Romer (1985) "Patterns of Political Action Committee Contributions to the 1980 Campaign for the United States House of Representatives," *Public Choice*, Vol. 47, No. 1, pp. 63–111.

Poole Keith T. and Howard Rosenthal (1997) *Congress: A Political-Economic History of Roll Call Voting*, Oxford: Oxford University Press.

Popkin, Joel (2005) "Cost of Employee Benefits in Small and Large Businesses," Small Business Research Summary, Office of Advocacy, United States Small Business Administration (August).

Posner, Richard A. (1975) "The Social Costs of Monopoly and Regulation," *Journal of Political Economy*, Vol. 83 (August), pp. 807–827.

Potter, David (1954) *People of Plenty: Economic Abundance and the American Character*, Chicago: University of Chicago Press.

Priest, George L. (2008) "The Abiding influence of the Antitrust Paradox," *Harvard Journal of Law and Policy*, Vol. 31, pp. 455–463.

Primeaux, Walter J. (1977) "An Assessment of X Efficiency Gained Through Competition," *Review of Economics and Statistics*, Vol. 59 (February), pp. 105–108.

Prindle, David F. (2006) *The Paradox of Democratic Capitalism*, Baltimore: Johns Hopkins University Press.

Pryor, Frederic L. (2001) "New Trends in US Industrial Concentration," *Review of Industrial Concentration*, Vol. 18, pp. 301–326.

——— (2002) *The Future of US Capitalism*, Cambridge: Cambridge University Press.

Public Citizen (2001) "Corporate Welfare" (June 21). www.citizen.org./congress/welfare/index.cfm.

Putterman, Louis, John E. Roemer, and Joaquim Silvestre (1998) "Does Egalitarianism Have a Future?" *Journal of Economic Literature*, Vol. 36 (June), pp. 861–902.

Rawls, John (1972) *A Theory of Justice*, Cambridge, MA: Harvard University Press.

Reder, Melvin (1982) "Chicago Economics: Preference and Change," *Journal of Economic Literature* Vol. 20 (March), pp. 1–38.

Reinsdorf, Marshall B. (2007) "Alternative Measures of Business Saving," *Survey of Current Business*, Vol. 87 (February), pp. 7–13: http://www.bea.gov/scb/pdf/2007/02%.

Reynolds, Paul Davidson (2005) "Understanding Business Creation: Serendipity and Scope in Two Decades of Business Creation Studies," *Small Business Economics*, Vol. 24, pp. 359–364.

——— (2007) *Entrepreneurship in the United States*, New York: Springer Science and Business Media.

Reynolds, Paul Davidson, Nancy M. Carter, William B. Gartner, and Patricia B. Greene (2004) "The Prevalence of Nascent Entrepreneurs in the United States: Evidence from the Panel Data Study of Entrepreneurial Dynamics," *Small Business Economics* (November) Vol. 23, pp. 263–284.

Rhine, Sherrie, L. W., William H. Greene, and Maude Toussaint-Comeau (2006) "The importance of Cash Checking Businesses to the Unbanked: Racial/Ethnic Differences," *Review of Economics and Statistics*, Vol. 88, pp. 146–157.

Rich, Frank (2005) "All the President's Newsmen," *New York Times* (January 16), p. 2.1. http://www.nytimes.com2005/01/16/arts/16rich.html.

Roemer, John E. (1998) "Why the Poor Do Not Expropriate the Rich: An Old Argument in New Garb," *Journal of Public Economics*, Vol. 70 (December), pp. 399–424.

Rosen, Sherwin (1981) "The Economics of ***Superstars,"*** *American Economic Review*, Vol. 71, No. 5 (December), pp. 845–858.

Roy, William (1997) *Socializing Capital*, Princeton: Princeton University Press.

Rueschmeyer, Dietrich, Evelyne Huber Stephens, and John D. Stephens (1992) *Capitalist Development and Democracy*, Chicago: University of Chicago Press.

Salamon, L. M. and J. J. Siegfried (1977) "Economic Power and Political Influence: The Impact of Industry Structure on Public Policy," *American Political Science Review*, Vol. 67 (September), pp. 1026–1043.

Samuelson, Paul and William D. Nordhaus (1998) *Economics* (sixteenth edition), New York: Irwin McGraw-Hill.

Sanes, Ken (2000). "Big Media and Bad Criticism," *Reform*, February 28, pp. 1–10. http://www.transparencynow.com/reform/slate.htm.

Sawhill, Isabel V. (1999) "Still the Land of Opportunity," *ABI Journal* (Spring), on the World Wide Web. www.igc.org/globalpolicy/socecon/inequal/sawhill.htm.

Scherer F. M. (1967) "Market Structure and the Employment of Scientists and Engineers," *American Economic Review*, Vol. 57 (June), pp. 524–531.

——— (1970, 1980) *Industrial Market Structure and Economic Performance* (1st and 2nd editions), Chicago: Rand McNally College.

——— (1992) "Schumpeter and Plausible Capitalism," *Journal of Economic Literature*, Vol. 30 (September), pp. 1416–1433.

——— (1996) *Industry, Structure, Strategy and Public Policy*, New York: Harper Collins.

——— (2008) Conservative Economics and Antitrust: A Variety of Influences in US Antitrust, in *How the Chicago School Overshot the Mark*, ed. Robert Pitofsky, New York: Oxford University Press.

Scherer, F. M. and David Ross (1990) *Industrial Market Structure and Economic Performance* (third edition), Boston: Houghton Mifflin.

Schiller, Bradley R. (2000) *The Micro Economy Today* (eighth edition), New York: Irwin McGraw Hill.

Schlesinger, Arthur Jr. (1945) *The Age of Jackson*, Boston: Little Brown.

——— (1988) Individualism and Apathy in Tocqueville's Democracy, in *Reconsidering Tocqueville's Democracy in America*, eds. Abraham S. Eisenstadt, New Brunswick, NJ: Rutgers University Press.

Schmalensee, Richard (2008) Thoughts on the Chicago Legacy, in *US Antitrust in How the Chicago School Overshot the Mark*, ed. Robert Pitofsky, New York: Oxford University Press.

Schumpeter, Joseph A. (1962) *Capitalism, Socialism and Democracy* (3rd edition), New York: Harper Torchbooks.

Schultz, Ellen E., and Theo Francis (2008) "Social Insecurity: High Interest Lenders Tap Elderly, Disabled," *Wall Street Journal*, February 12, p. A1.

Schwarz, John E. (2005) *Freedom Reclaimed*, Baltimore: Johns Hopkins University Press.

Scott, Janny (2005) "Life at the Top in America Isn't Just Better, It's Longer," *New York Times*, May 16, p. A1.

Scott, Janny and David Leonhardt (2005) "Class in America: Shadowy Lines that Still Divide," *New York Times*, May 15, p. 1.1.

Scott, John, C. (1984) Firm Versus Industry Variability in R&D Intensity, in *R&D, Patents and Productivity*, ed. Zvi Grilliches, Chicago: University of Chicago Press.

Sennett, Richard (2006) *The Culture of the New Capitalism*, New Haven: Yale University Press.

Servan-Schreiber, J. J. (1968) *The American Challenge*, New York: Atheneum.

Shafer, Jack (2000) "Big Is Beautiful," *Slate*, January 13. http://slate.msn.com.

Shane, Scott A. (2008) *The Illusions of Entrepreneurship*, New Haven: Yale University Press.

Shepherd, William G. (1967) "What Does the Survivor Technique Show about Economies of Scale?" *Southern Economic Journal*, Vol. 36 (July), pp. 113–122.

——— (1982) "Causes of Increased Competition in the U.S. Economy, 1939–1980," *Review of Economics and Statistics*, Vol. 64 (November), pp. 613–626.

——— (1991) *Public Policies toward Business* (eighth edition), Homewood, IL: Richard D. Irwin.

——— (1997) *The Economics of Industrial Organization* (fourth edition), Upper Saddle River, NJ: Prentice Hall.

Shiller, Robert J. (2001) *Irrational Exuberance*, New York: Broadway Books.

Shipler, David K. (2004) *The Working Poor*, New York: Alfred A. Knopf.

Shores, David F. (2001) "Antitrust Decisions and Legislative Intent," *Missouri Law Review*, Vol. 66, pp. 725–777.

Siconolfi, Michael, Anita Raghavan, and Mitchell Pacelle (1998) "All Bets Off: How Salesmanship and Brainpower Failed at Long Term Capital," *Wall Street Journal*, (November 16), p. A1.

Simons Henry C. (1947) *Economic Policy for a Free Society*, Chicago: University of Chicago Press.

Simpson, Glenn (2007) "Lender Lobbying Blitz Abetted Mortgage Mess," *Wall Street Journal*, December 31, p. A1.
Sloan, Allan (1998) "What Goes Around," *Newsweek*, New York, Vol. 132, No. 15 (October 12), p. 32.
Slotkin, Richard (1992) *Gunfighter Nation*, New York: Atheneum.
Smeeding, Timothy (2006) "Poor People in Rich Nations: The United States in Comparative Perspective," *Journal of Economic Perspectives*, Vol. 20, pp. 69–90.
Smith, Adam (1995) *An Inquiry into the Wealth of Nations*, Ottawa, Canada: World's Greatest Classic Books, Corel CD Home.
Solow, Robert M. (1957) "Technical Change and the Aggregate Production Function," *Review of Economics and Statistics*, Vol. 39 (August), pp. 312–320.
——— (1967) "The New Industrial State or Son of Affluence," *Public Interest*, Vol. 9 (Fall), pp. 100–108.
Spitzer, Eliot (2008) "Predatory Lenders' Partners in Crime," *Washington Post*, February 14, p. A.25.
Stegman, Michael A. (2007) "Payday Lending," *Journal of Economic Perspectives*, Vol. 21, No. 1 (Winter), pp. 169–190.
Stigler, George J. (1950) "Monopoly and Oligopoly by Mergers," *American Economic Review*, Vol. 40 (May), pp. 23–34.
——— (1971) "The Theory of Economic Regulation," *Bell Journal of Economics*, Vol. 2, (Spring), pp. 3–21.
——— (1982) "The Economists and the Problem of Monopoly," *American Economic Review*, Vol. 72 (May), pp. 1–11.
Stiglitz, Joseph (1991) "The Invisible Hand and Modern Welfare Economics," NBER Working Paper No. 3641.
Stokey, Nancy L. and Sergio Rebelo (1995) "Growth Effects of Flat Tax Rates," *Journal of Political Economy*, Vol. 103, No. 3 (June), pp. 519–550.
Stonebraker, Robert J. (1979) "Turnover and Mobility among the 100 Largest Firms: An Update," *American Economic Review*, Vol. 69 (December), pp. 968–973.
Temin, Peter (1978) "Chandler's The Visible Hand," *Bell Journal of Economics*, Vol. 9 (Spring), pp. 297–303.
Thoreau, Henry David (2004) *On the Duty of Civil Disobedience*, The Project Gutenberg EBook.
Thurow, Lester C. (1999) *Building Wealth*, New York: HarperCollins.
Tocqueville, Alexis De (1900) *Democracy in America* (revised edition), London: Colonial Press.
——— (1945) *Democracy in America*, Vol. 2 (revised edition), New York: Alfred A. Knopf.
Turrow, Joseph (1997) *Breaking Up America*, Chicago: University of Chicago Press.
Uchitelle, Louis (2006) *The Disposable American*, New York: Alfred A. Knopf.
U.S. Census Bureau (2005) Economic Census 2002.
——— (2000) *Historical Income Tables Households*. Washington, DC.
——— (2006) Statistical Abstract of the United States 2006. Washington, DC.
——— (2006) Educational Attainment in the United States: 2006. Washington, DC.

U.S. Census Bureau (2000) Supplemental Income Inequality Tables. Washington, DC. U.S. Department of Justice, Antitrust Division (2006) "Sherman Act Violations a Corporate Fine of $10 Million or More. www.usdoj.gov/atr/public/criminal/212901.htm/.

U.S. Department of Labor Bureau of Labor Statistics (2006) "Characteristics of Minimum Wage Workers: 2006. Washington, DC.

U.S. Department of State (2001) Small Business and the Corporation, Ch. 4 in, "An Outline of the U.S. Economy" prepared by Christopher Conte and Albert R. Karr (February). http://usinfo.state.gov/products/pubs/oecon/.

U.S. Small Business Administration, Office of Advocacy (2001) "Small Business—Frequently Asked Questions" (August).

Veblen, Thorstein (1997) *The Theory of the Leisure Class*, The Project Gutenberg EBook.

Waldman, Don E. (1986) *The Economics of Antitrust: Cases and Analysis*, Boston: Little, Brown.

Waldman, Don E. and Elizabeth J. Jensen (1998) *Industrial Organization* (second edition), Reading MA: Addison Wesley.

Walton, Gary M, and Hugh Rockoff (2005) *History of the American Economy* (tenth edition), Mason, OH: South-Western.

Weinberg, Daniel H. (2000) "A Brief Look at Postwar U.S. Income Inequality," Washington, DC: U.S. Census Bureau. www.census.gov/hhes/income/incineq/p60asc.html.

Weiner, Tim (1996) "Dwayne's World; Influence of Archer Daniels is Wide as Well as Deep" *New York Times*, January 16, p. D1. www.nytimes.com.

Weiss Leonard w. (1974) The Concentration—Profits Relationship and Antitrust, in *Industrial Concentration: The New Learning*, eds. Harvey J. Goldschmid, H. Michael Mann, and J. Fred Weston, Boston: Little Brown.

White, Lawrence (2002) "Trends in Aggregate Concentration in the United States," *Journal of Economic Perspectives*, Vol. 16 (Fall), pp. 137–160.

Whyte, William H. (2002) *The Organization Man*, Philadelphia: University of Pennsylvania Press.

Wiebe, Robert H. (1967) *The Search for Order 1877–1920*, New York: Hill and Wang.

Williams, Juliet (2006) The Road Less Traveled: Reconsidering the Political Writings of Friedrich von Hayek, in *American Capitalism: Social Thought and Political Economy in the 20th Century*, eds. Nelson Lichtenstein, Philadelphia: University of Pennsylvania Press.

Williamson, Jeffrey G. (1991) "Productivity and American Leadership: A Review Article," *Journal of Economic Literature*, Vol. 29 (March), pp. 51–68.

Williamson, Oliver E. (1975) *Markets and Hierarchies*, New York: Free Press.

——— (1981) "The Modern Corporation: Origins, Evolution, Attributes," *Journal of Economic Literature*, Vol. 19 (December), pp. 1537–1568.

Wilentz, Sean (1988) Many Democracies: On Tocqueville and Jacksonian America, in *Reconsidering Tocqueville's Democracy in America*, ed. Abraham S. Eisenstadt, New Brunswick: Rutgers University Press.

Winston, Clifford (1993) "Economic Deregulation: Days of Reckoning for Microeconomists," *Journal of Economic Literature*, Vol. 31 (September), pp. 1263–1289.

Wolff, Edward N. (2000) "Recent Trends in Wealth Ownership, 1983–1998," Working Paper No. 300, Jerome Levy Economics Institute.

Wright, Gavin (1990) "The Origins of American Industrial Success, 1879–1940," *American Economic Review*, Vol. 80 (September), pp. 651–668.

Wright, John R. (1990) "Contributions, Lobbying and Committee Voting in the U.S. House of Representatives," *American Political Science Review*, Vol. 84 (June), pp. 417–438.

Yergin, Daniel and Joseph Stanislaw (1998) *The Commanding Heights*, New York: Simon and Schuster.

Index

The manufacturer's authorised representative in the EU is Springer Nature Customer Service Centre GmbH, Europaplatz 3, 69115 Heidelberg, Germany. If you have any concerns regarding our products, please contact ProductSafety@springernature.com

Printed and bound by CPI Group (UK) Ltd, Croydon, CR0 4YY
30/10/2026
02242619-0011